DATE DUE

FREEDOM OR SECURITY

FREEDOM OR SECURITY
The Consequences for Democracies Using Emergency Powers to Fight Terror

Michael Freeman

Westport, Connecticut
London

Library of Congress Cataloging-in-Publication Data

Freeman, Michael, 1973–
    Freedom or security : the consequences for democracies using emergency powers to fight terror / Michael Freeman.
        p. cm.
    Includes bibliographical references and index.
    ISBN 0–275–97913–X (alk. paper)
    1. Civil rights. 2. Terrorism—Prevention—Government policy. 3. War and emergency powers. I. Title.

JC571.F6749 2003
323.44—dc21   2002029884

British Library Cataloguing in Publication Data is available.

Library of Congress Catalog Card Number: 2002029884
ISBN: 0–275–97913–X

First published in 2003

Praeger Publishers, 88 Post Road West, Westport, CT 06881
An imprint of Greenwood Publishing Group, Inc.
www.praeger.com

Printed in the United States of America

The paper used in this book complies with the Permanent Paper Standard issued by the National Information Standards Organization (Z39.48–1984).

10 9 8 7 6 5 4 3 2 1

Copyright Acknowledgments
The author and publisher gratefully acknowledge permission for use of the following material:
Extracts from Arturo Porzecanski, *Uruguay's Tupamaros: The Urban Guerrilla* (New York: Praeger Publishers, 1973). Reprinted by permission of Greenwood Publishing Group, Inc.

Contents

Acknowledgments

This project is only possible because of the family members, friends, and advisors who have provided me with spiritual, emotional, financial, and intellectual support. While at the University of Chicago, Charlie Glaser and Alex Wendt read and critiqued countless drafts, while Charles Lipson, Susan Stokes, and John Mearsheimer also provided valuable guidance. Seth Jones and Doowan Lee are great friends as well as supportive colleagues who were always there when I needed to try out a new idea.

This book would never have happened without my parents, Marc and Barbara, who have always encouraged and supported me, but also kept their distance when necessary. I also wish to thank Miriam Tai, who has had to listen to histories of the IRA and Shining Path during countless dinners and who has inspired me to be who I am.

I am indebted to all of you.

Chapter 1

The Tradeoff of Emergency Powers

While the September 11 attacks focused America's attention on terrorism, these attacks are only part of a broader pattern of violence in which the United States is the target of terrorists. For example, on April 19, 1995, Timothy McVeigh bombed the federal building in Oklahoma City, killing 168 people and injuring hundreds more. In addition, just two years earlier on February 26, 1993, an Egyptian terrorist attempted to topple the World Trade Center in New York. Although the bomb failed to bring down the buildings, six people were killed and thousands were injured.[1] After these earlier incidents, United States citizens demanded that the government "do something" in response to terrorism.[2] During the year after Oklahoma City, Congress debated legislation that became the Anti-Terrorism Bill, which was signed by President Clinton on April 24, 1996, almost exactly a year after the Oklahoma City bombing.[3] Although directed primarily at foreigners living in the United States and not United States citizens, this legislation generated considerable controversy, with some scholars claiming it contained "some of the worst assaults on civil liberties in decades."[4] Controversy has again erupted over the government's response to terrorism following the September 11 attacks. Congress quickly passed the Patriot Act, which allowed the government to detain foreign citizens for an extra 24 hours, tightened controls over student visas, and loosened wiretap restrictions. Additionally, the administration also decided to try suspected terrorists in military courts, rather than civilian courts. The controversy over these particular anti-terrorism measures illustrates the justified concern that governments will restrict liberties when confronted by a terrorist threat. Moreover, with the most recent attacks on New York and Washington, and with the ever-increasing possibility that terrorists might use weapons of mass destruction (chemical, biological, or nuclear), there is an even greater concern that the United States government will overreact to the threat from terrorism by restricting individual liberties.[5]

This concern for civil liberties is justified when one considers how the United States has restricted liberties in the past whenever national security was threatened—or at least believed to be. Supreme Court Justice Thurgood Marshall wrote in a 1989 decision, "History teaches that grave threats to liberty often come in times of urgency, when constitutional rights seem too extravagant to endure."[6] Historically, in the United States, civil liberties have been undermined most frequently during times of war—from the Revolutionary War, in which freedom of speech was undermined when people were arrested for criticizing the new government, to the Vietnam War, when the CIA allegedly conducted illegal domestic espionage.[7]

Many other democratic states have also restricted liberties by using so called "emergency powers" to deal with terrorism.[8] Emergency powers can best be thought of as a compromise that allows the government to ensure the security of the state while limiting the damage to liberty and democracy. As Paul Wilkinson notes, "In countering terrorism, the democratic state confronts an inescapable dilemma. It has to deal effectively with the terrorist threat to citizens and the state itself without destroying basic civil rights, the democratic process, and the rule of law."[9] Using emergency powers allows the state to provide immediate security and protect civil rights in the long term by *temporarily* suspending some rights and liberties. Emergency powers are just one countermeasure against terrorism; others might include increasing physical security, improving cooperation with allies, devoting more resources to intelligence agencies, increasing punishments for convicted terrorists, and adopting stiffer negotiation strategies. None of these measures, however, are as controversial as the enactment of emergency powers.

Emergency powers are controversial because they have "costs" as well as "benefits" for a democratic society. The assumed benefits of emergency powers are that a government will have an increased ability to arrest, convict, and imprison terrorists, while the costs of emergency powers may come from both their use and abuse.[10] The *use* of emergency powers entails some suspension of liberties; typically, the due process rights of suspected terrorists are suspended or diminished. In a country devoted to protecting individuals' liberties, any infringement of liberty is unwelcome, even if directed at suspected criminals. Many scholars recommend that states avoid using emergency powers because the restriction of any liberties runs counter to liberal traditions and political philosophy. Philip Heymann observes, "Changing the basic rules of law enforcement, even to combat terrorism … evokes substantial fears in democratic nations."[11] Paul Wilkinson goes further in arguing, "It must be a cardinal principle of liberal democracy in dealing with the problems of terrorism, however serious these may be, never to be tempted into using methods which are in-compatible with the liberal values of humanity, liberty, and justice."[12]

While these scholars point to the costs of *using* emergency powers, they may also be costly if they are *abused,* such as when an actor employs the emergency powers to permanently undermine individual liberties or seize greater powers within the state. This possibility is exemplified by Adolph Hitler's use of emergency powers in Weimar Germany, in which he used emergency powers to replace a democratic government with an authoritarian one. In addition, emergency powers can be abused to intentionally arrest and imprison citizens known to be unaffiliated with terrorism. For example, a government in power might turn against its political opponents, using the fight against terrorism as a justification for its actions.

The focus of this book will be on this second set of costs (from the abuse, rather than the use of emergency powers) for a variety of reasons. The costs to liberties from the use of emergency powers may be severe, but it is fairly straightforward to know and predict what the costs of emergency powers will be in terms of their *use* by looking at the specific measures of the emergency powers. For example, if emergency powers allow the police to search properties without a warrant, we should expect that the costs of these powers will be that suspected criminals will lose their right to be protected from searches without warrant.

Also, understanding the costs of *abuses* of emergency powers is much more problematic. When a government enacts emergency powers, there is usually no expectation that they will be abused.[13] Additionally, there is no consensus on when emergency powers will be abused within the scholarly literature on emergency powers.[14]

Lastly, while the costs of using emergency powers may be large, the costs from abuses of emergency powers can be much greater.[15] Any loss of liberty that comes from the *use* of emergency powers will be limited in time and will not, by definition, become permanent. Conversely, if emergency powers are *abused,* particularly in their duration, they may no longer be temporary and the government might permanently acquire greater powers at the loss of indi-vidual liberties. For example, in several cases, such as Weimar Germany, Peru, and Uruguay, abuses of emergency powers have been associated with the re-placement of democratic regimes with authoritarian governments.

THE TRADEOFF OF USING EMERGENCY POWERS

Throughout the scholarly literature on terrorism, it is commonly asserted that there is a tradeoff when states use emergency powers.[16] Many scholars as-sume that emergency powers will be effective, but will also be abused in ways that threaten democracy.[17] For example, Paul Wilkinson describes the conse-quences of emergency powers in the following manner:

In discussing special [emergency] powers any liberal will speak with strong distaste and reluctance ... Too many cases come to mind of ambitious politicians around the world who have exploited such measures for their own ends, or who would dearly like to do so. Mainly because of these abuses and the real dangers of permanent dictatorship emerging, liberals are right to insist that special powers should only be used if there is a fundamental threat to the political or economic system.[18]

This concern is echoed by Dermont Walsh, who argues that the use of emergency powers is a "question of balance—between the desirability of making this power available for the social good and the need to ensure that it is not abused."[19] J. C. Garnett similarly fears that "The powers necessary to suppress riot, insurrection, and revolution can easily be used to overturn democracy."[20] Robin Evelegh claims, "The means needed to defeat terrorism and suppress insurrection are the very ones needed to enforce a tyranny."[21] Finally, David Bonner admonishes his readers that "One does not save the liberal state from terrorism by trampling roughshod on its most precious values and postulates; that may change the nature of the state for the worse."[22] As a consequence of this supposed tradeoff, George Shultz posits that countries fighting terrorism "must steer their course carefully between anarchy and tyranny."[23]

Surprisingly, there is little disagreement among scholars that this tradeoff is likely to occur. Where scholars diverge, however, is on whether they choose to accept the tradeoff. This essentially entails deciding which is the more important of two goals—protecting democracy or maintaining the security of the state—that come into conflict when states confront terrorism. Irving Horowitz sees no middle ground between this tradeoff when he wrote, "This vicious dialectic can be broken down in two ways: by the absolute crushing of opposition, as in totalitarian systems, or by accepting the risks of terror as a permanent feature of developed, mobile, and liberal societies; as necessary evils along with prostitution, gambling, drugs, and other forms of deviance."[24] His two options are clearly too extreme: States can fight terrorism with existing laws with some success, and without becoming a totalitarian state. This quotation, however, highlights the choices that states must make.

Most scholars of terrorism argue that this tradeoff should be resolved in favor of protecting democracy. For example, Grant Wardlaw argues, "However serious the threat of terrorism we must not be tempted to use repressive methods to combat it. To believe that we can 'protect' liberal democracy by suspending our normal rights and method of government is to ignore the numerous examples in contemporary history of countries where 'temporary,' 'emergency' rule has subsided quickly and irrevocably into permanent dictatorial forms of government."[25] Richard Falkenrath, Robert Newman, and Bradley Thayer prescribe fully safeguarding democratic values even when terrorists might have weapons of mass destruction.[26] Philip Heymann also recognizes this tradeoff between fighting terrorism and protecting civil liberties, and argues that civil liberties must be protected. He claims that law enforcement agencies can be effective under normal laws, and that emergency powers add unnecessary risk. Consequently, he prescribes devoting more resources to law enforcement agencies, but not increasing their powers.[27]

Other scholars, most notably Benjamin Netanyahu, argue the tradeoff should be resolved in favor of fighting terrorism.[28] He claims that for democracies such as the United States, Britain, France, and Germany, "There is little choice but to adopt an active posture against terror." By active posture Netanyahu means emergency powers, and he prescribes them despite being cognizant of the dangers to democracy. He recognizes that, "Indeed, every one of the active steps that a democratic state can take against domestic terrorists constitutes a certain curtailment of someone's freedom to speak, assemble, or practice his religion without interference."[29]

The problem with all these positions on how to resolve the tradeoff between protecting democracy and fighting terrorism is that they all *assume* that there is such a tradeoff when emergency powers are used by a state. The subsequent debate on how to resolve the tradeoff between anarchy and tyranny is largely a normative question about what a state or scholar values most—democracy or survival (at the extremes). This book, rather than enter this normative debate, will challenge the assumption that underlies it by asking the theoretical question of when and why does this assumed tradeoff occur.

Governments that use emergency powers often assume a different set of consequences than those just discussed. For governments, emergency powers are expected to be effective, but should not lead to abuses of power. This book challenges these sets of assumptions as well. Not only does the tradeoff assumed by terrorist scholars (effective but dangerous) often fail to materialize, but the high benefits (effective) and low costs (safe) of emergency powers assumed by governments are often too optimistic.

THE QUESTION

The central question of this book is: What are the consequences for democratic states of using emergency powers to fight terrorism?[30] The consequences can be divided into two dimensions: Emergency powers can be effective or ineffective, and they can be abused or not abused. (The two dependent variables are discussed as dichotomous only for purposes of simplicity. Also, I will refer to the abuse or non-abuse of emergency powers as dangerous and safe, respectively, although I have earlier pointed to the costs from even the safe use of emergency powers.) This leads to two specific questions regarding the consequences of emergency powers: When are emergency powers effective, and when are emergency powers abused?[31] By looking at both the costs (abuses) *and* benefits (effectiveness) of emergency powers, I will be able to offer policy prescriptions that take both sets of consequences into account.[32] Before looking at possible theoretical answers to these questions, I will first define and describe emergency powers more thoroughly as well as explain what is meant by effectiveness and abuse.

First, what are emergency powers? Emergency powers are the extra powers wielded by a government when its normal abilities to cope with a crisis are inadequate.[33] Frederick Watkins, in his analysis of emergency powers in Weimar Germany, claims "There is always a danger that constitutional systems will prove incompatible with effective action in periods of exceptional difficulty. From ancient Rome down to the present, most constitutional states have therefore considered it wise to provide some regular means for the suspension of normal political procedures in the face of temporary crises."[34] The means provided can vary from suspending specific liberties to the entire constitution. As Brian Loveman puts it, "A regime of exception enhances or reassigns normal government authority while curtailing temporarily certain civil liberties and rights ... In accordance with the constitution, all or part of existing constitutional procedures and individual guarantees are suspended."[35] In Clinton Rossiter's historical study of emergency powers (which he calls constitutional dictatorship), he describes the need for emergency powers in the following manner:

The complex system of government of the democratic, constitutional state is essentially designed to function under normal, peaceful conditions, and it is often unequal to the exigencies of a great national crisis ... Therefore, in time of crisis a democratic, constitutional government must be temporarily altered to whatever degree is necessary to overcome the peril and restore normal conditions. This alteration invariably involves government of a stronger character; that is, the government will have more power and the people fewer rights.[36]

While emergency powers may grant wide command to the government, they are also limited in several key aspects. Most importantly, they are limited in their duration; they are to be used for either a specific length of time or until the government deems the emergency to be over. The Roman dictator, appointed for six months, is an example of a limit on duration by design, whereas the suspension of habeas corpus in the United States is an example of emergency powers that can be used for as long as the government decides that an emergency exists. The limit on the duration of the emergency powers (whether for a specific time limit or at the discretion of the government) is what makes them *emergency* powers. If a state permanently suspends some individual rights to fight terrorism, this would be a serious blow to the liberal state, but not an example of emergency powers.[37] Emergency powers are also frequently, but not necessarily, limited in their scope. At one extreme, emergency powers can suspend all liberties for all people. At the other end of the spectrum, emergency powers may only suspend just a few liberties of particular citizens, such as suspected terrorists. While emergency powers may lie anywhere on this spectrum, they are usually limited to some degree in terms of their scope.

Emergency (or extra-constitutional or exceptional) powers have a long history. In the Roman Republic, in times of emergency, the Senate proposed that the consuls appoint a dictator (without the modern connotations), who would hold absolute power for six months and had the tasks of ending the emergency and restoring the constitutional order.[38] Other, more modern examples of emergency powers include President Lincoln's suspension of habeas corpus during the Civil War and Article 48 in Weimar Germany, which Hitler used to his advantage in his rise to power.[39] With the increase in terrorism in the 1960s and 1970s, various states such as Britain, Italy, Spain, Uruguay, Canada, and Israel have used emergency powers as one strand of their counter-terrorist efforts.

Britain's emergency powers under the Northern Ireland Act of 1973 and the Prevention of Terrorism Act of 1974 serve as a specific example of both the content and limits on emergency powers. These measures allowed the police to arrest suspects without a warrant, allowed prisoners to be detained without an arrest, gave police broad authority for search and seizure, and denied prisoners the right to trial by jury.[40] The emergency powers used by Britain were limited in duration because they had to be renewed yearly by Parliament, and in scope because free speech, the right to vote, and other such freedoms were unaffected.

Emergency powers are effective when they reduce the violence caused by terrorism. While some scholars and government officials look at the statistics that count the number of suspects arrested or imprisoned using emergency powers, I look at whether the number of attacks, the number of deaths, or the number of injuries has decreased after the enactment and implementation of the emergency powers. At their most effective, emergency powers will eliminate a terrorist group altogether. For emergency powers to be coded as effective, though, not only must the level of violence decrease after the implementation of the emergency powers, but also the emergency powers must be shown to be causally connected to the change in the level of violence. In Italy, for example, the government passed anti-terrorism legislation in 1975, which included the temporary suspension of individual liberties. The subsequent decrease in terrorist violence, however, was due to aspects of the legislation that would not be classified as emergency powers. This case, therefore, would *not* be coded as one of effective emergency powers.

There are two distinct but related types of abuse of emergency powers, depending on whether they are abused in their scope or their duration. If the state takes advantage of the emergency powers to arrest political opponents known to be unaffiliated with terrorism, or violates additional liberties not covered by the emergency powers, these would be abuses in the scope of the powers. Abuses of this type are usually carried out by the security forces of the state and pose a danger to the individual liberties of citizens. On the other hand, if the government changes the emergency powers from temporary to permanent, this would be an abuse of the duration of the powers.[41] Abuses of this type are typically coup d'états, are usually undertaken by the military or the executive, and are threats to the very democratic nature of the state.[42] Both types of abuse constitute a danger to the democratic state, and so together comprise the dangers of emergency powers. Analytically and theoretically, however, the two types of abuse have somewhat different explanations for when they occur and how they can be prevented, which will be discussed later.

Answering the questions that are central to this book is important for several reasons. First, I challenge the contention within much of the terrorism literature that there is a tradeoff for states that use emergency powers (they are always effective but abused). Also, I question the assumption of many states and policymakers that expects emergency powers to be safe and effective. I challenge these assumptions by looking at four cases with different combinations of the dependent variables. One case will be where emergency powers were effective but abused (Uruguay), as predicted by the conventional wisdom; however, the other cases will show that the conventional wisdom misses much of the variation and possible combinations in the consequences of emergency powers. The other three cases will be states where emergency powers were used effectively and not abused (Canada), ineffectively and abused (Peru), and ineffectively but not abused (Britain).

Second, beyond challenging the conventional wisdom by showing there is more variation than expected, this book also goes beyond the descriptive nature of the literature that deals specifically with this issue by offering a theoretical argument on when (under what conditions) there is a tradeoff between protecting democracy and fighting terrorism. In 1983, Martha Crenshaw wrote, "There are no general studies that document the concrete effects of policies against terrorism on individual freedoms."[43] Since then, several other authors have performed case studies on the effects of terrorism on democracy. These include a book edited by David Charters with case studies of Britain/Ireland, Germany, Italy, France, Israel, and the United States,[44] as well as a volume edited by Peter Janke with chapters on the consequences of emergency powers in Italy, Germany, Japan, the Netherlands, and Canada.[45] These books, however, do not offer theoretical, or causal, arguments about why there is or is not a tradeoff, and when we should expect the tradeoff to be a concern. Instead, these accounts offer descriptive, case-by-case studies on the effects of counter-terrorist policies on democratic values in particular countries.

Third, while many authors are concerned with fighting terrorism, their prescriptions of which measures to undertake are usually presented as a comprehensive list.[46] No space is devoted to the theoretical task of whether and under what conditions different counter-measures are effective. This study looks at one specific measure—emergency powers—and whether this measure is effective in fighting terrorism. Moreover, by examining both sides (the costs as well as benefits) of emergency powers, this study can offer implications that are more complete than studies that only examine one side of the tradeoff.

Lastly, and most importantly, this study has tremendously important policy implications. For democratic states confronted by terrorism, there are two great dangers. One danger is from the terrorist violence itself; the other danger comes from the state's response to terrorism and how this affects the democratic character of the state. This study, by seeking to understand when there is a tradeoff from using emergency powers, seeks to minimize both of these dangers. By showing in certain instances that emergency powers can be effective without being abused, leaders in democratic states can make informed decisions on whether using emergency powers are valuable in the fight against terrorism.

EXPLAINING THE CONSEQUENCES OF EMERGENCY POWERS

While this book challenges the conventional wisdom that sees a tradeoff when states use emergency powers to fight terrorism, it is not enough to simply show that emergency powers can lead to different combinations of effectiveness/ineffectiveness and abuse/no abuse. The fact that this variation occurs begs the question, "Why are emergency powers effective or abused in some cases, and not in others?" The following is a brief overview of my answers to each question, while Chapter 2 is devoted in its entirety to developing these arguments more fully.

So, when are emergency powers abused? My answer is based on an understanding of constitutionalism, which is essentially a theory of how states constrain power. Liberal, constitutionalist, democracies are founded on three principles: equality, liberty, and the separation of powers—each of which constrains against arbitrary uses of power. Equality guarantees that all citizens of a state can participate as equals in the political process through regular and open elections. Individual liberties establish clear limits on the power of government by protecting individuals and activities (speech, religion, assembly, due process, and so on) from government intervention. The separation of powers divides the power of government into multiple branches (usually an executive, legislature, and judiciary), with each one capable of checking the other branches and thereby protecting against abuses of power.

Emergency powers, however, suspend many of these constitutional safeguards that would ordinarily protect against abuses of power. The key to whether the emergency powers will be abused is whether specific constitutional safeguards remain intact. Specifically, the important safeguards are those that can monitor abuses and enforce compliance with the law if abuses occur. While emergency powers may be broad in scope, the likelihood that emergency powers will be abused depends on whether the safeguards that can perform the monitoring and enforcement functions continue to operate even during times of emergency. I will focus primarily on two sets of safeguards that can monitor abuses and enforce compliance with the law: a free press/free speech, and the separation of powers. Other aspects of emergency powers, such as the restrictions on due process rights, restrict individual liberties, but are less important for whether emergency powers will be abused. Due process rights can protect against abuses within the criminal justice system on a case-by-case basis, but cannot protect against abuses on a larger scale. A free press and the separation of powers, however, can protect against widespread abuses.

A free press is critical to monitoring abuses of power. Even when due process rights are suspended, as they typically are under emergency powers, an uncensored press can publicize abuses that normally would be rectified within the judicial process. If the state abuses its power by arresting innocent citizens and denies them their due process rights, those arrested can air their grievances in the press. Obviously, the press has the power to monitor and publicize abuses but does not have the institutional capability of ending abuses; however, public discussions concerning the use or abuse of emergency powers may force the government to respond to domestic pressure. The right to free speech more broadly is also crucial if abuses are to be monitored. Individuals, whether ordinary citizens, members of government, or members of the media, must all have the right to criticize the government without fear of reprisal. If their speech is censored in any way, there cannot be an open and public debate of government policies.

The separation of powers improves the capability of one branch of government to check other branches if emergency powers are abused. In constitutional systems, whether a parliamentary or a presidential system, the different branches of government have the capability to constrain other branches. In parliamentary systems, the prime minister rules with the backing of his party and a coalition of other parties in Parliament. If emergency powers are abused at the hands of the executive, he may lose support from the coalition parties in the government and possibly even the backing of his own party. In presidential systems, the legislature has the power to pass laws modifying the emergency powers if they are seen to be abused and can even impeach the president if necessary. Likewise, the judiciary can declare the emergency legislation unconstitutional or overturn verdicts in terrorist trials. For the different branches of government to be able to check abuses of power, they must not only remain separate and strong, but the political opposition must retain its right to criticize the government. In many countries, the different branches of government can also perform important monitoring functions in investigating abuses of power. In several of the cases that follow, the legislative bodies conducted investigations or inquiries into abuses of power by the executive branches (including the military). The continued existence of a clear separation of powers, even during an emergency, is therefore important in terms of both monitoring abuses and enforcing compliance if abuses occur.

An additional factor that contributes to when emergency powers will be abused is the normative commitment to democracy of particular actors within the government. Abuses of power do not just occur; someone or some group has to act to abuse their power. If the commitment to democracy is strong, no actor will be willing to abuse power for his own personal or organizational gain. In general, then, abuses of power occur when both constitutional safeguards and the normative commitment to democracy are weak. If both are strong, actors will have neither the desire nor the ability to abuse power. If the normative commitment to democracy is weak but the constitutional safeguards are strong, some actors might want to abuse power but will be institutionally constrained if they try. Alternatively, if norms are strong but the institutions are weak, abuses will not occur because no one will want or try to abuse their power; however, had they tried, they would have succeeded.

In sum, abuses of emergency powers can be divided into two types—abuses in their scope, and in their duration. Emergency powers are usually abused in terms of their scope by the security forces. In protecting against such abuses, a free press and government commissions can monitor potential abuses, while the various branches of government can enforce compliance with the laws if abuses of occur. Abuses in the duration of emergency powers are usually perpetrated by the executive or the military. To protect against this type of abuse, a strong commitment to democracy is important. Also, the existence of a strong separation of powers allows opposing branches (although usually the legislature) to check any abuses of power by the executive branch or the military.

When are emergency powers effective? My argument is based on an understanding of the strengths and weaknesses of terrorist movements and predicts that emergency powers will be most effective when used quickly against terrorist groups with low levels of support. Terrorist groups have many advantages in their fight against the state: they are secretive, highly motivated, and hold the initiative entirely in their hands. Despite these strengths, they also have several weaknesses that can be exploited by the state. The state holds an overwhelming advantage in terms of resources compared to the terrorist group; the state can mobilize tens of thousands of policemen and other security forces in order to combat terrorism waged by a few hundred terrorists. Moreover, the security forces have access to the best weapons, the most technologically advanced tools, and usually the widespread support from the general population. Despite these advantages, the state often sees the need to use emergency powers to fight terrorism. Emergency powers, particularly the suspension of due process rights, are designed to attack the membership of a terrorist organization. By allowing the police to conduct searches without warrant, or hold suspects without bringing them to trial, the state hopes to imprison large numbers of terrorists to eventually eliminate the terrorist organization. Terrorist groups, however, can recruit new members to sustain the movement. If the state can move quickly against terrorists with little support, emergency powers are the most likely to be successful.

The emergency powers will be most effective when the state can imprison terrorists faster than new recruits can join the organization and take their place. Two factors are critical: the speed with which the government employs the emergency powers, and the level of support enjoyed by the terrorists. There is no hard and fast measure for how fast a government must act in imprisoning terrorists; the key measure is whether the state imprisons terrorists faster than the remaining terrorists in the organization can train new recruits. Typical training periods for terrorist groups take several weeks to several months. Only after going through training and indoctrination are new recruits allowed to fully operate as terrorists. In many cases of success, states have arrested hundreds, if not thousands, of suspected terrorists in a matter of days or even a few months, well before they could train their replacements.[47] Two factors that contribute to the speed of the government's operations against the terrorists are the quality of the intelligence held by the government and the skill of the terrorist leaders in forming an organization that is difficult to penetrate or locate.

In addition to the speed of the government's anti-terrorism campaign, the ability of terrorist groups to replace imprisoned members is also affected by the level of support (including active supporters and passive sympathizers) relative to the size of the terrorist group. Terrorists and their support groups can be thought of as a pyramid. At the top are the active terrorists who plan and carry out the operations. Below them are active supporters who are not officially members of the terrorist group, but offer them financial support, information, or safe houses. At the bottom of the pyramid are the passive sympathizers who do not actively do anything to help the terrorists, but who sympathize with their general goals and methods. When emergency powers begin to arrest and imprison active terrorists, the organization must recruit new members from the supporters and sympathizers. If the terrorists' goals are widely supported, they will find it easy to recruit new members and the supply of potential recruits will be nearly inexhaustible. If the terrorist group lacks widespread support, the state can effectively arrest and imprison terrorists faster than new recruits can fill their positions. Both the size of the terrorist group and its level of support are important, but especially in relation to each other. Even large groups will have difficulty maintaining their operations if they do not have a large number of supporters. Note, however, that size alone may trump other variables for very small groups (on the order of dozens) or very large groups (with thousands of members). The underlying reasons for *why* some groups have larger support bases will not be explained from a theoretical standpoint, although I will describe the sources of support on a case-by-case basis. Some explanations for the level of support will include the ideology and tactics of the terrorist group, as well as how the response of the government is perceived.

MEASURING VARIABLES AND SELECTING CASES

Several methodological issues need to be addressed, including how the independent and dependent variables will be measured, how the cases will be selected, and whether the conclusions generated by the following analysis can be applied to additional cases.

The two dependent variables are the effectiveness and abuses of emergency powers. For measuring the effectiveness of emergency powers, I will use an approach similar to that of Christopher Hewitt, who measures the effectiveness of several counter-terrorism policies by looking at several indicators for the level of terrorist violence (including numbers of attacks and numbers of deaths) and analyzing whether these indicators change after a particular counter-measure is introduced.[48] At their most effective, some measures might eliminate the terrorist group altogether, which is easy to observe, but using the indicators mentioned above will allow me to assess smaller changes in the level of terrorism.

Measuring abuses of emergency powers will consist of observing whether emergency powers are unconstitutionally extended in their duration or scope. For example, if a president legally disbands the legislature for a limited time period but then uses the opportunity of not being constrained by the separation of powers to indefinitely suspend the constitution, this would be an abuse of the time limit of the emergency powers. Likewise, emergency powers used intentionally against civilians known to be innocent would be an abuse of their scope. Determinations of what constitutes an abuse of emergency powers are based on the emergency powers used for each state. In this way, abuse is a relative term rather than an absolute one. For example, while the suspension of habeas corpus is bad for civil liberties in an absolute sense, it would only count as an abuse if the emergency powers do not allow it. Contrasting the cases of Britain and Peru highlights this point. In Britain, the right to habeas corpus was suspended by the emergency powers, while in Peru habeas corpus was still protected. Consequently, when Britain interned suspected terrorists without trial this did not constitute an abuse of the emergency powers, but in Peru, it did. The somewhat perverse result of classifying abuses in relative terms is that states that enact broader emergency powers could do similar, illiberal acts as other states, but these acts would not be classified as abuses of the emergency powers. The alternative would be to use an absolute measure for what counts as an abuse of emergency powers. The abuses then, though, would not be of the emergency powers themselves, but of civil liberties more generally. The problem with this alternative approach is that it would require a theory predicting the exact content of the emergency powers because even properly used emergency powers would be classified as abuses. By using a measure of abuses that is relative to each state's emergency powers instead, I can simplify this process by taking the content of the emergency powers as exogenous.

To compare abuses across cases, though, the measurement of the *severity* of the abuse needs to be measured in an absolute sense. In other words, after I assess whether or not an abuse has occurred (based on the relative content of that country's emergency powers), the severity of that abuse will be assessed on an absolute scale. In practice, an absolute measure for the severity of abuse is possible, in part because certain actions are never allowed by emergency powers. For example, torture and extra-judicial killings (in which the security forces kill a suspect instead of using the judicial system) are always illegal, even during times of emergency. Furthermore, the most dangerous abuse of emergency powers is when they are abused in their duration to such an extent that an authoritarian regime takes power. When this happens, all aspects of the liberal state are cast aside, and the citizens lose all their rights and freedoms. To compare abuses across cases, I can put the severity of abuses on a spectrum on which authoritarian coups count as the worst abuse, followed by extra-judicial killings and torture. Following these abuses, which do not depend on the content of the emergency powers, would be restrictions of due process rights, which count as abuses or not depending on the content of the emergency powers. The illegal, indefinite internment of suspects would be the worst due process abuse because it denies the suspect all other due process rights. The least severe abuses would be unlawful searches and arrests, or extended detention periods, assuming once again that these are not allowed by the emergency powers. If they were permitted, then they would not count as abuses. In addition to looking at the type of abuse, their severity can be assessed by looking at the frequency of abuse. Clearly, the extra-judicial killing of 5,000 suspects is worse than the killing of 500 or just 5 suspects. Of course, even with an absolute measure of the severity of abuse, comparing cases is not completely objective because different cases will have different combinations and degrees of abuse. For instance, some subjective judgments are needed to assess whether one hundred suspects illegally detained for an extra few days is better or worse than the extra-judicial killing of five or ten people. Practically, though, the cases that follow are fairly easy to rank in terms of the severity of abuse (I will explain how I rank each case shortly). To repeat, what counts as an abuse is assessed relative to the content of the emergency powers, while the severity of the abuses is measured on an absolute scale by assessing the type and quantity of abuses that occurred.

The independent variables are relatively easy to measure. The sizes of terrorists groups, as well as their bases of support, are fairly well known and easily accessible.[49] Also, the speed with which the security forces move against the terrorists, the strength of unaffected liberties, and whether power remains separated are readily observable.

In terms of measuring the strength of the institutional constraints, this variable can be measured in several ways.[50] First, do the institutions capable of protecting against abuses of power even exist after the invocation of the emergency powers? Some emergency powers allow the executive to simply disband the legislature, for example. Second, do these institutions have the legal capacity to check abuses of power? Third, are these institutions comprised of individuals who have the desire to use their position to check abuses? If the individuals in the legislature or judiciary lack a strong normative commitment to democracy, for instance, they will be unlikely to use their constitutional and institutional power to constrain the executive or the military. Finally, what is the institution's history as a constraint on abuses of power? In some countries, the legislature and press actively monitor various organizations and activities within the government, while in other countries these institutions lack this traditional role.

In this book, I will use four case studies as plausibility probes to illustrate the validity of my causal claims. For the sake of simplicity, the dependent variables can be thought of as dichotomous: Emergency powers are either effective or ineffective against terrorists, and they are either safe or dangerous to democracy.[51] (The term safe does not mean "cost-free" but is used as the equivalent as the term "not-abused.") Combining these values for the dependent variables yields a two-by-two table (Table 1.1). Where each case is placed within each cell of the table depends on a more nuanced assessment of the consequences of the emergency powers than simply whether they were effective or ineffective or abused or not abused.

The list of possible cases is limited to democratic states that have used emergency powers against terrorist groups.[52] The most notable cases would include Britain, Israel, Italy, Uruguay, Canada, Spain, and Peru.[53] Allow me to briefly describe each case. Great Britain has used emergency powers to fight the Irish Republican Army (IRA) in Northern Ireland since 1973. Liberty and democracy have been maintained, albeit with some unnecessary abuses, while the IRA continues to conduct terrorist operations without hindrance. Canada responded to the kidnappings by the Front de Libération du Québec (FLQ) in 1970 with emergency powers that effectively eliminated the FLQ as a terrorist group with arguably no permanent cost to democracy. Uruguay used emergency powers against the Tupamaros group from 1968 until 1972. When the army took over anti-terrorist operations, they effectively eliminated the Tupamaros; however,

Table 1.1
Democratic States That Have Used Emergency Powers Against Terrorism

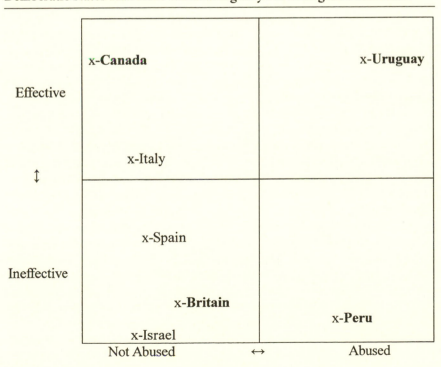

the emergency powers allowed a greater role for the military and allowed it to attack the constitutional pillars of Uruguay, thereby enabling the military to successfully take over power in 1973. In Peru, the Sendero Luminoso began their campaign in 1980, just as Peru was returning to democracy. The government responded by declaring emergency zones across large portions of Peru. The security forces, despite the emergency powers, were unable to counter the terrorists until they captured Abimael Guzmán, the leader of the Senderos, through normal police work (that is, not due to the emergency powers). During the campaign against the Sendero Luminoso, the security forces committed widespread abuses in the emergency zones and supported the coup of Alberto Fujimori in 1992. In Spain, Basque nationalists (Euzakadi ta Askatasuna [ETA]) have used terrorism against the state since 1959 and increased the tempo of their operations after the transition to democracy in 1977. Using special anti-terrorism laws, Spain has been able to reduce the level of violence only slightly, although liberties and democracy have been relatively well protected. Italy used emergency powers, beginning in 1975, to effectively combat terrorism from the Red Brigade and other smaller groups. Assessing the effectiveness of the emergency powers is difficult because much of the success against the Red Brigade was a result of the state encouraging terrorists to confess, turn state's witness, and forswear future terrorist attacks. These measures, while part of the broader anti-terrorism legislation, are not defined as emergency powers because they did not restrict any liberties; however, the additional powers given to the police under the emergency legislation did contribute in some degree to the success of the Italian efforts against the Red Brigade. Liberties and democracy were safeguarded in Italy, and the different pieces of emergency legislation were allowed to lapse in 1982 and 1984. Faced with frequent wars and domestic terrorism, Israel has used emergency powers almost continuously since its independence in 1948. Despite using emergency power, democracy continues to function within Israel. The emergency powers, however, have had little impact in Israel's efforts against terrorism. Each case can be placed on a table with one axis for effectiveness and the other for abuse.

Other countries, such as the United States, France, Japan, Germany, and Belgium, have faced terrorism, but have not chosen to use emergency powers. Still other countries, such as Taiwan and South Korea, have used emergency powers, but for economic or traditional security concerns, and not to fight terrorism.

From the list of democratic countries that have used emergency powers against terrorism, I will look at the cases of Canada, Uruguay, Peru, and Britain primarily because each case has different values of both dependent variables, which allows for explanatory completeness. Some choices were made in deciding which case to choose from each cell, although Peru and Uruguay were the only cases in their respective cells. The case of Britain was chosen from the cell of ineffective/safe because it is the best-documented case of terrorism.[54] Moreover, the prominence of this case within the literature on terrorism would make it odd if this case were not included. The case of Canada was chosen from the safe/effective cell because it is better documented than the Italian case and also because it provides geographic diversity. The four cases examined here cover terrorism in North America, South America, and Europe.

Overall, besides providing geographic variation, the four cases provide variation on the timing and the duration of the terrorist threat. The IRA has existed as a terrorist threat for nearly a hundred years, while the Provisional IRA has operated Northern Ireland for the last 30 years. On the other hand, the Tupamaros and the FLQ arose as Marxist and nationalist groups, respectively, in the early 1960s and were effectively defeated by the early 1970s. Most recently, the Shining Path of Peru was formed in 1970, did not begin its attacks until 1980, and was only defeated in the early 1990s after twelve years of probably the most deadly and costly terrorist campaign ever.[55]

All four cases that I have selected are cases of democratic states using emergency powers, thereby raising the potential for selection bias. The concern would be that the emergency powers are more likely to be effective or safe because the states would not use them if they thought they would be dangerous or ineffective. In other words, states are not naïve—they respond to terrorism aware of the likely costs and benefits of their policies. Table 1.1, however, shows that there is much more variation than states would expect. Nevertheless, it is possible that there are some cases where countries have not used emergency powers because they feared that they would be too costly. Several countries, such as the United States, France, and Japan, have not (so far) resorted to using emergency powers against terrorism. Consequently, if states do not use emergency powers because of the likely consequences, there may be some problems of selection bias in the cases that are available. I am, however, willing to tolerate this bias because I am concerned with the consequences of emergency powers used to fight terrorism and not in trying to determine under what conditions states use emergency powers to fight terrorism. I do acknowledge that the variation in the consequences of emergency powers might be skewed because states might not use them unless beneficial results are expected; however, I am not making arguments about the overall pattern of distribution for the consequences of emergency powers. Instead, the four cases are designed to validate the logic of my arguments for when emergency powers have particular sets of consequences.

The lessons learned from these cases can be generalized to other cases. Of course, not every country faces the same dangers from terrorism, nor does each share a common political system through which to respond to terrorism. Nevertheless, many countries share basic democratic institutions and values, allowing them to be compared in fruitful ways.[56] The conclusions of this study can be applied to cases like the United States or even Russia, in which nearly 300 people were killed in four terrorist attacks in September 1999. In addition to these hypothetical cases, the arguments developed in this study are also applicable to the other countries from the universe of cases that are not analyzed here.

The remainder of this book will be organized in the following manner. Chapter 2 develops the theoretical arguments in more detail. I will discuss the threat that terrorism poses to the state and why the state might choose to use emergency powers to counter this threat. Following this, I will present the logic for why emergency powers used quickly against terrorist groups with low levels of support are the most likely to be effective. Turning to the other set of consequences, the literature on emergency powers will be reviewed, followed by a discussion of constitutionalist theory. From these literatures, I will develop an argument on the abuses of emergency powers used against terrorism. I will argue that institutional constraints, such as the separation of powers and a free press, are critical in protecting democracy from abuses of emergency powers.

Chapter 3 explores Britain's use of emergency powers to combat IRA terrorism beginning in the early 1970s. The British Parliament passed the Northern Ireland Act in 1973 and the Prevention of Terrorism Act in 1974, and has renewed and modified these measures annually. The British government used widespread internment without trial, denied suspected terrorists the right to be judged by a jury of their peers, and allowed the police to search and arrest suspects without warrants. These measures were largely ineffective, as indicated by the number of terrorist bombings and shootings that have continued at essentially a constant tempo since 1972. The reason that the emergency powers were ineffective is that they did not enable the security forces to arrest terrorists faster than they could be replaced by new recruits. At times, the security forces moved quickly to arrest large numbers of people, but these arrests were based on poor intelligence and failed to hinder IRA operations. In addition, the IRA enjoyed widespread support from most of the Catholic population of Northern Ireland. This resulted in a constant supply of new recruits to the IRA, particularly after perceived abuses by the security forces. The emergency powers were used relatively safely in Britain, although some abuses did occur. Many innocent people were interned in the early 1970s; prisoners frequently reported that they were tortured in prison, and several people were killed when the government allegedly adopted a shoot-to-kill policy in the 1980s. Despite these abuses, Britain has remained a democratic state committed to the rule of law, even in Northern Ireland. These abuses were limited because of the constitutional constraints in Britain. The emergency powers did not affect the separation of powers or curtail the right to free speech (for the most part). Consequently, the press and Parliament could monitor potential abuses and act accordingly. In fact, after each alleged abuse, Parliament revised the emergency powers to protect citizens from further abuses. In sum, Britain's use of emergency powers was safe, but ineffective.

Chapter 4 discusses Uruguay's use of emergency powers to deal with the threat from the Tupamaros. Emergency powers were invoked almost continuously from 1968 until 1973. The emergency powers were initially ineffective because the Tupamaros enjoyed widespread support and the police failed to move quickly in arresting large numbers of suspected terrorists. In 1972, however, both of these factors changed when the army moved rapidly in arresting thousands of suspected Tupamaros and when the Tupamaros lost much of their support after a change in their tactics. By the end of 1972, the Tupamaros were completely eliminated as a terrorist organization. The effectiveness of the emergency powers was matched, however, by their abuse. Allegations of torture were commonplace and the security forces also arrested politicians in opposition to the government. Most importantly, the president and military used the emergency powers to consolidate their power before launching a coup in 1973. These abuses occurred for several reasons. Emergency powers gave the military complete autonomy in fighting the terrorism. Also, the government's attacks on political opponents under the pretense of fighting terrorism undermined the ability of the legislature to act independently. Lastly, the emergency powers allowed the government to censor and even shut down media outlets that published anything mentioning the Tupamaros or criticized the government. Overall, emergency powers were effective in Uruguay, but were abused and led to a military dictatorship.

Chapter 5 examines Canada's use of emergency powers in October 1970 in response to the kidnapping crisis initiated by the FLQ. The FLQ had existed since 1963, but had been responsible for only periodic bombings that caused few deaths. That changed when the FLQ kidnapped James Cross and Pierre Laporte in October 1970. Facing what they believed to be a serious threat to the security of Canada, the government responded by invoking the War Measures Act. These emergency powers did not end the crisis (the kidnappers were located through normal police work), but they were effective in eliminating the FLQ as a terrorist group. The government acted quickly to arrest hundreds of suspected terrorists in the first few hours after the emergency powers were declared. This kept the FLQ from escalating the crisis through additional kidnappings. Furthermore, the emergency powers were nearly universally supported in Canada, and undermined the support for the FLQ. Finally, the emergency powers allowed the government to bring in the armed forces to provide physical security against future attacks, thus allowing the police to focus their resources on looking for the kidnappers. The War Measures Act was also employed with practically no abuses. Only a few hundred innocent citizens were detained after the early arrests, but they were quickly released. Democracy was maintained and all liberties were restored six months after the crisis. The emergency powers were used safely because they did not infringe on the powers of Parliament or the ability of the press to monitor potential abuses. Parliament voted on the War Measures Act immediately after they were invoked, approving them by an overwhelming margin. In addition, the use of emergency powers was widely debated and monitored throughout the media. In sum, Canada is a case where emergency powers were used safely and effectively.

Chapter 6 focuses on the use of emergency powers by Peru against the Sendero Luminoso (Shining Path). The Senderos launched their first operation in 1980, and thereafter proceeded to conduct one of the most deadly and costliest terrorist campaigns in history. Between 1980 and 1992, approximately 30,000 Peruvians were killed in the crossfire between the terrorists and security forces. Beginning in 1982, several provinces of Peru were placed under a state of emergency, which allowed the army to act without worrying about civil liberties. Despite the use of emergency powers, the Sendero Luminoso continued its terrorist campaign in the countryside and stepped up the campaign in Lima. By 1992, the state was close to collapse, with frequent power and water shortages, daily bombings in Lima, and effective terrorist control of the countryside. In September 1992, however, the leader of the Senderos, Abimael Guzmán, was captured by the police and sentenced to life in prison. Almost immediately thereafter, the Shining Path began to disintegrate and the state was able to reassert its authority. The emergency powers did not contribute to the success against the terrorists because the Senderos were adept at developing widespread support among the peasants and workers of Lima. Moreover, the emergency powers were widely abused. The security forces frequently killed innocent citizens and basic liberties were completely violated in areas that were declared states of emergency. In addition, the military supported the coup of Alberto Fujimori in April 1992. These abuses occurred because the normal institutional constraints against abuses of power had been eroded by the state of emergency. In provinces under emergency powers, there was strict press censorship and the provinces were administered by the security forces. With no safeguards capable of monitoring or overseeing the armed forces, the military used its power to conduct the anti-terrorism campaign as it saw fit, instead of according to the constraints of the law. Peru, therefore, is the case with the worst possible consequences; emergency powers were ineffective and dangerous.

Chapter 7 concludes by returning to the assumption that emergency powers lead to a difficult tradeoff. Based on the four case studies, I will offer policy guidelines for when states should use emergency powers, specifically when they should expect them to be effective and when they might be abused. I will argue that the assumed tradeoff rarely occurs; emergency powers may be used effectively and safely given the right conditions, but may also be ineffective and be abused. I will then offer an analysis of the possible use of emergency powers in the United States given the events of September 11, 2001.

NOTES

1. Philip Heymann, *Terrorism and America: A Commonsense Strategy for a Democratic Society* (Cambridge, MA: MIT Press, 1998), xiii.

2. James X. Dempsey and David Cole, *Terrorism and the Constitution: Sacrificing Civil Liberties in the Name of National Security* (Los Angeles: First Amendment Foundation, 1999), 106. Dempsey and Cole argue that the Oklahoma City and World Trade

Center bombings "overwhelmed all rational discussion, and the law was enacted as an effort to do something in response to these two crimes."

3. Dempsey and Cole, *Terrorism and the Constitution*, 116.

4. Dempsey and Cole, *Terrorism and the Constitution*, 117.

5. See Richard A. Falkenrath, Robert D. Newman, and Bradley Thayer, *America's Achilles Heel: Nuclear, Biological, and Chemical Terrorism and Covert Attack* (Cambridge, MA: MIT Press, 1998), for more on the threat of terrorists using weapons of mass destruction.

6. Quoted in Michael Linfield, *Freedom under Fire: U.S. Civil Liberties in Times of War* (Boston: South End Press, 1990), 1.

7. See Linfield, *Freedom under Fire*.

8. Paul Wilkinson, *Terrorism versus Democracy: The Liberal State Response* (London: Frank Cass Publishers, 2000), 115 points out that "most democratic states which have experienced prolonged and lethal terrorist campaigns of any scale within their borders have at some stage introduced special anti-terrorist measures aimed at strengthening the normal law in order to deal with a grave terrorist emergency."

9. Paul Wilkinson, "Maintaining the Democratic Process and Public Support," in *The Future of Political Violence: Destabilization, Disorder and Terrorism*, ed. Richard Clutterbuck (New York: St. Martin's Press, 1986), 177.

10. I am not using the term "costs" to refer to the monetary or other costs associated with emergency powers. I am concerned solely with how emergency powers undermine liberty and democracy.

11. Heymann, *Terrorism and America*, 113.

12. Wilkinson, *Terrorism versus Democracy*, 115.

13. Some leaders, though, may use emergency powers with the intention of abusing them for their own personal gain.

14. See Frederick Mundell Watkins, *The Failure of Constitutional Emergency Powers under the German Republic* (Cambridge, MA: Harvard University Press, 1939); Clinton L. Rossiter, *Constitutional Dictatorship: Crisis Government in the Modern Democracies* (Princeton: Princeton University Press, 1948); and Carl Friedrich, *Constitutional Government and Democracy* (Boston: Ginn and Company, 1946) as examples. Watkins looks at three aspects of emergency powers that determine whether they will be abused, while Friedrich examines four, and Rossiter identifies eleven.

15. Christopher Hewitt, *Consequences of Political Violence* (Aldershot, England: Dartmouth Publishing Company, 1993), 123 posits that "the most severe disruptions are produced not by political violence itself but by the governments' response to it."

16. The tradeoff of emergency powers is one where their implementation leads to costs and benefits that a state must weigh against each other. The tradeoff is not one where the two sets of consequences are causally connected. It is not the case that emergency powers must always be abused and effective, or not abused and safe, for example.

17. Ron Haggart and Aubrey Golden, *Rumours of War* (Toronto: new press, 1971), 213 put it succinctly: "the price for achieving efficiency is abuse."

18. Paul Wilkinson, *Terrorism and the Liberal State* (London: Macmillan Press 1977), 159–160.

19. Dermont P. J. Walsh, "Arrest and Interrogation," in *Justice under Fire: The Abuse of Civil Liberties in Northern Ireland,* ed. Anthony Jennings (London: Pluto Press, 1990), 27.

20. J. C. Garnett, "Emergency Powers in Northern Ireland," in *Coping with Crises: How Governments Deal with Emergencies,* ed. Shao-chuan Leng (Lanham, MD: University Press of America, 1990), 55.

21. Robin Evelegh, *Peace-Keeping in a Democratic Society: The Lessons of Northern Ireland* (Montreal: McGill-Queen's University Press, 1978), 60.

22. David Bonner, "United Kingdom: The United Kingdom Response to Terrorism," in *Western Responses to Terrorism,* ed. Alex Schmid and Ronald Crelinsten (London: Frank Cass Publishers, 1993), 178.

23. George Shultz, "The Challenge to the Democracies," in *Terrorism: How the West Can Win,* ed. Benjamin Netanyahu (New York: Farrar, Straus, Giroux, 1986), 19.

24. Irving Louis Horowitz, "The Routinization of Terrorism and Its Unanticipated Consequences," in *Terrorism, Legitimacy, and Power: The Consequences of Political Violence,* ed. Martha Crenshaw (Middletown, CT: Wesleyan University Press, 1983), 51.

25. Grant Wardlaw, *Political Terrorism: Theory, Tactics, and Counter-measures* (Cambridge: Cambridge University Press, 1989), 69.

26. Falkenrath, Newman, and Thayer, *America's Achilles Heel,* 8.

27. Heymann, *Terrorism and America,* 80 and 156.

28. Wilkinson, *Terrorism and the Liberal State,* 152 and 156; and Ken Robertson, "Intelligence, Terrorism, and Civil Liberties," in *Contemporary Research on Terrorism,* ed. Paul Wilkinson and Alasdair Stewart (Aberdeen: Aberdeen University Press, 1987), 561 argue that there is need for a balance between the protection of civil liberties and the protection of the political entity itself.

29. Benjamin Netanyahu, *Fighting Terrorism: How Democracies Can Defeat Domestic and International Terrorists* (New York: Noonday Press, 1995), 29.

30. This issue applies only to democracies because authoritarian states are not concerned with protecting liberties. Furthermore, emergency powers do not exist in an authoritarian state because the state can act as it wishes without having to declare an emergency as justification.

31. Rossiter also is concerned with both the effectiveness and dangers of emergency powers. He describes the central question as "In short, how are they [democracies] to maximize the efficiency and minimize the dangers of constitutional dictatorship. See Rossiter, *Constitutional Dictatorship,* 297.

32. This is not a completely thorough policy analysis because I do not examine *all* costs and benefits from emergency powers, but just specifically whether they are dangerous for liberty and democracy and whether they are effective against terrorism.

33. This definition assumes a democratic, constitutional state in which the powers of government are limited by law (as in the United States) or by custom (such as in Great Britain). In authoritarian regimes, there is no need for the government to seize greater powers in times of emergency. Brian Loveman, *The Constitution of Tyranny: Regimes of Exception in Spanish America* (Pittsburgh: Pittsburgh University Press, 1993), 19 points out that the notion of emergency powers is "irrelevant in an absolute monarchy, ... or totalitarian regime."

34. Watkins, *The Failure of Constitutional Emergency Powers*, 3.

35. Loveman, *The Constitution of Tyranny*, 12–13. Loveman goes further in observing that the implementation of what he calls "regimes of exception" might include the suspension of specific rights, the declaration of a state of siege or state of war, blanket suspension of the constitution, the delegation of authority to an actor or body within the government, or the declaration of martial law.

36. Rossiter, *Constitutional Dictatorship*, 5.

37. For example, is a state permanently infringed on the right of privacy by allowing the police to monitor phone conversations without a warrant, this would be a loss of individual liberty but not emergency powers unless this power were only temporary.

38. Rossiter, *Constitutional Dictatorship*.

39. Watkins, *The Failure of Constitutional Emergency Powers*.

40. Cindy C. Combs, *Terrorism in the Twenty-First Century* (Upper Saddle River, NJ: Prentice Hall, 1997), 188.

41. Some person, group, or institution might take advantage of the emergency powers to lawfully extend their use after the emergency powers remove many of the constraints on abuses of power. This would still be classified as an abuse of the emergency powers because it would violate the intention of the initial invocation of the emergency powers as temporary provisions.

42. For the most part, abuses of duration are more serious than abuses of scope because the latter undermines individual liberties while the former undermines democracy as well as all liberties. The case of Peru, however, will show that abuses in scope can be quite damaging as well, considering the thousands of people unlawfully killed by the Peruvian security forces.

43. Martha Crenshaw, "Introduction: Reflection on the Effects of Terrorism," in *Terrorism, Legitimacy, and Power: The Consequences of Political Violence*, ed. Martha Crenshaw (Middletown, CT: Wesleyan University Press, 1983), 14.

44. David Charters, ed., *The Deadly Sin of Terrorism: Its Effect of Democracy and Civil Liberties in Six Countries* (Westport, CT: Greenwood Press, 1994).

45. Peter Janke, ed., *Terrorism and Democracy: Some Contemporary Cases* (New York: St. Martin's Press, 1992). Other books dealing with how different states respond to terrorism and other emergencies include Alex P. Schmid and Ronald Crelinsten, eds., *Western Responses to Terrorism* (London: Frank Cass Publishers, 1993); Shao-chuan Leng, ed., *Coping with Crises: How Governments Deal with Emergencies* (Lanham, MD: University Press of America, 1990); and Juliet Lodge, ed., *The Threat of Terrorism* (Boulder, CO: Westview Press, 1988).

46. See G. Davidson Smith, *Combating Terrorism* (London: Routledge, 1990); Neil C. Livingstone, *The War against Terrorism* (Lexington, MA: Lexington Books, 1982); and John B. Wolf, *Fear of Fear: A Survey of Terrorist Operations and Controls in Open Societies* (New York: Plenum Press, 1981).

47. See chapters 4 and 5 on Uruguay and Canada.

48. Christopher Hewitt, *The Effectiveness of Anti-Terrorist Policies* (Lanham, MD: University Press of America, 1984). Other measurers of effectiveness might include the number of terrorists arrested or imprisoned. The police frequently use these indicators to assess their effectiveness. See Peter Taylor, *Beating the Terrorists: Interrogation in*

Omagh, Gough, and Castlereagh (New York: Penguin Books, 1980), 80; and Paul Wilkinson, "British Policy on Terrorism: An Assessment," in *The Threat of Terrorism*, ed. Juliet Lodge (Boulder, CO: Westview Press, 1988), 37 for examples of police forces touting increases in terrorists arrested, houses searched, and weapons confiscated as evidence of their success. In the end, however, the numbers of arrests and convictions do not matter much if terrorist violence continues. For this reason, I look at the level of violence and not the number of arrests.

49. See, for example, Schmid, et al., *Political Terrorism: A New Guide to Actors, Authors, Concepts, Data Bases, Theories, and Literature* (Amsterdam: North-Holland Publishing Company, 1988).

50. For scholars that monitor the strength of institutional constraints on power and rank the political freedom of different countries, see the Polity 98 Database; Mike Alvarez et al., "Classifying Political Regimes," *Studies in Comparative International Development* 31, no. 2 (summer 1996); and Kenneth Bollen, "Issues in the Comparative Measurement of Political Democracy," *American Sociological Review* 45 (1980).

51. Clearly, this simplification obscures the variation along a continuum for both dependent variables.

52. Only democratic states are in the universe of cases because totalitarian states simply would not face the tradeoff with which this paper is concerned.

53. For good summaries of how democratic states have responded to terrorism, see Charters, *Deadly Sin of Terrorism*, with chapters on Britain, Germany, Italy, France, the United States, and Israel; Schmid and Crelinsten, *Western Responses to Terrorism*, with chapters on the Netherlands, Spain, France, Germany, Italy, and Britain; Peter Janke, *Terrorism and Democracy*, with chapters on Canada, Germany, Italy, and Japan; Leng, *Coping with Crises*, with chapters on Israel, Northern Ireland, Italy, Korea, and Taiwan; and Lodge, *The Threat of Terrorism*, with chapters on Britain, Germany, Italy, Spain, the Netherlands, Belgium, and France.

54. By some estimates, the literature on terrorism in Northern Ireland numbered 7,000 items by 1989. See Alan O'Day, ed., *Terrorism's Laboratory: The Case of Northern Ireland* (Aldershot, England: Dartmouth Publishing Company, 1995), 1.

55. Approximately 30,000 deaths were associated with the Sendero Luminoso (Shining Path) from 1980 to 1992. For comparison, in Ireland from 1970 to 1981, a little over 2,000 casualties were related to terrorism. From Alfred McLung Lee, *Terrorism in Northern Ireland* (Bayside, NY: General Hall, 1983), 170; and David Scott Palmer, ed., *The Shining Path of Peru* (New York: St. Martin's Press, 1994).

56. See Rossiter, *Constitutional Dictatorship*; Leng, *Coping with Crises*; Combs, *Terrorism in the Twenty-First Century*; and Charters, *Deadly Sin of Terrorism* as examples of other comparative case studies.

Chapter 2

Explaining the Consequences of Emergency Powers

This book will ask two questions about the consequences of using emergency powers to fight terrorism: When are emergency powers effective, and when are they abused? I will offer one theory for each question, combining both arguments to yield a more complete picture on the consequences and possible trade-off of using emergency powers.

EFFECTIVE EMERGENCY POWERS

Answering the question of when are emergency powers effective requires exploring some preliminary issues, including: a definition of terrorism; the challenge terrorism poses for the state (and democracies in particular); the methods the state uses to combat terrorism; and the expected benefits of using emergency powers. After discussing these issues, I will present my explanation for when emergency powers are effective.

Defining terrorism is no simple task. Practically every book on terrorism begins with a definition of terrorism, with every author having a unique definition.[1] Terrorism is hard to define because it is a value-loaded term carrying with it political, legal, moral, and practical implications, connotation, and consequences. The phrase, "One man's freedom fighter is another man's terrorist" captures the ambiguity, politicization, moral judgment, and high stakes involved in defining terrorism. For example, the Jewish groups that fought the British in Palestine were seen as terrorists by the British, but as heroic freedom fighters to Zionist sympathizers. A definition of terrorism, therefore, must cut through all this ambiguity to establish clear criteria that can be applied across locations and time.

Instead of falling into this definitional morass, I will use a definition that is fairly commonsensical and reflective of what we commonly call terrorism. I define terrorism as the threat or use of violence to spread fear to lead to political change.[2] This definition allows us to differentiate terrorism from other types of violence, such as guerrilla movements, inter-state war, and organized crime. War between states is the use of violence for political goals,[3] but is different from terrorism because states use violence according to a military logic, not primarily to cause fear (although states have occasionally used fear as a weapon in war). Organized crime syndicates share many of the attributes of terrorists (small, secretive groups using violence and intimidation), but their aims are to make money and not to change the policies of the government.[4]

Guerrilla groups are the most similar to terrorists, and the two are often used synonymously in press reports, academic writing, and government documents. Guerrillas use violence or the threat of violence to cause a change in policy. In this respect, guerrilla violence is similar to interstate war. The difference between war and guerrilla conflict is that guerrillas operate on a smaller scale than states, and consequently use different tactics. Whereas states attack other states' deployed military forces, guerrilla groups use ambushes, sniper attacks, sabotage, and bombings to target their enemy's supply lines, arms depots, or leadership bunkers. A common mischaracterization is that guerrilla groups target military forces, while terrorists target civilians. This distinction, however, is misleading. In any armed conflict, distinctions between military and civilian targets are blurred. For the terrorist or guerrilla, the factories that supply the state with weapons, the civilian leadership that leads the war effort, and civilians that support the state's policies are all legitimate military targets. Even in interstate war, countries target one another's factories and leadership bunkers; therefore, the fact that a military target was attacked gives no information as to whether it was attacked by terrorists or guerrillas. The real difference between terrorists and guerrillas is the use of fear, or terror, to achieve political change. Guerrilla attacks are based on a military logic, whereas terrorist attacks are based on psychology. Guerrillas try to defeat the enemy using military means, while terrorists try to force the government to change its policies out of fear.

Problems with these definitions arise when groups could easily be classified as both guerrillas and terrorists. For example, the Provisional IRA can claim it is a guerrilla group because it frequently fought British and Protestant military, paramilitary, and police forces that they viewed as occupiers of Northern Ireland in street battles typical of urban warfare. The IRA attacks on off-duty security forces and bombings of hotels and pubs, however, were all designed to terrorize the security forces and the Protestant civilian population. The solution to this definitional problem is to avoid labeling a group at the exclusion of other definitions. In other words, the IRA is a group that engages in *both* terrorist and guerrilla attacks, and so should be labeled as both a terrorist group and guerrilla movement. Using only one label would fail to capture much of the complexity of the IRA and other groups.

The threat that terrorism poses to a state has usually been exaggerated and misunderstood. Most people in government, academia, and the press focus on the physical damage caused by terrorism. The common indices of terrorism are the number of people killed and wounded, and the costs of repairing damage caused by the attack. Historically, though, terrorist attacks have caused relatively little damage. For example, a former head of Israel intelligence points out that in 1980, 28 Israelis were killed by terrorists, while about 700 Israelis were killed in road accidents during the same period.[5] Similarly, more people die of road accidents each year in Northern Ireland than from terrorism.[6] On the other hand, there are some notable exceptions where terrorism has caused a great deal of damage. Obviously, the attack on the World Trade Center and the Pentagon on September 11, 2001, was one of the bloodiest days in United States history. Likewise, terrorists might inflict incredible damage if they acquire and successfully use weapons of mass destruction. Also, some groups, such as Peru's Sendero Luminoso, have been tremendously destructive. They were responsible for 30,000 deaths in twelve years and caused the economic loss of billions of dollars.[7]

For the most part though, looking at the numbers of deaths or costs of repairs misses the uniqueness of terrorism. Terrorists use violence not to defeat the enemy, but to create a climate of fear that is out of proportion to the actual damage caused by terrorist attacks. The state is then forced to respond and the response itself may be the greatest danger caused by terrorism.

Calibrating an appropriate response is not an easy task for the government of a state. On one hand, if the state does not respond vigorously enough, the legitimacy and credibility of the government may be called into question. Citizens will not feel safe and can lose faith in the ability of the government to protect them from random attacks.[8] Also, choosing to ignore the threat from terrorism might encourage the terrorists. Terrorist groups are often poorly organized or trained in their early years; a quick and decisive initial response might be the most effective way of countering terrorism. For example, the Peruvian government mostly ignored the dangers from the Sendero Luminoso in the early 1980s. The Senderos used this window of opportunity to strengthen their organization through better training and recruitment. When the government of Peru finally acted, the Senderos were a much larger and more capable opponent than they had been a couple years earlier.[9] On the other hand, a state may over-react to a terrorist group. Severe measures may seem illegitimate to terrorist sympathizers, and may actually increase support for the terrorist group. Furthermore, as this analysis will show, states that use emergency powers run the risk of undermining democracy.[10] The second half of this chapter explores the dangers of over-reaction, specifically the danger that emergency powers will be abused.

When a state is faced with a terrorist threat, there are a variety of counter-measures that may be implemented. States might impose stricter border controls, increase security around key targets, improve cooperation with other states, increase coordination among domestic agencies, control media coverage, focus intelligence assets on terrorist groups, lengthen mandatory sentences for terrorist offenses, or initiate political and economic reforms as demanded by the terrorists, to name a few. None of these measures are controversial, however, in the way that emergency powers are. Only emergency powers promise the benefits of defeating terrorism while also imposing costs on a democratic society. As articulated in Chapter 1, even if they are used as intended, emergency powers entail temporary curtailments of individual liberties. At worst, the emergency powers can lead to the end of democracy. It is for these reasons that this countermeasure deservedly receives so much attention.

Given the dangers of emergency powers (which will be discussed later in this chapter), what do governments hope to gain by using emergency powers? Why are emergency powers thought to be necessary to effectively combat terrorism? States often feel pressured to use emergency powers to fight terrorism because doing so is a clear and strong countermeasure that looks good in the eyes of a public that demands that the government "do something" against the terrorists.

Emergency powers, however, are more than just cosmetic measures to assuage public fears; they also are intended to be effective against the terrorists. Emergency powers can increase the power of the state along many dimensions. They can suspend normal due process laws, allowing the police to conduct searches without warrant, arrest citizens without charge, hold them in jail without bringing them to trial (denying them the right of habeas corpus), and use abusive interrogation methods. Emergency powers may also limit other liberties, such as the right to free speech or assembly (by establishing curfews). Finally, emergency powers may suspend the political separation of powers in which power is formally and institutionally separated between different branches of government.

Each dimension of emergency powers is expected to contribute to the anti-terrorism effort. Relaxing or modifying due process laws, for example, is designed to improve the ability of the police and judicial system in arresting and convicting suspected terrorists. To facilitate the arrest of suspected terrorists, emergency powers can allow the police to conduct searches without a warrant or require less evidence to obtain a warrant from a judge. This allows the police to search for evidence unconstrained by any limits. In addition, police often are allowed to arrest suspects without charging them with a crime, which lets the police remove any suspect from the population and enables them to interrogate suspects while they are held in prison to gain information or a confession. Convicting terrorists in a court of law is often difficult under normal legal situations because witnesses are intimidated by testifying against the terrorists. To counter this, emergency powers relax the evidence requirements in a trial, allowing, for example, uncorroborated confessions of other terrorists as sufficient evidence to convict a suspect. Emergency powers can eliminate trials by jury if states fear that sympathetic juries in terrorist trials would return perverse verdicts. In addition, if convictions are unlikely, emergency powers might overturn the right of habeas corpus and allow the police to detain a suspect without bringing him to trial. Coupled with the power to arrest a citizen without bringing charges, the ability to indefinitely detain a suspect essentially allows the police to imprison any citizen they want without the suspect having any recourse to his rights to due process.

Restrictions on other individual liberties are frequently part of emergency legislation because they also are expected to assist the state in its fight against terrorism. By suspending the right to free speech, for example, the state hopes to control the public's discussion over terrorism and the government's response. Without free speech or a free press, criticism of the government can be eliminated. Many scholars argue that the attention paid to terrorism by the media is counterproductive because terrorists often plan their operation to gain as much publicity as possible. If the media, whether voluntarily or because of emergency powers, does not cover the terrorist attacks, the terrorists will not receive the attention they need if they are to win the sympathy and support of the general population.

The suspension of the separation of powers is also thought to be helpful in fighting terrorism. In a constitutional democracy, the separation of powers makes the process of government less efficient, at least compared to authoritarian systems. When power is separated, legislation is passed after a lengthy process of negotiation and consensus building. In times of emergency, this process may become too unwieldy if the state is to respond quickly and effectively. Consequently, emergency powers often allow the executive branch to rule by decree, thereby bypassing the legislature. Also, emergency powers sometimes allow the executive to disband the legislature until new elections are held.

Taken together, all of these aspects of emergency powers have one goal in common: to end or diminish the threat of terrorism. The suspension of liberties, due process rights, and the separation of powers are all designed to assist the state in imprisoning terrorists while undermining support for terrorism. Emergency powers, like all countermeasures, however, are empirically not always effective at fighting terrorism, which leads to one of the questions that is central to this book: When are emergency powers effective? The existing literature does not offer any clear logic for when emergency powers are effective.[11] In fact, the conventional wisdom in the literature on terrorism is simply that states should adopt a variety of countermeasures when fighting terrorism.[12] They assume that all these policies will work and should be pursued at all times. The fact that variation exists in the effectiveness of emergency powers, however, is sufficient evidence to indicate that the optimism of the conventional wisdom is misplaced.

Why are countermeasures not always effective? In many ways, the ineffectiveness of the state in fighting terrorism is surprising. After all, in relation to a terrorist group, the state has an overwhelming preponderance of resources. Whereas terrorist groups number in the hundreds or sometimes thousands of members, even small states control security forces (including police, internal troops, and regular army personnel) that number in the hundreds of thousands, if not millions. Also, while terrorist groups have to steal money, guns, and explosives, the state can devote millions or billions of dollars towards fighting terrorism. In addition, the state has access to the best technology, including surveillance equipment and computer databases. Finally, the state has the advantage of being on the right side of the law.[13] Because terrorism is illegal, the terrorists must constantly be in hiding from the security forces.

Despite these advantages, states often have great difficulty in dealing with terrorism because terrorist groups have several advantages as well. The small size of terrorist groups makes it hard for the state to infiltrate or gather information on the terrorists. Also, terrorist groups, because they are small, are easy to form. It takes only a few like-minded individuals to come together and bomb some target in the name of a cause for a new terrorist group to be formed. Additionally, terrorist organizations are usually organized with secrecy as a paramount concern. Terrorists are typically organized into small cells consisting of a few individuals and each individual uses a pseudonym to keep his or her identity hidden from the other members. The leader of the cell is the only one who is in contact with any other terrorists, and usually only with his or her direct superior. Consequently, a captured terrorist will be unable to give the police any information on the identities of anyone else in the terrorist organization. Also, terrorists are usually highly motivated by an ideology (religion, nationalism, and so on) that encourages them to fight and die for a cause. In contrast, the personnel of the security forces often come from lower-class backgrounds and join the police or the army, less for any ideological reason but rather as a way out of their socioeconomic status. Terrorists enjoy the advantage of only having to cause a small amount of damage to gain the attention of the state and possibly cause political change. Lastly, terrorists are not encumbered by the constraints of the law. They can bomb and assassinate as they see fit without constraints. The security forces, on the other hand, are required to fight the terrorists while fully respecting and following the law.

Given these different strengths and weakness of both the terrorists and the state, it is not too surprising that countermeasures are not always effective. What frequently occurs is a stalemate between the state and the terrorists, where the terrorists are incapable of conducting more than periodic bombings or assassinations, while the state is incapable of eliminating the terrorist group altogether. The state spends vast resources against terrorism, which results in frequent arrests of individual terrorists, yet the terrorist organization remains intact.

Emergency powers are designed to break this stalemate by providing the security forces and the judicial system greater powers to arrest and imprison terrorists. The emergency powers are designed to exploit a potential weakness of the terrorist organization: the need to recruit new members. Recruiting and training new members takes time. New members must be identified and indoctrinated into the group's ideology, and trained to operate according to specific methods.[14] All of this takes a matter of several weeks to several months, during which the state can continue to capture and arrest known terrorists with the aid of the emergency powers. Emergency powers will be successful against terrorist groups when they can imprison and remove the terrorists from society faster than they can be replaced. Emergency powers will be ineffective if the terrorists can easily replace captured or imprisoned members of the organization with new recruits. Two factors influence the effectiveness of the emergency powers: the size of the support network of the terrorists, and the speed with which the emergency powers are implemented.

Emergency powers will be more likely to be ineffective if a terrorist group has a large base of supporters and sympathizers, relative to the size of the active terrorist group. The size of the group, as a variable by itself, is particularly salient when the group is very small, such as a few individuals, or very large, such as several or even tens of thousands. When a terrorist group numbers only a few single or dozen individuals, the terrorist group itself is limited in its capabilities. It lacks the organizational robustness to compensate when dealt a severe blow by the state. Imprisoning ten members of a group that numbers two dozen is more damaging than if 100 terrorists were arrested out of group of 250 terrorists. With a larger group, even with arrests of this scale, there will still be numerous active cells remaining, as well as a core of individuals from the leadership of the group. In a smaller group, though, a similar ratio of arrests might disrupt every cell in the organization and is more likely, just from chance, of arresting the core leadership group. In addition, members in smaller groups are more likely to know everyone in the organization. As a result, a few arrests can lead the police to the entire terrorist network. In Canada, for example, the FLQ only numbered a few dozen terrorists. When the police tracked down the identity of a few of the FLQ kidnappers, they were able to find the entire active FLQ, which only consisted of two cells.

When terrorist groups are very large, numbering in the tens of thousands of members spread out throughout a country, emergency powers are unlikely to be effective. In these instances, the capabilities of most states' security forces will be tested. These large terrorist groups also frequently conduct more traditional insurgency or guerrilla campaigns in addition to terrorism. The Sendero Luminoso in Peru, for example, numbered in the tens of thousands of members and conducted operations across most of Peru. With such a large membership, the organization was capable of surviving the arrests and imprisonment of thousands of its members.

In most cases, though, the size of the terrorist organization does not affect the success of the state. In general, the state enjoys a preponderance of power against most terrorist groups, which typically number in the few hundred to few thousand. With the large numbers of security personnel, vast amounts of money and technology to spend against terrorism, ample room in prisons and courts, and the increased powers derived from the emergency legislation, states should be equally effective (or ineffective) against various sized terrorist groups.

For most terrorist groups, then, the key variable to their continued existence in the face of state pressure is the ability to replace captured members with new recruits. For these groups, the level of support for the terrorists determines the availability of new recruits. The level of support should be understood as the ratio of support relative to the size of the active terrorist group. For example, a group with 100 active members and 500 supporters has a lower level of support than a group with 10 members and 100 supporters, in spite of the differences in size of the active group. In understanding the relationship between the size of the terrorist group and its level of support, it is useful to think of a terrorist group as a pyramid or iceberg, with the active terrorists at the point, the supporters below them, and a large number of sympathizers at the base or below the surface of the water. Active terrorists are those who are members of the terrorist organization and involved in the terrorist activity—they are the bombers, shooters, drivers, commanders, recruiters, and so forth. The supporters are the people who help the terrorists by providing safe homes or information on targets or other forms of passive support. Sympathizers are people who are not involved in any way with the terrorists, but agree with their goals and methods.[15]

If the state tries to crack down on a terrorist group, the terrorists will attempt to replace the arrested members with new recruits. If the terrorist group has a large support base, emergency powers are likely to be seen by those that support and sympathize with the terrorists as unnecessary and threatening. As a result, many passive supporters will look to take a more active role, and many of the sympathizers will look to join the terrorist cause to right the wrongs that they perceive. For example, Martha Crenshaw claims that the large support network for the ETA gave it the "stable source of recruitment it needed to survive government repression and heavy attrition of membership ranks."[16] Conversely, if the terrorist group lacks a large support and sympathizer base, it will have a much more difficult time replacing the terrorists that have been captured and imprisoned. Unfortunately for the state, this argument suggests that when terrorists are better supported, and therefore a more serious threat, emergency powers will be less effective.

This argument, while focusing on the level of support for terrorist groups, does not theorize as to why some groups are larger or smaller in size, or have higher or lower levels of support. To *explain* these factors, instead of just observing their causal importance, would require an entire theory on the origins of terrorism and would go beyond the practical scope of this study. Nevertheless, although these factors are treated as exogenous to this study, there are several possible causes or reasons for why different groups have different sizes and levels of support. Some plausible factors might include the terrorists' ideology, their skill at communicating that ideology, the methods or tactics of the terrorist groups, whether the government's response to terrorism is viewed as appropriate, or whether the government responds or even acquiesces to the terrorists' demands. In later chapters, many of these factors will play a prominent role in the descriptions of the terrorist groups.

Another factor that determines the effectiveness of emergency powers is the speed with which the state moves against the terrorists. If the state moves quickly, arresting terrorists in large numbers relative to the size of the organization, the state might be able to remove terrorists faster than they can be replaced by new recruits. There is no concrete measure for what qualifies as "fast" or "slow" actions by the security forces. Rather, the speed of the government's response is in proportion to how quickly the terrorists can recruit new members. Empirically, it is fairly easy to observe this factor. For example, when the army took over anti-Tupamaro operations in Uruguay, they arrested thousands of suspected terrorists in only a few months. The Tupamaros numbered only a few hundred terrorists and a few thousand supporters. With most of the active terrorists *and* supporters quickly imprisoned, the organization was unable to recruit new members to replace those that were imprisoned. Conversely, the British forces in Northern Ireland have not, for the most part, tried to quickly arrest large numbers of suspected terrorists. The one time they did was during the internment raids of 1971. Over 2,000 suspected IRA members were arrested in six months, but these arrests were based on outdated intelligence and consequently failed to diminish the threat from the IRA.

This argument about the speed of the government's response raises the question of why some states at certain times are able to move quickly and others are not. Answering this question, similar to the question of why some terrorist groups are large and well supported, is beyond the scope of this project. Nevertheless, one factor that seems to contribute to the speed of the government's response is the quality of intelligence available to the security forces. This is a function of the skill of the security forces and the skill of the terrorists. The security forces need to be able to recruit informers from within the terrorist group, infiltrate their own personnel into the terrorist group, obtain information through interrogation of captured terrorists, and coordinate and cross-reference all the information that they gather if they are to gain the information on who the terrorists are and where they are located. On the terrorists' side, they can do several things to make it harder for the security forces to gain information about them. Typically, terrorists are recruited on a personal basis, which makes infiltration and the development of informers more difficult. Also, most terrorists are organized into cells, which limits any individual terrorist's contact with other terrorists. This limits the amount of information that can be gained from a successful interrogation. Overall, when intelligence is lacking, the state will be unable to move quickly to capture terrorists. When the quality of intelligence is good, the security forces can use their knowledge of the identities and locations of the terrorists to quickly capture large numbers of them.

To summarize, two factors are important in whether the emergency powers will be effective. Both the speed with which the state acts and the level of support for the terrorist group affect the ability of the terrorist group to replace imprisoned members with new recruits. These two factors, however, do not always point in the same direction; sometimes states move quickly against well-supported groups, or move slowly against poorly supported groups, for example. In total, there are four combinations if we simplify speed and support into dichotomous variables. The greatest chance of success will occur when the terrorist group does not have a large support base and when the state acts quickly, by arresting (and convicting) a large portion of the terrorists. Next best would be the scenario of a small support base and slow implementation. In this case the terrorists would have time to recruit new members, but the population of potential recruits would be too small to replace the imprisoned terrorists and the terrorist movement would slowly be destroyed. The second worst combination would include a large support network and a quick implementation of emergency powers. The state will be temporarily effective in arresting large numbers of terrorists and disrupting the terrorist's organization. Over time, however, the terrorist organization will rebuild itself with new recruits eager to join the cause. The least likely scenario under which emergency powers would be effective is when the terrorists have a large support base, and the government acts slowly in implementing the emergency powers. In this scenario, the government does not arrest enough terrorists to even disrupt the organization; moreover, the terrorists that are arrested are easily replaced.

Note that this theory for when emergency powers will be effective does not include the scope of the emergency powers as part of the explanation for their effectiveness. Many people might assume or even argue that if the state wants to be more effective against terrorism, it must be allowed to violate as many individual liberties as possible; however, the following analysis will highlight several problems with assuming that more extensive emergency powers correlates with more effective emergency powers. In brief, some aspects of emergency powers increase the ability of the state, but many others do not. In particular, the suspension of many due process rights allows the police to more easily search, arrest, detain, and imprison terrorists. Other aspects of the emergency powers—such as the suspension of the right to free speech or the suspension of the separation of powers—might make the act of governance easier for the state, but these powers cannot help the security forces in quickly capturing large numbers of terrorists. Including provisions that restrict the right to free speech or the separation of powers would increase the scope of the emergency powers, but would not increase their effectiveness.

DANGEROUS EMERGENCY POWERS

When are emergency powers likely to be abused? Before answering this, I will first reiterate what I mean by abuse. I will then look to the literatures on emergency powers and constitutionalism in developing my theory for when emergency powers are abused.

As mentioned in Chapter 1, abuses of emergency powers can occur in their duration and scope. Emergency powers can be made permanent, thereby abusing the limits on the duration of the powers. Emergency powers are, by definition, temporary powers. If individual liberties and the normal process of government (the separation of powers) are not restored after the emergency passes, the emergency powers have been abused. In several instances, emergency powers have been permanently extended after the emergency has passed. In these cases a military or presidential coup replaced a democratic regime with an authoritarian government. Emergency powers can also be abused if the limits on their scope are violated. The scope of emergency powers is limited by the content of the emergency powers to the suspension of only particular liberties and particular processes of government. These powers are abused if additional liberties are violated. For example, if emergency powers are used to arrest and imprison people not suspected of terrorism, abuses have occurred. A government may also abuse emergency powers to imprison and thereby silence the political opposition. Additionally, emergency powers might be abused if they restrict liberties beyond what was legislated by the emergency powers. For instance, the security forces may take advantage of relaxed due process rights to torture prisoners arrested for terrorist offenses.[17]

One way of explaining when emergency powers are abused would be to look at some of the scholarly work already written on emergency powers. Carl Friedrich, Frederick Watkins, and Clinton Rossiter have all written on the subject of emergency powers, including analyses of ancient Rome, Weimar Germany, France, Britain, and the United States. These three authors, however, are more concerned with defining what constitutes emergency powers rather than explaining when they might be abused.[18]

A better explanation for abuses of emergency powers comes from the study of constitutionalism, which focuses on how states constrain power generally, but which has insights for how emergency powers might be constrained. Constitutionalism, as described by Jan-Erik Lane, is "the political doctrine that claims that political authority should be bound by institutions that restrict the exercise of power."[19] To create a state where power is constrained, a constitutional state can try to limit the abuse of power in three important ways: through equality (which gives all citizens some share of the political process), liberty (which places limits on the power of government vis-à-vis individual citizens), and the separation of powers (which separates the state's power within government while creating checks and balances).[20] In simple terms, equality diffuses power, liberty limits power, and the separation of powers checks power.[21] According to constitutional theory, abuses of power are the least likely when the state is constrained in all three ways.[22]

A constitutional state is, first and foremost, a political society based on the notion of equality. Decision making should be a collective effort (popular control), and citizens must participate in the political process as equals (political equality).[23] In other words, all citizens have an equal right to participate in the political process, and when they do participate they have equal power within the process. Equality is one path to constitutionalism because if all citizens participate in and control the political process, the will of one individual cannot rule tyrannically and power is constrained by the collective power of all citizens. Although the principle of equality constrains power in important ways, further constraints are necessary because a society based solely on equality is susceptible to the tyranny of the majority.[24] To protect against this situation, constitutional states limit the power of the government by creating rights for the individual that cannot be violated, even by a majority of the citizens.[25] For example, the rights guaranteed to United States citizens by the Bill of Rights and other amendments cannot be violated by any legislation except by further amendments (which require more than a majority vote). Liberty and equality are not perfectly compatible, however, because liberty limits the power of the democratic majority.[26] Ian Shapiro points out that, "Whereas democracy [based on equality] revolves around infusing the law with the will of the majority, the appeal of the rule of law [meaning liberty] is an appeal to its supremacy over the wills of persons."[27] This conflict between liberty and equality results in the constitutional state being based neither solely on the idea of equality or on liberty, but includes a measure of both. The constitutional state cannot survive without both liberty and equality. As Beetham argues, "Liberalism has historically provided both a necessary platform for democracy and a constraint upon it."[28] Political scholars, consequently, often use the term democracy to describe *liberal* democracies because democracy cannot last without liberty.[29]

The term "democracy" is therefore a confusing term when discussing political regimes. While democracy should be defined strictly as the actualization of political equality, many scholars define democracy according to both liberty *and* equality.[30] In practice, though, democracy is usually used as the opposite of authoritarianism. In this respect, democracy is understood to encompass equality, liberty, and the separation of powers, and is essentially a synonym for the constitutional state.[31] It is this broad definition of democracy that I will use for the remainder of the analysis. When I write of threats or dangers to the democratic character of the state, I mean dangers to all aspects of the constitutional state. In some instances, though, the dangers may be to a specific aspect of the state, and I will try to highlight these instances as they occur.

A final safeguard against the abuse of power is the separation of legislative, judicial, and executive powers within a government.[32] Recognizing that power concentrated in a central government can still be abused, constitutional scholars seek to further constrain power by diffusing and separating governmental functions within the government. The concept of separation of powers was originally developed by Montesquieu, and adopted by Madison in the design of the United States Constitution.[33] The separation of powers not only diffuses power, but also gives each branch of government the ability to check abuses by other branches. Scott Gordon claims, "A number of societies have succeeded in constructing political systems in which the power of the state is constrained. The key to their success lies in recognizing that *power can only be controlled by power.* This proposition leads directly to the theory of constitutional design founded upon the principle most commonly known as 'checks and balances'."[34] Therefore, the safest form of democratic government—the one least likely to see power abused—is one in which the powers of government are separated into distinct branches that are largely independent except for certain checks and balances. Governments where the legislature can pass laws without being subject to judicial review or where the president can disband the legislature if he chooses to would be much more likely to see abuses of power, including emergency powers. A parliamentary state with a weak executive, or a state that follows the Latin American model of a strong executive and weak legislature, would both be less stable than a state modeled after the United States Constitution with its strong separation of powers.[35]

To review, to replace the arbitrariness of authoritarian government with a system in which power is constrained, constitutional states are based on political equality, the protection of individual liberties, and the separation of powers within the government with its concomitant checks and balances. I will now turn to applying the general theory of constitutionalism to the specific question of when emergency powers are abused by democratic states.

During times of emergency, the constraints imposed on the government—which are ordinarily so valued—limit the ability of the government to respond to the emergency. The inability of a state to use normal procedures to deal with an emergency and the dangers of emergency powers are recognized by A. M. Gallagher, who writes, "The need for emergency government arises when a state is under some threat. Under such conditions the two main priorities of a democratic government, to protect the civil liberties of its citizens and to maintain the integrity of the state, may come into conflict since pursuit of the latter may require some derogation from the former."[36] Constitutional states use emergency powers to deal with emergencies because the ordinary power of government is thought to be insufficient to deal with the emergency.[37] Constitutional governments are limited in their coercive power because power is constrained in the ways mentioned above—through equality, liberty, and the separation of powers. During emergencies, however, the government can more effectively deal with the threat if it suspends certain aspects of the constitutional state, specifically individual liberties and the separation of power.[38]

Emergency powers can take many forms, depending on whether they are in response to a war, invasion, economic depression, or a natural disaster. For example, faced with an invasion, a country may forcibly draft citizens into the army, place the economy on a war footing, and criminalize activities that would harm the war effort even though they would normally be protected during peacetime. During economic emergencies, the state might enter the normally free market to ensure employment, wage, production, or price levels. Against terrorism, emergency powers typically restrict or suspend due process rights, limit the freedom of the media and free speech generally, and suspend the separation of powers in favor of a stronger executive.

Compared with the other justifications for invoking emergency powers, such as times of economic emergency or invasion, emergency powers directed at terrorism are particularly likely to be abused for three reasons. In other types of emergencies, the enemy is the foreign country, the economy, or nature. Against terrorism, though, emergency powers allow the state to label individual citizens as "the enemy" and target them for terrorist offences. As a result, it is much more likely that innocent individuals will be intentionally accused or imprisoned in the name of fighting terrorism. Also, terrorism is difficult to define for governments and scholars. The decision to define groups as terrorists is often co-opted by political concerns; labeling an opposition group as terrorists gives the state more legitimacy and support in its fight against them.[39] Strict definitions help, but states might label any group opposed to it as a terrorist group and use emergency powers to oppress it. Finally, the emergencies caused by terrorism are likely to last longer than other emergencies. Terrorist movements, while sometimes extremely brief, also have the potential to last for decades, such as the British experience in Northern Ireland. When the emergency becomes almost normal, the use of emergency powers becomes normalized as well. As a result, the public becomes accustomed to the use of the emergency powers and their abuse is a smaller step away from what the public perceives as an acceptable or legitimate use of power.

So far, I have discussed the abuse of emergency powers without an account of agency—somehow abuses just occur. Abuses, however, require some agent to actually commit the abuses. There are actually several possible actors in a state that might abuse the emergency powers, depending on which type of abuse is under consideration. Abuses in the duration of emergency powers occur when some actor permanently acquires greater powers than are normally allowed by the constitution. For this type of abuse, the most likely actors would be the president (or executive more generally) or the military. The president might use his increased powers during the emergency to bypass the legislature and rule by decree or to even suspend the legislature entirely. In addition, the president might abolish the judiciary or appoint new justices that are loyal to him. The military, on the other hand, might abuse the emergency powers by keeping their additional powers after the emergency has passed. They might exploit their new anti-terrorism mission to attack those opposed to them or even the political institutions of the state. The armed forces could also seize power in a coup d'état, in which they eliminate the institutions of constitutional rule altogether.

For abuses of the scope of the emergency powers, the security forces—including the police and military—are the key actors who would commit these abuses. Typically, abuses in the scope of the emergency powers occur when the security forces overstep their legal powers in their effort to defeat the terrorists. Often, for example, they will use abusive interrogation methods, including torture, to obtain confessions or intelligence from prisoners. In addition, they might conduct widespread sweeps in which they arrest hundreds of citizens they know are not terrorists in the hope of having a better chance of finding the true terrorists. These examples are illegal under emergency powers and constitute an abuse in the scope of those powers.

For these different actors to abuse emergency powers there must be some desire on their part to do so. The more that the executive, military, and police are committed to upholding democracy and all of its associated values, the less likely that they will abuse the emergency powers. Intuitively, some countries seem more committed to the norm of democratic rule than others. For instance, Paul Sniderman et al. ask, "How can countries like Canada and the United States weather political storms without jettisoning their democratic principles and practices? Because adherence to democratic values is strongest and most steadfast precisely among those with the most direct influence on and responsibility for public decisions."[40] Undoubtedly, having individuals in power who are committed to upholding democracy is better than the alternative. At the minimum, the absence of these norms is at least necessary for abuses to occur. If no single actor wants to take advantage of their increased power, abuses cannot occur. On the other hand, abuses are more likely to occur if the president has a weak commitment to upholding democracy, if civil-military relations are bad (in the sense that the military is willing to enter the political arena), and if the security forces are more committed to capturing terrorists than working within the laws of the country.

From a theoretical standpoint, norms play an important role in affecting whether emergency powers are abused or not. Empirically, though, it is often difficult to know or measure how committed certain groups or individuals are to upholding democracy. All leaders, for example, claim to be committed to democracy. It is only after the fact—after they seize power in a coup, for instance—that we can know whether their public pronouncements about their commitment to democracy can be believed. In Peru, we might think that President Fujimori was committed to democratic principles based on his address to the nation in the beginning of his presidency. He declared, "The unrestricted respect and promotion of human rights will be a firm line of action by my government... The terrorist violence our fledgling democracy currently faces cannot justify, in any way, the occasional or systematic violation of human rights."[41] Yet, two years later, he seized power in a coup d'état and ruled Peru without any consideration for human rights. Even though we might not be able to assess the normative commitment to democracy with any sense of confidence, this does not detract from its importance theoretically. Clearly there is variation between states along this dimension. Intuitively, at least, it would seem that the leaders of some countries such as Canada or Britain would simply be less likely to even consider the idea that they might use the emergency situation to seize greater powers for themselves than would leaders of other countries.

In terms of the quality of civil-military relations, this variable is easier to measure before a crisis occurs, although still not with complete confidence.

After all, military coups often come as a surprise to many observers. Nevertheless, certain institutional mechanisms that limit the military's role in politics and in domestic law enforcement can be observed. In the United States, for example, civilians maintain strong control over the military. Additionally, the armed forces have no jurisdiction over domestic affairs, unlike other states where the military is an extension of the police forces. In contrast to civil-military relations, the normative commitment of the security forces (the police, armed forces, and other agencies responsible for domestic security) is empirically less important. Whether the security forces abuse emergency powers in the case studies that follow has less to do with the norms of these organizations and more with whether they are constrained by outside actors. In every case except Canada, there were widespread allegations of abusive interrogation methods, forced disappearances, and indefinite internment. In other words, in most cases, the norms of the security forces seem to be fairly constant. The difference in the outcomes between Britain and Peru, for example, is a result of the external constraints on the security forces. In Britain, the press, Parliament, international organizations, and private groups all monitored and publicized abuses by the security forces; in Peru, none of these constraints existed, and abuses were widespread and often deadly.

In the remaining chapters, I acknowledge the importance of weak norms as a necessary condition for abuses to occur; however, measuring this variable with any confidence before a crisis occurs proves too difficult. As a result, although unsatisfying from a theoretical standpoint, the commitment to democracy will be only observed and described as much as possible, but not incorporated into my theory.

Assuming there is some actor who wants to abuse the emergency powers, there are still aspects of the constitutional state that can protect the state from possible abuses of power. At first glance, however, protecting the state from the abuse of emergency powers seems difficult. Many of the safeguards commonly used to check power during normal times are either weakened or suspended during an emergency. Emergency powers need not undermine all constitutional constraints, however; some aspects of constitutionalism are often left intact. In particular, I will focus on whether the aspects of constitutionalism that monitor potential abuses and enforce compliance with the laws are maintained even during the emergency. (Note that these safeguards might be weakened because of the emergency powers, but they also might be weak even before the emergency arises because of the constitutional design of the country. In either case, abuses of power are more likely when these institutions are weak.)

Why are monitoring institutions important? These institutions can provide information on whether abuses have occurred. In many cases, knowing whether abuses have occurred is difficult for several reasons. When the security forces commit abuses, these abuses are still illegal (even though an emergency exists) and so the security forces will try to hide any signs of abuse. Also, the public often prejudges citizens who have been victimized by the security forces as terrorists. As a result, their allegations of abusive treatment are usually dismissed as terrorist propaganda efforts.[42] Finally, victims of abuse are often intimidated by the security forces from publicizing their stories.[43] Because of these difficulties in monitoring abuses, the ability of outside and independent institutions to do so is critical if abuses are to be uncovered. When abuses are uncovered, public reaction will usually turn against those that committed the abuses. Moreover, information about abuses of power also enables other institutions in government to enforce the law and punish those who have committed the abuses.

Why are institutions capable of enforcing the law important? Even in a state with a strong commitment to democratic procedures, some actors might try to abuse their power. Usually, the laws themselves provide protection from these abuses. If a policeman is corrupt, for example, the courts can punish him accordingly. In times of emergency, though, these laws are often insufficient. What is needed is an institution that can check the power of other actors. In constitutional systems, the final check on power is the principle and practice of the separation of powers. If the executive branch abuses its power, the legislature and judiciary can revoke the emergency powers, declare them unconstitutional, or call for new elections.

The specific mechanisms that provide these monitoring and enforcement functions include the right to free speech (including a free press) and a government with power separated into different branches. The stronger these two safeguards, the less likely that abuses of emergency powers will occur. The right of free speech is a cornerstone of any democratic society. This right is enjoyed by individual citizens, members of the political opposition within the government, and by the media, which investigates and reports possible abuses of power. Individuals who feel they have been wronged can make their grievances public. Without the right to free speech, however, the government can silence individuals and control the spread of information about potential government abuses. In addition, the right of free speech is central to the concept of a loyal opposition. In a democracy where government is in the hands of the people, the opposition party or parties have the right and obligation to criticize the government's policies. The debates between the majority and opposition parties create the public forum where issues can be decided. If the opposition does not or cannot act freely, it can no longer monitor, provide information, and debate the actions of the government, including potential abuses of power. Lastly, the media also serves to monitor and debate potential abuses of power. Often the media is the first place citizens turn when they feel that their rights have been violated. From local news reporters doing investigative journalism into city politics to the role of the *Washington Post* in the Watergate scandal, a free press has often provided a safeguard against abuses of power. In examining the role of the press in Northern Ireland, for example, J. C. Garnett observes, "The glare of publicity is a powerful constraint on those who may be tempted either to break the law or interpret it too harshly. Police and security officials are held in check by the possibility of exposure, criminal charges, and dismissal from their jobs."[44]

The right to free speech is important in monitoring and publicizing abuses of power, but cannot actually enforce compliance with constitutional procedures. The ability to provide information, however, should not be underestimated. In many states, the existence or non-existence of a free press and free speech influenced whether emergency powers were abused or not. In the cases of emergency powers that were used safely, the right to free speech was protected. For example, in Britain, some very mild and voluntary censorship was implemented, but the press had essentially free access to the conflict in Northern Ireland. Debates over potential abuses, including allegations of torture and alleged shoot-to-kill policy, were frequent and public. Individuals who believed they had been mistreated could and did turn to the press to publicize their stories. Moreover, the opposition in Parliament voiced its opposition to the policies of the government and frequently debated the usage of the emergency powers in Northern Ireland. In contrast, when the government of Uruguay imposed emergency powers, the media was forbidden to discuss the Tupamaros terrorist movement, and dozens of radio station and newspapers were closed down when they refused to comply. Also, the military tried to arrest members of the legislature who criticized the government by claiming the congressmen were assisting the terrorists.

While the right of free speech is important in monitoring, providing information, and debating potential abuses of power, the separation of power allows different branches of government to both monitor abuses and enforce compliance with the law if abuses occur. The separation of powers, as mentioned earlier, constrains power in a state by diffusing and dividing governmental power between several branches of government.[45] In times of an emergency, the constitutional arrangement of separation of powers can be cumbersome; the executive branch could act far more quickly and decisively if it could bypass the legislature by ruling by decree and not be subject to judicial review. Consequently, during times of emergency, emergency powers frequently suspend the constitution by empowering the executive branch with the emergency powers at the expense of the power of the other branches.

In a political system based on the separation of powers, only one branch can decide whether an emergency exists and whether it warrants the use of emergency powers. Carl Schmitt has argued that emergencies prove that the separation of powers is not really possible because whoever "decides on the exception" is the true sovereign power within the state.[46] The sovereign power, in other words, is held by the one branch that is capable of declaring that an emergency exists.[47] The separation of powers can, however, be maintained if one branch decides whether emergency powers are warranted and a different branch wields the emergency powers. The separation of powers can also be maintained if the wielder of the emergency powers is prohibited from suspending the government as part of the emergency powers.

If the separation of powers remains intact, there are several ways that abuses of power can be checked. Different branches of government can monitor abuses by other branches or by the security forces. The legislature, in particular, often commissions investigations into potential abuses. In Britain, for example, Parliament investigated the implementation of the emergency powers with almost yearly reports from various committees and commissions. In Peru, the legislature was less capable of monitoring abuses in the emergency zones because the emergency powers enabled the military to control all access into the province placed under a state of emergency.

The separation of powers can also protect against abuses by enforcing compliance with the laws. If the security forces abuse the scope of the emergency powers or if the executive tries to extend the duration of the powers indefinitely, then the legislature can pass legislation revoking the emergency powers or even impeach the executive, while the judicial branch can declare that the emergency powers are unconstitutional. If, however, the emergency powers suspend the legislature and judiciary, power will no longer be constrained by any of these checks or balances. The British use of emergency powers in Northern Ireland, for instance, has strengthened the ability of the police and courts to arrest and convict suspected terrorists but has not suspended the parliament in Great Britain. Although a parliamentary system is not one where power is formally divided, power in Britain is still constrained. In particular, the emergency powers have to be approved by Parliament on a yearly basis. As a result, there are annual debates before the emergency powers are renewed. If there were reasons to end the emergency powers or alter their content because of allegations of abuse, a coalition of opposition parties or an empowered opposition following an election would have the opportunity to do so.

One aspect of the constitutional state that is not included as a safeguard against abuses of emergency powers is the protection of individual liberties in the form of due process rights. In normal times, due process rights are important in protecting individual citizens from abuses of power. The police cannot conduct a search without a warrant, citizens cannot be arrested without charge, a suspect cannot be held indefinitely without trial, a prisoner cannot be tortured into confessing, and a defendant is entitled to a trial by jury (in many countries). Emergency powers, however, often curtail many of the due process rights of suspected terrorists, but not always all of them. The remaining due process rights can protect individual citizens from abuse in several ways. For example, a citizen unlawfully detained can file a writ of habeas corpus to bring his case to trial. Similarly, if a confession is obtained through torture, a jury at the trial can decide whether to admit the confession as evidence or dismiss it. The unaffected due process rights, however, can protect individuals only on a case-by-case basis and cannot protect society as a whole. All that due process rights can do is rectify past abuses against individuals, but they cannot stop the security forces from conducting further abuses in the future. Due process rights have also no bearing on abuses in the duration of the emergency powers. Consequently, while this factor may be important in some individual cases, as a whole, I would expect it to play only a limited role in the empirical analysis that follows.

My argument, to review, is that emergency powers used to fight terrorism are most likely to be abused when the emergency powers suspend the right to free speech and end the separation of powers. For protecting against abuses in the duration of the emergency powers, which are typically military or presidential coups, the separation of powers is the best defense. For abuses in the scope of the emergency powers, which occur when the security forces infringe on liberties that were protected, a free press and independent legislature are critical for monitoring abuses and enforcing the laws when abuses occur.

Note that this explanation for the abuses of emergency powers does not include some other factors that some might think are important. Many people might expect that more extensive emergency powers would be more likely to be abused. This line of argument is actually consistent with my own, but not as specific. My argument points to particular elements of the emergency powers (whether monitoring and enforcement mechanisms remain strong), rather than the overall scope of the emergency powers in explaining when abuses are more likely.

Additionally, some observers might expect that emergency powers are more or less likely to be abused depending on the strength of democracy within a country. "Stronger" democracies might have stronger norms and institutions than weak democracies such that they would be less likely to abuse emergency powers, let alone even use them. As the following analyses show, however, our intuitions about which states are the most democratic do not necessarily correspond to how these states have fought terrorism in their country. For example, compare the cases of Peru and Britain. Intuitively, we would expect Britain to be the more democratic state with stronger norms and institutional safeguards; however, Britain also has a long history of using emergency powers to fight Irish Republicanism. Many of Britain's current emergency provisions can be traced back to the Special Powers Act of 1922, which allowed for internment without trial, relaxed requirements for searches and arrests, and several other regulations that are part of the later emergency powers.[48] Moreover, these measures were well supported in Britain, even though we would expect British citizens to be strongly committed to upholding civil liberties. Laura Donohue writes, "At a time when the Western World appears increasingly concerned with the dissemination of liberal, democratic thought, Britain, one of the countries leading the establishment of liberal norms, repeatedly derogates from the standards it sets."[49] Britain, then, has arguably used emergency powers for *eighty* years, and to a degree greater than most other states. Peru, on the other hand, waited almost three years from the beginning of terrorist violence to use emergency powers. Moreover, Peru's emergency powers only allowed for four specific liberties to be suspended and for the military to have complete jurisdiction over the emergency zones. Whereas Britain suspended the right of habeas corpus by instituting internment without trial, Peru's constitution protected this right—

even during the emergency. In sum, looking at the level of democracy, instead of the specific factors I have described, would lead to some misleading results.

In the coming chapters, I will test my arguments about the effectiveness and abuse of emergency powers in four case studies. The following chapter will examine the use of emergency powers in Northern Ireland, with subsequent chapters devoted to the use of emergency powers to fight terrorism in Uruguay, Canada, and Peru.

NOTES

1. See Paul Wilkinson, *Terrorism versus Democracy: The Liberal State Response* (London: Frank Cass Publishers, 2000); Bruce Hoffman, *Inside Terrorism* (New York: Columbia University Press, 1998); Philip Heymann, *Terrorism and America: A Commonsense Strategy for a Democratic Society* (Cambridge, MA: MIT Press, 1998); Richard A. Falkenrath, Robert D. Newman, and Bradley Thayer, *America's Achilles' Heel: Nuclear, Biological, and Chemical Terrorism and Covert Attack* (Cambridge, MA: MIT Press, 1998); and Cindy C. Combs, *Terrorism in the Twenty-First Century* (Upper Saddle River, NJ: Prentice Hall, 1997) for some examples.

2. This definition is basically borrowed from Hoffman, *Inside Terrorism*, 43, who defines terrorism as "the deliberate creation and exploitation of fear through violence or the threat of violence in the pursuit of political change." This definition avoids labels such as legitimate or illegitimate because these labels carry moralistic value judgments that only serve to politicize any categorization of a group as terrorists.

3. See Carl von Clausewitz, *On War* (Princeton: Princeton University Press, 1976) for this famous characterization of war.

4. Many scholars also distinguish between domestic, transnational, and international groups depending on where the terrorists operate and whether states offer them support. For my purposes, I focus on terrorist groups that are domestic or internal to a state. For external groups, it is more likely that a state will respond with tighter border security, for example, than with emergency powers.

5. Shlomo Gazit, "The Myth and the Reality of the PLO," in *International Terrorism: Challenge and Response*, ed. Benjamin Netanyahu (New Brunswick, NJ: Transaction Books, 1981), 346.

6. Alfred McLung Lee, *Terrorism in Northern Ireland* (Bayside, NY: General Hall, 1983), 170. Caroline Kennedy-Pipe, *The Origins of the Present Troubles in Northern Ireland* (London: Longman, 1997), 162, points out that the *yearly* death toll from terrorism in Northern Ireland is less than the *weekly* total of automobile accidents in the United Kingdom.

7. David Scott Palmer, ed., *The Shining Path of Peru* (New York: St. Martin's Press, 1994), 2.

8. Martha Crenshaw, "Introduction: Reflection on the Effects of Terrorism," in *Terrorism, Legitimacy, and Power: The Consequences of Political Violence* (Middletown, CT: Wesleyan University Press 1983), 18.

9. Gustavo Gorriti, *The Shining Path: A History of the Millenarian War in Peru*, trans. Robin Kirk (Chapel Hill, NC: University of North Carolina Press, 1999).

10. Crenshaw, "Reflection on the Effects of Terrorism," 20.

11. One exception is the literature on counterinsurgency operations. In this literature, the importance of "winning the hearts and minds" is often highlighted. In some ways, my theory echoes this literature's emphasis on winning support; however, terrorism poses a slightly different threat to the state than does an insurgency movement. Against terrorism, it is less important for the state to win the support of the civilian population; rather, it is more critical that the terrorists, themselves, lack support. Against terrorism, all the government needs from the general population is acquiescence, not support.

12. See G. Davidson Smith, *Combating Terrorism* (London: Routledge, 1990); Neil C. Livingstone, *The War against Terrorism* (Lexington, MA: Lexington Books, 1982); and John B. Wolf, *Fear of Fear: A Survey of Terrorist Operations and Controls in Open Societies* (New York: Plenum Press, 1981).

13. J. Bowyer Bell, *A Time of Terror: How Democratic Societies Respond to Revolutionary Violence* (New York: Basic Books, 1978), 229, includes legitimacy as one of the government's assets in fighting terrorism.

14. See Eamon Collins and Mick McGovern, *Killing Rage* (London: Granta Books, 1997) for his personal account as an IRA member, including his recruitment process.

15. See Tim Pat Coogan, *The IRA: A History* (Niwot, CO: Robert Rinehart Publishers, 1994) for a reprinting of the IRA's *Green Book* in which support is characterized as active (what I call supporters) and passive (what I call sympathizers).

16. Martha Crenshaw, "An Organizational Approach to the Analysis of Political Terrorism," *Orbis* 29, no. 3 (fall 1985), 468.

17. A. M. Gallagher, "Policing Northern Ireland: Attitudinal Evidence," in *Terrorism's Laboratory: The Case of Northern Ireland*, ed. Alan O'Day (Aldershot, England: Dartmouth Publishing Company, 1995), 49, offers similar criteria for abuses of emergency powers: "Special powers may be used to suppress legitimate opposition groups. Individual abuses of power may be more likely to occur under conditions of crisis because of pressure on the security forces for results, because of the sheer volume of power being used or because those abusing power go unpunished. There is a danger of habituation, both on the part of government and the public: government may come to use emergency powers simply because they seem to work, without giving due attention to less drastic alternatives; public opinion may become desensitized to human rights abuses."

18. Frederick Mundell Watkins, *The Failure of Constitutional Emergency Powers under the German Republic* (Cambridge, MA: Harvard University Press, 1939); Clinton L. Rossiter, *Constitutional Dictatorship: Crisis Government in the Modern Democracies* (Princeton: Princeton University Press, 1948); and Carl Friedrich, *Constitutional Government and Democracy* (Boston: Ginn and Company, 1946).

19. Jan-Erik Lane, *Constitutions and Political Theory* (Manchester: Manchester University Press, 1996), 19. For Lane, these institutions include three types: human rights, the separation of powers, and international law. See also Friedrich, *Constitutional*

Government and Democracy, 4; and Scott Gordon, *Controlling the State: Constitutionalism from Ancient Athens to Today* (Cambridge, MA: Harvard University Press, 1999), 5, for similar definitions of constitutionalism.

20. See Lane, *Constitutions and Political Theory,* 25 and 244.

21. Note that constitutionalism does not require that states have formalized, written constitutions. See Gordon, *Controlling the State,* 5; and Lane, *Constitutions and Political Theory,* chapter 1.

22. The rule of law is often associated with constitutionalism. I do not include it in my review of constitutionalism because there does not seem to be a consensus on defining the term. Some scholars, such as Francis Sejersted, "Democracy and the Rule of Law: Some Historical Experiences of Contradictions in the Striving for Good Government," in *Constitutionalism and Democracy,* ed. Jon Elster and Rune Slagstad (Cambridge: Cambridge University Press, 1988), 131, define the rule of law as a synonym for constitutionalism (minus democracy). Others, such as Ian Shapiro, ed., *The Rule of Law* (New York: New York University Press, 1994), 2, define the term as the protection of individual liberties through laws. Still other scholars define the rule of law as something different from but important to constitutionalism. Jon Elster, "Introduction," in *Constitutionalism and Democracy,* ed. Jon Elster and Rune Slagstad (Cambridge: Cambridge University Press, 1988), 3, for example, defines the rule of law as the requirement that laws be stable and predictable.

23. David Beetham, *Defining and Measuring Democracy* (Cambridge: Polity Press, 1994), 5.

24. Elster, "Introduction," 3, posits that the purpose of the constitutional state (which does not include democracy for him) is to constrain the will of the majority and to protect individual rights.

25. See Beetham, *Defining and Measuring Democracy,* 93; and John Stuart Mill, *On Liberty* (London: Penguin Books, 1974). Stephen Holmes, "Precommitment and the Paradox of Democracy," in *Constitutionalism and Democracy,* ed. Jon Elster and Rune Slagstad (Cambridge: Cambridge University Press, 1988), 196, argues that constitutionalism (characterized by the separation of powers and individual liberties) is "essentially antidemocratic."

26. This conflict is well studied; see Jon Elster and Rune Slagstad, eds., *Constitutionalism and Democracy* (Cambridge: Cambridge University Press, 1988); I. Shapiro, *Rule of Law,* chapters 1–4; and Beetham, *Defining and Measuring Democracy.*

27. I. Shapiro, *Rule of Law,* 2.

28. Beetham, *Defining and Measuring Democracy,* 34.

29. Bollen, "Comparative Measurement of Political Democracy," 375, posits that democracy is based on two principles: equality and political liberty.

30. Alex Inkeles, ed., *On Measuring Democracy: Its Consequences and Concomitants* (New Brunswick, NJ: Transaction Publishers, 1991), ix, summarizes the literature as defining democracy according to political structures (equality) and civil liberties (liberty).

31. See Inkeles, *On Measuring Democracy,* viii.

32. See Charles de Secondat, baron de Montesquieu, *The Spirit of the Laws* (Cambridge: Cambridge University Press, 1989), 156–166; and Alexander Hamilton, James

Madison, and John Jay, *The Federalist Papers* (New York: Penguin Books, 1961) for arguments for checks and balances.

33. Lane, *Constitutions and Political Theory.* The key difference between the two men was that Madison added the concept of checks and balances to Montesquieu's separation of powers. If the powers of government are truly and distinctly separated along the lines advocated by Montesquieu, each branch of government will have no overlapping authority with the other branches. Madison proposed that each function of government be separated out to free-standing branches, but that their powers should be intertwined in certain ways that would allow other branches to check or balance against the abuse of power by one of the other branches.

34. Gordon, *Controlling the State,* 15.

35. See Robert A. Dahl, *On Democracy* (New Haven: Yale University Press, 1998) and Juan J. Linz and Alfred Stepan, eds., *The Breakdown of Democratic Regimes: Latin America* (Baltimore: Johns Hopkins University Press, 1978).

36. Gallagher, "Policing Northern Ireland," 49.

37. Clearly, authoritarian states do not need to use emergency powers because the ruler is not constrained by any protected liberties.

38. The principle of equality is only rarely threatened by the use of emergency powers. Equality is manifested in regular, open elections. Emergencies either begin and end before new elections can be held or elections occur in the middle of an emergency situation. See Canada during the October Crisis as an example.

39. See Alex P. Schmid, et al., *Political Terrorism: A New Guide to Actors, Authors, Concepts, Data Bases, Theories, and Literature* (Amsterdam: North-Holland Publishing Company, 1988), part I; and Hoffman, *Inside Terrorism,* Chapter 1 for discussions on the difficulty and variations in defining terrorism.

40. Paul Sniderman, et al., *The Clash of Rights: Liberty, Equality, and Legitimacy in Pluralist Democracy* (New Haven: Yale University Press, 1996), 18.

41. Amnesty International, *Peru: Human Rights in a Climate of Terror* (New York: Amnesty International, 1991), 26.

42. Terrorist claims often lack credibility for good reason. In Northern Ireland, IRA prisoners often inflicted wounds on themselves to claim that their confessions were obtained only through torture. See Peter Taylor, *Beating the Terrorists: Interrogation in Omagh, Gough, and Castlereagh* (New York: Penguin Books, 1980).

43. This monitoring function is particularly important in protecting against abuses in the scope of the emergency powers. Recall that these abuses are typically carried out by the security forces and are difficult to know about for the reasons mentioned previously in this chapter. Abuses in the duration of emergency powers are essentially coups and are far easier to observe. Information about whether a coup has occurred is obviously easier to come by than whether the police, for example, tortured a prisoner.

44. J. C. Garnett, "Emergency Powers in Northern Ireland," in *Coping with Crises: How Governments Deal with Emergencies,* ed. Shao-chuan Leng (Lanham, MD: University Press of America, 1990), 62.

45. A separation of powers, in its strictest sense, would mean each branch is completely independent (separate) of the others and would be a poor safeguard against

abuses of power. (See Montesquieu, *Spirit of the Laws.*) What is needed is for powers to be separated but also overlapping, as Madison proposed in creating a system of checks and balances between the separate branches of government.

46. Carl Schmitt, *Political Theology: Four Chapters on the Concept of Sovereignty* (Cambridge, MA: MIT Press, 1985), 5.

47. For more on Schmitt's criticism of constitutionalism, see Rune Slagstad, "Liberal Constitutionalism and Its Critics: Carl Schmitt and Max Weber," in *Constitutionalism and Democracy,* ed. Jon Elster and Rune Slagstad (Cambridge: Cambridge University Press, 1988), 103.

48. Laura Donohue, *Counter-terrorist Law and Emergency Powers in the United Kingdom 1922–2000* (Dublin: Irish Academic Press, 2001).

49. Donohue, *Counter-terrorist Law,* xxiv.

Chapter 3

Northern Ireland and the IRA

Britain has used special legislation and emergency powers to fight Irish republicanism for decades. The history of Irish terrorism is a long and bloody one, but this chapter will examine the consequences of emergency powers only in the last thirty years. In the late 1960s, the civil rights movement in Northern Ireland turned bloody, with sectarian violence erupting between the Catholic and Protestant populations. The British army moved in and was later armed with emergency powers, as legislated by the Northern Ireland Act 1973 and the Prevention of Terrorism Act 1974. Over the next several decades, the emergency powers took slightly different forms, but they were mostly ineffective in diminishing the threat of terrorism because the British police and army forces were unable to cut into the support base of the Provisional Irish Republican Army. In terms of the dangers of using emergency powers, British democracy and civil liberties have been maintained despite frequent outcries and allegations of abuse. The constant vigilance by individuals, the press, non-governmental organizations, and Parliament has constrained any individual or group that might have abused the emergency powers for its own ends.

BACKGROUND OF IRISH TERRORISM

The origin of the conflict in Northern Ireland is conventionally traced back to the 1600s when Scottish Protestants were settled in the Northern Ireland provinces of Ulster.[1] In the years after the initial settlement, there were conflicts between British and Irish forces, but these were battles of expansion between the British colonizers who were Protestant, and local Irish defenders who were Catholic. The fact that a minority of Protestants lived within a Catholic majority in Ireland did not become a sectarian issue until the late nineteenth century, when Irish self-governance and independence from Britain became a legitimate hope for the Irish. Ireland appeared to be headed into civil war in the early 1900s as the desire for Home Rule became increasingly popular among Irish Catholics. Ulster Protestants responded by preparing to defend their continued union with Britain. World War I temporarily marginalized the issue, although 1916 saw the Easter Rising and the formation of the Irish Republican Army (IRA).[2] The IRA was formed out of the Irish Republican Brotherhood, founded in 1859, and the Irish Volunteers, founded in 1913.[3]

After the end of World War I, British attention returned to Ireland. In the December 1918 Parliamentary elections, the Sinn Fein party won seventy-three out of eighty Irish seats, but refused to sit in the British Parliament. Instead, they formed a government in Dublin and declared Irish independence in January 1919; however, this was not immediately recognized by Britain. On December 23, 1920, Ireland was partitioned under the Government of Ireland Act, creating Northern Ireland out of the six counties of Ulster (Antrim, Armagh, Down, Londonderry, Fermanagh, and Tyrone), while the southern twenty-six counties formed the Republic of Ireland. In 1925, the border between Northern Ireland and the Irish Free State was formally and legally registered with the League of Nations. Irish independence was far from a bloodless political event. Forces in Ireland opposed to any partition of Ireland, led by the IRA, fought a bitter civil war against both Republican forces in the south (who wanted to compromise with Britain) and Unionist forces in the north. Michael Collins, leader of the South and founder of the IRA, was killed by the IRA in 1922 because he had failed to achieve independence for all of Ireland. Between 1920 and 1922, thousands of IRA and British security forces were killed and wounded in ambushes, bombings, and assassinations.[4]

Ireland was relatively peaceful from 1922 until 1939, when the IRA renewed its bombing campaign. This campaign soon ended after the IRA leadership was weakened by arrests and disagreement over strategy.[5] After a long lull of inactivity, bombs again exploded throughout Ireland on December 12, 1956, marking the beginning of what was to become the Border Campaign. After several years of violence, however, the IRA was forced to call an end to the campaign because a rift in the leadership structure within the IRA weakened the movement, and the campaign failed to generate much support within Ireland.[6]

By 1962, it appeared the IRA was finished as a viable opposition force within Ireland.[7] When the civil rights movement started to garner worldwide attention in the late 1960s, the IRA was no longer a powerful actor in Ireland. As a result of its military weakness and lack of popular support, the IRA changed its ideology in the early 1960s from Irish nationalism to Marxism under the influence of Roy Johnston.[8] Furthermore, the IRA demilitarized, selling off practically all of its weapons to Welsh nationalists.[9]

The spark that set off the current round of violence in Northern Ireland was the civil rights movement of the 1960s that focused on the discrimination in housing and employment against Catholics in Northern Ireland. The situation turned violent when peaceful marchers in Londonderry were batoned by the Royal Ulster Constabulary (RUC) on October 5, 1968. A year later, on August 12, 1969, the Protestant Apprentice Boys marched through the Bogside area of Londonderry. When some Catholic hooligans began throwing stones at the watching RUC, the RUC charged them. The Bogsiders set up barricades and were besieged for days by the RUC.[10] Responding to the violence, the Irish Prime Minister announced that he would send Irish army units up to the border to treat wounded Catholics. Protestant extremists reacted by rioting in Belfast, after which London decided to send British army troops into Northern Ireland.[11]

Throughout the rioting and violence in 1968 and 1969, the IRA was nowhere to be found. Graffiti on walls pronounced that the IRA stood for "I Ran Away." To many IRA members, the rioting and violence demanded that the IRA should act in its traditional role and protect the Catholic communities against Protestant hooliganism, but the Marxist leadership refused to take sides in what they saw as a conflict *within* the working class. In January 1970, the IRA split into two groups: the Official IRA, which continued its Marxist orientation, and the Provisional IRA, which returned to its traditional, republican cause, willing to use violence as necessary.[12] Since the split, the Provisional IRA has been the largest and most active guerrilla and terrorist group in Northern Ireland.[13] Consequently, this chapter focuses on the Provisional IRA as the primary terrorist group in Northern Ireland.[14]

When the British army arrived in August 1969, its mission was to separate the two sides and restore order to Northern Ireland.[15] Several incidents, however, soon signaled to the Irish Catholics that the purpose of the British army was primarily to protect the union with Britain, and that British forces were sympathetic to the Protestant groups and opposed to the republican Catholic groups. In particular, the brutality and violence of British actions drove many Irish Catholics into the arms of the IRA.[16] Hadden, Boyle, and Campbell argue that heavy-handed British army tactics "so alienated the Catholic community … that a continuing flow of new recruits was ensured."[17]

In July 1970, the army established a curfew in the Lower Falls area of Belfast and engaged in rough-handed searches of people and property. Several people were killed and dozens wounded in what came to be known as "The Rape of the Falls."[18] In February 1971, the Provisional IRA killed its first British soldier, and later killed three more soldiers in March when an IRA woman lured the soldiers from a bar into an ambush outside. The new Unionist Prime Minister, Brian Faulkner, demanded that the British government respond more vigorously to the violence.[19] Under the authority of the Public Order Act of 1951 and the Civil Authorities Act of 1922–33, the army responded by introducing internment without trial on August 9, 1971. On the first night, 342 people were arrested; all of them Republican supporters, but only a handful were connected to the IRA. The lists of people to be interned were based on outdated intelligence; consequently, the leadership of the Provisional IRA was not affected.[20] Most of those arrested were quickly released, but twelve were interrogated in depth with the aid of what is known as the "five techniques"—hooding, wall-standing, continuous noise, and the deprivation of sleep and food.[21] The use of these five techniques was reviewed by the Compton Committee, which ruled that they constituted ill treatment, but not torture; however, the European Commission on Human Rights later ruled that the interrogation methods used by the British in autumn 1971 *did* constitute torture.[22] The Provisional IRA responded to internment with an escalation of violence. The number of IRA bombings rose to over 100 in August, and reached a peak of 146 in January 1972, killing 231 people in six months.[23]

On January 30, 1972, in what has become known as "Bloody Sunday," soldiers from the British Army Parachute Regiment shot thirteen civilians marching in a civil rights protest in Londonderry after earlier getting into a gun battle with the IRA. The following Widgery Committee report found that most of the victims were innocent and that some of the shootings were reckless.[24] The British government, responding to international pressure, sought to regain control of the British army in Northern Ireland, which up until then had been subordinate to the direction of the Stormont (Northern Ireland) government. When the Prime Minister of Northern Ireland refused to grant Westminster control over the security forces, Britain disbanded the Stormont Parliament and instituted direct rule of Northern Ireland.[25]

In this environment of sectarian violence and British occupation, the Provisional IRA moved in as the protector of Irish Catholic communities. The IRA gained supporters from those who felt victimized by Protestant militia groups, the Unionist police force (RUC), and the British army. Christopher Hewitt points out, "In the Catholic ghettos of Belfast the IRA functions as a defense force, patrolling its borders and protecting the inhabitants from Protestant assassins or rioters. Those areas of Belfast attacked by Protestant rioters in 1968 continue to be IRA strongholds. A vicious cycle also maintains sympathy for the IRA. IRA attacks on the British Army result in Army searches; in turn leading to further alienation of the public, to more IRA attacks and so on."[26] Attacks from Protestant paramilitary groups also serve to maintain the spiral of violence in Northern Ireland.

The IRA has three aims: weaken the commitment of the British government for administering Northern Ireland; terrorize the Protestant community and weaken support for their militia groups; and weaken support for their Republican rivals, the Official IRA.[27] Their long-term goal is the creation of an Irish Republic on the whole island of Ireland. To achieve these goals, the IRA has sought to persuade the British to leave, the Protestants to stop fighting, and the Catholics to support them (rather than the Officials who espoused non-violent political solutions).[28]

IRA tactics mainly consist of bombings and assassinations of British and Protestant security forces, whether on duty or not, and often without consideration of any collateral damage.[29] Attacks within Northern Ireland have been frequent over the past thirty years with hundreds of deaths and thousands of injuries on all sides occurring every year.[30] Some of the more noteworthy IRA attacks include a 1973 car bombing in London; bombings in Birmingham and Guildford in 1974 in which twenty-four people died and hundreds were injured; two bombings in London in 1982 in which eleven soldiers were killed; a December 1983 bombing of Harrod's department store; an attack on the Tory conference in Brighton in 1984 that killed five and could have killed most of the British cabinet; a 1985 attack on the Newry Barracks of the RUC that killed nine and injured thirty-two; a rocket attack on 10 Downing Street at the height of the Gulf War; and a 1993 bombing of the City of London that caused extensive financial damage.[31]

As the perpetrators of these acts and many more like them, the IRA deserves to be labeled as a group that uses terrorist methods.[32] Recall that terrorism is the use of violence to create a climate of fear that will lead to political change. All of these attacks, whether on civilians or soldiers, were designed to use terror to convince the British government to change its policies in Northern Ireland. Even the attacks on the security forces were not planned by the IRA according to a military logic because they were not trying to defeat the British forces. Instead, they hoped to exploit the psychological impact of the attacks to convince British leaders to withdraw the British forces from Ireland.

Besides violence, the IRA also used hunger strikes as a tactic. Six different times during the current conflict, IRA prisoners have gone on hunger strikes while in prison, demanding to be treated as political rather than criminal prisoners.[33] The most famous hunger strike was the H-block hunger strike that began on March 1, 1981, in which the leader of the hunger strike, Bobby Sands, won a seat in the British Parliament on April 9, a month before his death in prison. The use of hunger strikes points to the complexity of the IRA. While they should be characterized as a terrorist group because of their use of assassinations and bombings, they also operated more like a guerrilla group in the first few years of the conflict and used non-violent protests with the hunger strikes.

EMERGENCY POWERS WITHIN THE BRITISH POLITICAL SYSTEM

To respond to the terrorism of the IRA, the British government enacted and implemented several pieces of emergency legislation. Before describing the history of emergency powers in Northern Ireland, I will first lay out the political background and structure of the British political system.

Britain has a long and robust tradition of liberty and democracy.[34] Britain is one of the oldest democracies in the world, and has maintained its regime type without interruption at least since 1880.[35] Elections are frequent, open, and contested, while voter participation is high. Also, civil liberties are a cornerstone of British political society. Due process rights, such as trial by jury and the right of habeas corpus, are central elements of the British legal system. The strength of democracy in Britain has resulted in a strong commitment to democratic norms. As mentioned in Chapter 2, the stronger this normative commitment, the more unlikely it is for abuses of power to occur. The idea that a prime minister or the army might seize power in Britain through a coup d'état is practically unthinkable.

Power is also constrained in Britain by a political system of checks and balances. Although Britain does not have a formal, written constitution, it is universally characterized as a liberal, constitutional, parliamentary democracy.[36] Power is constrained in Britain by its diffusion to several governmental bodies. There is no formal separation of executive, legislative, and judicial powers, as in the United States; instead, by tradition and custom, power is shared by the prime minister and the cabinet, the Parliament, the House of Lords and the monarchy, and the judiciary.[37] At first glance, it may appear that the Parliament holds the greatest power and is the true sovereign in Britain.[38] This is largely the result of the battles between the Crown and Parliament in the seventeenth century, which culminated in the 1688 settlement that established Parliament's central role in British politics. Moreover, the British parliamentary system, in which the majority party forms the government, seems to lack the checks and balances that normally constrain power when there is a separation of powers. In fact, in Britain, the executive and legislative functions are both contained within one institution—the prime minister and his appointed cabinet. The prime minister, unlike the United States president, does more than execute the laws; he also initiates practically all legislation. Scott Gordon writes, "Virtually all important legislative proposals are introduced by the government. Private members' bills seldom get as far as being voted on. The role of the House of Commons in modifying government bills is, by all accounts, almost negligible. In sum then, the Cabinet, as the representative of the majority party in Parliament, is the central legislative and executive organ in the British political system."[39]

This type of political system is susceptible to the tyranny of the majority. A party that holds a majority in the House of Commons can form a government and pass legislation as it desires, without the check of a presidential veto. There is also little that Parliament can do to check the power of the prime minister if he maintains the backing of his party. Because of the power of the prime minister and his party, it is plausible to characterize the British system as an "elected dictatorship."[40]

While there is no formal separation of powers, power is still constrained in the British political system by several institutions within the government that constrain the power of the prime minister.

For example, the government must retain its majority in the House of Commons. The prime minister can always be voted out of office if his party loses in an election. Also, the prime minister can lose his office if there is a rift within the party and a rival assumes the leadership of the party.[41] Parliament can also constrain the prime minister and his cabinet by conducting investigations into the actions of the executive branch. The House of Commons has improved its ability to monitor the government through its system of select committees, established in 1979. These committees are composed of eleven members selected from both parties, and have broad powers to "inquire into the administrative activities as well as the policy decisions of the executive agencies" much like House and Senate committees in the United States.[42] Next, the monarchy and the House of Lords have some ability to constrain the power of the prime minister and his government. Formally, these historical remnants have little power; the House of Lords has not affected any legislation since 1909, while the monarch has not vetoed legislation in almost three hundred years.[43] Informally, though, the monarchy and the House of Lords can draw attention to an issue and influence popular opinion about it. Lastly, the judiciary is an independent check on government power, much as it is in the United States. Cases can be appealed to the Law Lords (formally the Lords of Appeal in Ordinary) where the relevant law is subject to review.[44]

Within this political context, emergency powers are legislated by an act of Parliament. The fact that Parliament enacts the emergency powers, but the executive branch (in the form of the security forces) wields the power maintains the separation of power in a way that Rossiter and Friedrich recommend (as argued in Chapter 2). The content or scope of the powers is unconstrained by any laws or constitution. This is because civil liberties in Britain are not codified in a "bill of rights" or any other legislation, but instead are based on tradition and common law. Parliament has the ability to pass emergency legislation without having to worry about legally or constitutionally protected liberties; without a written constitution, new legislation simply overrides any previous legislation.[45] As a result, in times of crisis, the Parliament can restrict individual liberties without having to revoke or suspend any laws protecting particular freedoms. This has led many people in Britain to support the enactment of a bill of rights that would protect certain rights even during an emergency.[46]

Historically, emergency powers in Northern Ireland have been contained in several overlapping pieces of legislation.[47] The British Parliament first passed emergency powers for Northern Ireland with the Civil Authorities (Special Powers) Act of 1922.[48] From 1922 until 1973, several other acts of emergency powers were legislated by Parliament,[49] but all of these were superseded by the two acts of emergency powers that have been used in the current conflict: the Northern Ireland (Emergency Provisions) Act of 1973 and the Prevention of Terrorism (Temporary Provisions) Act of 1974.[50] Both of these acts have been renewed and re-enacted with minor changes several times.[51]

The use of these acts by the British security forces in Northern Ireland can be broken up into four phases: internment (1968–1972), Diplock Courts (1972–1975), criminalization (1976–1981), and the supergrass[52] system

(1981–1987).[53] Taken together, these phases actually show a decrease in the scope of the emergency powers, with an increased emphasis on using normal judicial processes to fight terrorism. In 1985, a peace process began, with frequent cease-fires and greater cooperation between Britain and Ireland.[54] Despite these attempts at peace, however, violence has continued and emergency powers are still used to search, arrest, and imprison suspected terrorists in Northern Ireland. The following paragraphs examine the four phases of emergency powers.

Internment without trial was the primary tactic used to fight terrorism in Northern Ireland in the beginning of the current conflict. The goal was simply to remove all terrorists from the population by placing them in internment camps. Whenever internment is used by a state, the government essentially abandons all aspects of due process and simply decides on the guilt of an individual without giving the citizen recourse to the law, including the right to be tried in a court by a jury of one's peers. Implicit in the use of internment is the recognition that the criminal and legal systems of the state are inadequate to the task of imprisoning terrorists through normal means.

When the civil rights movement first began in the late 1960s, the security forces in Northern Ireland, including the RUC and the British army, still relied on the Civil Authorities (Special Powers) Act of 1922 to wage their campaign against terrorism. This act granted the government of Northern Ireland the powers of internment without trial, arrest without charge, search without warrant, and detention for up to 48 hours for interrogation. These powers were originally intended to be used as a temporary measure to deal with the violence of the Irish Civil War; however, they were renewed annually until 1928, extended for five years in 1928, and then made permanent in 1939, although hardly ever used until the current round of violence.[55] Internment was used most dramatically when the British army and Northern Irish security forces conducted the internment sweeps of 1971. On the first day, 342 suspects were detained, while 2,375 people were arrested over the following six months, although the vast majority of those detained were quickly released.[56] The IRA claimed that only fifty-six of its members were interned in these raids.[57] This internment operation failed to stem the tide of Republican violence for several reasons, which will be discussed later in this chapter.

Following the disbanding of the Stormont Parliament and the imposition of direct rule in 1972, the British Parliament took up the question of whether internment should be used against suspected terrorists. Faced with domestic and international criticism, Parliament commissioned Lord Diplock to assess the security situation in Northern Ireland and recommend security and legal measures for the British army to use in fighting terrorism without having to resort to internment.[58] In his report in 1972, Lord Diplock recommended that internment without trial be continued temporarily, but a gradual return to the court system should take place. Lord Diplock was aware of the problems with trials by jury; several largely Protestant juries had returned perverse acquittals against Loyalist paramilitaries,[59] and several juries had been threatened and intimidated.[60] Consequently, the Diplock Report recommended that trial by jury be suspended in favor of courts (later known as Diplock courts) where a tribunal of judges would decide the guilt of the accused suspect. The goal of the Diplock recommendations was to put as many terrorists behind bars as possible, whether through the courts or internment.

The recommendations of the Diplock commission became the basis of Britain's counter-terrorism policy when they were legislated as the Northern Ireland (Emergency Provisions) Act 1973.[61] This act continued to allow indefinite internment, suspended the right to trial by jury, increased the time suspects could be detained before a decision had to be made to bring them to trial, release them, or intern them from 48 hours to 72 hours, and relaxed the evidentiary requirements to allow confessions obtained under interrogation to be sufficient for conviction.[62]

Terrorism from Northern Ireland spilled over into Britain proper in 1973 and 1974, prompting Parliament to consider more comprehensive emergency powers to apply to all of Britain. (The EPA only applied to Northern Ireland.) In October 1973, the IRA bombed two pubs in Guildford, killing seven and injuring hundreds, followed in November by a bomb in Birmingham that killed twenty-one and injured several hundred. *The Times* called the attacks an "act of war," and Parliament immediately began debating new emergency legislation.[63] On November 29, 1974, Parliament passed the Prevention of Terrorism (Temporary Provisions) Act.[64] The PTA proscribed specific terrorist organizations, excluded suspected terrorists from entering Great Britain, allowed the police to search and make arrests without warrant, and extended the time prisoners could be detained to seven days.[65] The PTA was originally due to expire after six months, although this was changed to yearly renewals in 1976. This act was revised with minor changes in 1976, 1984, 1989, and 1996.[66]

Although the Diplock Report and the subsequent EPA 1973 and PTA 1974 marked the beginning of the turn to criminalization (by using courts), they still relied on internment if a guilty verdict was not expected in a court of law. Internment had been widely criticized, especially after the large-scale internment operations of 1971. Moreover, the number of bombings increased in 1972 and 1973, raising doubts as to the efficacy of the internment strategy. In a 1976 meeting, the Chief Constable of the Royal Ulster Constabulary (RUC) told his police, "The only way to defeat the IRA was the rigorous application of the law to put them behind bars."[67] In 1974, the incoming Labour government appointed the Gardiner Committee to examine the use of internment as a strategy to fight terrorism.[68] The committee concluded in 1975 that internment could not be maintained as a long-term strategy; instead, "Trial by jury is the best form of trial for serious cases and that it should be restored in Northern Ireland."[69] The committee, however, went on to recognize that juries would be intimidated; therefore, Diplock courts would still be necessary.[70] The Gardiner

Report therefore suggested that internment should be ended, while the jury-less Diplock courts should be maintained.

The recommendation to end internment was gradually adopted in 1975; by the end of the year, all interned suspects were released in Northern Ireland.[71] With internment no longer an option, obtaining convictions in a court of law became critical if terrorists were to be imprisoned; however, convicting terror-ists in a court of law was difficult for several reasons. As previously mentioned, jury trials were difficult because the juries were intimidated or biased.[72] Diplock courts solved this problem. Also, evidence was hard to come by if no one was willing to come forward to testify against the suspect. To counter this problem, the EPA 1973 relaxed the evidentiary requirements such that uncor-roborated confessions were sufficient evidence to convict a suspect. Confes-sions, however, were difficult to obtain in a constitutional society in which suspects could not be tortured and when the suspects were highly motivated terrorists trained in the ways to protect themselves under interrogation. To counter this, the army and police were allowed to detain and interrogate a sus-pect for up to seven days under the statutes of the PTA 1974. The difference be-tween two or three days of detention and seven days enhanced the ability of the police to more effectively undermine a suspect's physical and psychological well being to obtain a confession.[73]

Security personnel understood that the only way to convict a terrorist was to obtain a confession, which increased the likelihood that they would use abusive methods to obtain the confession. Not surprisingly, soon after this new policy of criminalization took effect, more complaints began to be made by prisoners of beatings and abusive treatment. For example, of the thirty-eight terrorist sus-pects charged at one police station, thirty complained of police brutality.[74] These complaints were initially dismissed with the explanation that the injuries were self-inflicted for propaganda purposes;[75] however, an Amnesty International re-port and the Bennett Committee report both found that there was clear evidence that the injuries of suspects could not have been self-inflicted and were, in fact, the result of abusive interrogation methods.[76] These conclusions were echoed by the Parker Commission and the European Commission and Court.[77]

In response to the Bennett Committee report, the government instituted "strict internal controls on interrogation procedures. The introduction of these administrative controls during 1979 and an increased commitment to their en-forcement on the part of senior officers led to a dramatic decline in the number and seriousness of complaints."[78] Instead of forcing suspects to confess and im-plicate themselves, the police began to try to convince suspects to inform on other terrorists in exchange for immunity. Those that implicated others were called supergrasses.[79] Hadden, Boyle, and Campbell write, "The decision to rely on evidence from first-hand informers, or 'converted terrorists,' as a means not only of identifying but also securing convictions against others was almost cer-tainly related to the perceived difficulty in obtaining confessions following the implementation of the Bennett recommendations."[80]

In November 1981, Christopher Black implicated thirty-eight other terrorists in exchange for immunity. While supergrasses had existed prior to Black's
arrest, this marked the beginning of a large increase in their use. In the two
years after his arrest, seven Loyalist and eighteen Republican supergrasses led
to nearly 600 arrests.[81] The use of supergrasses largely died out after 1983, with
only one supergrass in 1985 and one in 1987.[82] In the first ten supergrass trials,
120 out of 217 of the defendants were found guilty, although 67 of those found
guilty had their verdicts overturned after appeal. Overall, the conviction rate
was only around 42 percent, in large part because many of the judges in the
Diplock courts were unwilling to convict suspects based only on uncorroborated evidence. Moreover, many supergrasses also withdrew their evidence before their cases came to trial.[83]

INEFFECTIVE EMERGENCY POWERS

The emergency powers were largely ineffective in helping the state fight terrorism. The reason for their ineffectiveness is that the security forces were unable to arrest and imprison terrorists faster than new recruits could replace
those that were captured. Two factors influenced the ability of the British state
to do so: The IRA enjoyed fairly widespread support among the Catholic population and, except for the internment raid of August 1971, the British security
forces did not move quickly to imprison large portions of the IRA.

To be judged effective, emergency powers must be responsible for the decrease in the level of violence related to terrorism. At their most effective,
emergency powers have the potential to eliminate terrorist groups completely.
If this is not possible, however, emergency powers can still reduce the violence
from terrorism, as measured by the number of attacks (bombings and shootings) or by the number of deaths and injuries to civilians and security forces.
Table 3.1 is a partial breakdown of these statistics from 1971 to 1993.

As this data indicates, there was a sharp increase in all types of violence in
1972, followed by a drop and then stabilization in the number of deaths, explosions, and shooting incidents. For example, looking at the data provided in Table
3.1, the total number of deaths per year peaked at 468 people in 1972, but then
roughly between 75 and 100 people were killed in almost every year from 1977
until 1992. This pattern is seen most clearly when plotted on a graph, as shown
in Figure 3.1.

What explains this pattern of violence? Were emergency powers effective in
at least reducing the level of violence? To assess the effectiveness of emergency
powers, Christopher Hewitt compares the level of violence with the level of
emergency powers in five cases, including in Northern Ireland.[84] He plots the
level of emergency powers against deaths, explosions, and all attacks on security forces and concludes that, in all cases, "[there is no] recognizable pattern
whereby violence declines following the introduction of emergency powers.

Table 3.1
Violence in Northern Ireland, 1971–1993

	1971	1972	1973	1974	1975	1976	1977	1978	1979*	1980	1981	1982
Shootings	1,756	10,628	5,018	3,206	1,803	1,908	1,081	755	189*	642	1142	547
Explosions	1,022	1,382	978	685	399	766	366	455	90*	400	529	332
Civilian deaths	115	322	171	166	216	245	69	50	7*	50	57	57
Security deaths	59	146	79	50	31	52	43	31	3*	26	44	40
Civilian injuries	1,838	3,813	1,812	1,680	2,044	2,162	1,027	548	113*	--	--	--
Security injuries	705	1,063	839	718	430	567	371	391	73*	--	--	--

	1983	1984	1985	1986	1987	1988	1989	1990	1991	1992	1993#
Shootings	424	334	237	392	674	537	566	559	499	506	211#
Explosions	367	248	215	254	384	458	420	287	367	371	106#
Civilian deaths	44	36	25	37	66	54	39	49	75	76	24#
Security deaths	33	28	29	24	27	39	23	27	19	9	7#
Civilian injuries	--	--	--	--	--	--	--	--	--	--	--
Security injuries	--	--	--	--	--	--	--	--	--	--	--

Source: These figures are from Michael A. Pool, "The Spatial Distribution of Political Violence in Northern Ireland," in *Terrorism's Laboratory: The Case of Northern Ireland,* ed. Alan O'Day (Aldershot, England: Dartmouth Publishing Company, 1995), 30; and Tim Pat Coogan, *The IRA: A History* (Niwot, Colorado: Robert Rinehart Publishers, 1994), 287 and 503.

*Figures from January to March.

#Figures from January to May.

- -No data on injuries after 1979.

Sometimes violence declines, sometimes it increases, but most times the legislation has no discernible impact."[85] In the case of Northern Ireland, violence actually increased after the use of internment and the enactment of the emergency powers. J. C. Garnett observes, "It is quite clear that the emergency legislation has not enabled the British army either to destroy the IRA, or to prevent sectarian violence, or to free the province from terrorist activity."[86]

Logically, if emergency powers were effective, we should expect a drop in violence following their implementation. Undoubtedly, emergency powers *were* used to arrest thousands of suspects and search hundreds of thousands of homes. For example, over 3,000 suspects were arrested under the provisions of the PTA or EPA in 1981,[87] while 75,000 houses were searched in 1973;[88] however, the eventual drop in the level of violence was not a result of the emergency powers. In fact, following the British internment raid of 1971, and the passage of the Northern Ireland (Emergency Provisions) Act in 1973 and the Prevention of Terrorism (Temporary Provisions) Act in 1974, terrorist inci-

Figure 3.1
Deaths and Explosions in Northern Ireland

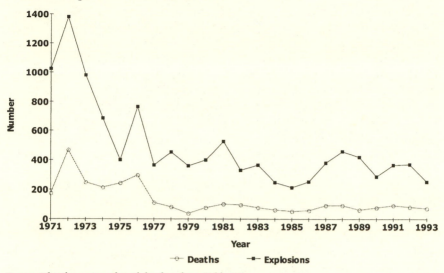

Source: This figure is a plot of the data from Table 3.1.

dents were at their highest levels. Clive Walker, in *The Prevention of Terrorism in British Law,* observes, "A quick survey reveals that enactment [of the PTA in 1974] had no immediate discernible effect. Thus the I.R.A.'s campaign continued during the remainder of 1974, through 1975 and into 1976, broken only by two lulls when 'ceasefires' were arranged."[89]

The quick increase and gradual decrease in the level of violence reflects a shift away from the traditional IRA tactics of leading riots and protests in the streets of Belfast. These tactics, more in line with urban guerrilla warfare, were necessary in the beginning of the current conflict because of the scope of the violence. In fact, in 1972, Northern Ireland was almost in a state of civil war with Protestant and Catholic gangs controlling the streets, blockading neighborhoods, and organizing riots. Operating as the traditional protector of Catholic communities, however, proved tremendously costly to IRA in terms of volunteers, guns, supplies, and ammunition. The IRA was simply too small and too unprepared for an open, guerilla-type conflict with the Protestant militia groups and the British security forces. It was the IRA's inability to conduct this campaign—and not because of the use of emergency powers—that forced them to change their operations to the more traditional terrorist tactics of targeted bombings and assassinations.[90] The IRA gradually began to plan fewer but more focused and lethal attacks. Between 1977 and 1992, the number of explosions remained fairly constant. Between 1973 to 1983 the proportion of deaths from assassination rose from 25 percent to 50 percent, while deaths resulting from riots, explosions, and gun battles dropped in both absolute and relative terms.[91] Over time, the IRA has been able to maintain the initiative in conducting operations at the time and place of its choosing. There has developed a type of stalemate in which the IRA can do no more than periodic bombings and assassinations while the security forces can hinder but not eliminate the IRA. This suggests that the only viable solution to the problem of violence in Northern Ireland is a political one. Garnett writes, "Every writer on the subject of counterinsurgency is at pains to emphasize that suppressing terrorism is fundamentally a 'political' rather than a 'security' problem."[92]

The emergency powers were ineffective at combating terrorism because of the widespread support for the IRA and because the security forces were unable to quickly arrest large numbers of terrorists. The result was that there was always a wave of new recruits eager to join the IRA and continue its fight against Britain.[93]

The level of support relative to the number of active numbers is critical for understanding the ability of any terrorist movement to sustain itself in the face of government pressure. In Northern Ireland, the numbers of active IRA members (gunmen, bombers, commanders) is best estimated as fluctuating for most of the conflict between 300 and 500 people.[94] In 1972, the IRA probably briefly reached a maximum strength of 2,000 members,[95] but soon dropped back to around 500 members.[96] Other estimates put the strength of the IRA as between 250 and 600 members since the mid-1980s.[97]

Potential recruits for the IRA are plentiful within the Catholic population of Northern Ireland. IRA members are predominantly volunteers or recruits from urban, working-class neighborhoods in Belfast, Londonderry, and other northern towns and cities.[98] Even those in the leadership of the IRA come from working class backgrounds, which is rare for terrorist or other social movements.[99] Typically, volunteers or recruits join the IRA after they have suffered or witnessed some abuse at the hands of the British army or have been a victim of Loyalist violence.[100] For example, one of the hunger strikers, Francis Hughes, joined the IRA after he had been beaten by the security forces.[101] Similarly, Eamon Collins, the supergrass and author, turned to the IRA after he had been brutally searched and interrogated along with his brother and father.[102]

Throughout the current troubles, the IRA has had no problem attracting recruits or volunteers.[103] An anonymous commander in the IRA claimed in an interview that they "have waiting lists [of recruits] waiting to join up."[104] In the early years of the conflict, the IRA needed as many recruits as they could find to fight the street battles that were so common at the time;[105] however, in the late 1970s, the IRA restructuring led to a lessening demand for new recruits, despite the government's efforts to imprison terrorists under the emergency legislation.[106] With the changes in IRA strategy and tactics, "There were fewer opportunities to serve and so fewer recruits: the secret army became more secret, more skilled, less open to volunteers too young to have served in the first influx."[107] Moreover, David Bonner argues that recruits for the IRA will always be forthcoming into the future. "They have a permanence transcending the membership at any given time, and there seems a cultural permanence with little shortage of new recruits or leaders to replace those imprisoned."[108] The ease of recruitment is due to the high level of support enjoyed by the IRA. As long as sectarian violence continues and the British army remains in Northern Ireland, the IRA will have high enough support to ensure a continuous supply of volunteers ready to join the organization.

Support for the IRA comes from both active supporters and passive sympathizers. The IRA is aided by large numbers of active supporters who are "involved in maintenance, communications, intelligence, and supply"[109] and "provide propaganda support, collect funds, and provide safe houses."[110] According to Paul Wilkinson, these active supporters number around 2,000 people.[111] In a much higher estimate of support, Christopher Hewitt cites British army sources that claimed one quarter of the Catholics in Belfast and Londonderry supported the IRA.[112] Along similar lines, Conor Cruise O'Brien similarly claims that at least 20 percent of the Catholic population in Northern Ireland gives varying levels of support to the IRA.[113] Regardless of the precise level of support, which is clearly difficult to measure precisely, it is clear that the number of supporters vastly exceeded the number of active members.

The IRA also enjoyed widespread tacit support from those sympathetic to their cause.[114] Hewitt claims that half of the Catholic population sympathized with the IRA in 1972 at the peak of the violence.[115] Tim Coogan writes, "The I.R.A. benefited from the traditional passive support given to the movement. The bed for the night, the blind eye, the co-operation in money or services. For instance, the I.R.A. are not invulnerable, bullets do wound them, but one very rarely hears of a doctor or a hospital reporting the fact that a wounded man is receiving treatment—'traffic accidents' are widespread."[116] The financial support given to the IRA by those sympathetic to it was key to its continuing operations.[117] The IRA financed itself through levies on Catholic businesses, given willingly in the vast majority of cases.[118] In addition to donations, the IRA obtained funds "through illegal means such as protection rackets, tax fraud, robberies, smuggling, and illegal gaming machines, and legal means such as drinking clubs, taxi firms, shops and other legitimate businesses."[119]

Support for the IRA was not static or constant; it responded to events. When the British army moved in and began the internment operation in 1971, support for the IRA skyrocketed, volunteers flooded the organization, and the level of violence increased.[120] The IRA organized a rent and tax strike and most of the Catholic areas of Belfast and Londonderry became "no-go" areas for the security forces. Northern Ireland was racked by rioting and gun battles in the streets.[121] In the five months after internment began in August 1971, there were 729 explosions, 1,437 shooting incidents, and 143 people were killed, including 46 members of the police and army.[122]

While this level of violence was not maintained beyond a few years, the hostility generated by internment proved to have a lasting impact on the ease of recruitment for the IRA. New recruits had been joining the IRA in response to other British actions, particularly the Falls Road incident and Bloody Sunday; however, the increase in recruits after these other events "was dwarfed by the supply of manpower and support generated by internment."[123] These new volunteers also made gathering intelligence on the IRA more difficult because they were unknown to the intelligence services.[124] Internment was also counterproductive beyond the increased hostility that it generated among the Catholic population who had been ill-treated. It also gave the IRA a propaganda weapon, created training centers for the IRA in prison, and gave the IRA some legitimacy by treating them as political rather than criminal prisoners.[125]

Internment did have some benefits for the British security forces. It allowed them to gain useful intelligence through the interrogation of those who were interned. This intelligence allowed the security forces to arrest and imprison a large proportion of several active IRA units. J. C. Garnett writes, "Internment ... undoubtedly removed many dangerous men from the community, and the intelligence community learned a good deal from the interrogation of detainees in the newly created interrogation centers."[126] By some accounts, the Provisional IRA was on the ropes by 1974. According to Paul Wilkinson, by 1974,

The Provisionals' main explosives experts were inside Long Kesh and the Belfast Brigade of the Provisionals was denuded of leadership by the arrest of three leading officers in September 1974. By December 1974 the Belfast Brigade was in such weak shape that it comprised only fifteen or so active bombers and marksmen, mostly boys aged between fourteen and seventeen. Internment had begun literally to throttle the I.R.A.'s organization on the ground *because the army's intelligence had become so accurate that it had been able to identify the terrorists. The I.R.A.'s main force of bombers was, by November 1974, either interned or imprisoned.*[127]

Despite these successes of internment, the assessment by Wilkinson was premature because he did not take into account the skill of the IRA leadership in adapting to these new policies. The IRA was able to recruit new members and reorganize into a more secretive and better trained organization to better counteract the government's use of interrogation while suspects were interned or detained.[128] The IRA recognized that its brigade-style, hierarchical organization was vulnerable to interrogation because suspects under interrogation could give information on the membership and organization of large segments of the IRA. Consequently, the IRA began to reorganize in a cell structure with individual cells consisting of four volunteers who would have no contact with other cells.[129] The need for better training was recognized in an IRA 'Staff Report' that began, "The three-day and seven-day detention orders are breaking volunteers and it is the Republican Army's fault for not indoctrinating volunteers with the psychological strength to resist temptation."[130] To better prepare volunteers for interrogation, the IRA issued the *Green Book* to new recruits as its doctrinal guidebook. A large portion of the book deals with anti-interrogation tactics, with sections on arrest, interrogation, physical torture, psychological torture, and humiliation. It also warned recruits against many of the psychological tactics used by the police.[131] In sum, while internment may have resulted in some benefits from an intelligence standpoint, the increased support for the IRA made the policy of internment counterproductive overall.

Support for the IRA similarly increased after other violent clashes with security forces. In May 1987, the British Special Air Service (SAS) ambushed and killed eight IRA members who were about to attack the RUC barracks in Loughall. This incident angered many Catholics who justifiably believed that the British had adopted a "shoot-to-kill" policy, rather than rely on the courts.[132] Consequently, Tim Coogan speculates that the ambush was only a short-term victory for the security forces. "Each of the dead eight's funerals probably drew more than fifty replacements for the IRA."[133] Hunger strikes by IRA prisoners also proved to be an effective means of garnering support for the IRA.

However, the IRA also lost support after several incidents when Republican sympathizers viewed IRA actions as unnecessarily brutal. For example, on November 8, 1987, an IRA bomb exploded without warning at Enniskillen, killing eleven.[134] This attack showed "how, even for supporters of the IRA, the terrorist line of acceptable targets can be crossed into unacceptability."[135] The IRA also lost support after the "Bloody Friday" bombings on July 21, 1972, in which nineteen bombs went off in Belfast, killing 9 people and injuring 130. Richard Clutterbuck argues that these attacks "proved disastrous for the Provisional IRA. Reaction everywhere was hostile especially amongst Catholics."[136] As a final example, a bombing in August 1999 in Omagh "engendered horror and fierce public opposition."[137] Nevertheless, despite these fluctuations in support, the IRA has always maintained a sufficient level of support to continue its campaign and recruit new members.

If the IRA had not enjoyed such widespread support, it is unlikely that they would have been able to continue their campaign. The history of the IRA during its Border Campaign of 1956–1962 shows what happens when a terrorist movement lacks widespread support. Emergency powers would be more effective if support is low because the terrorist group would have difficulty in replacing imprisoned members with new recruits. During the border campaign, emergency powers were used on both sides of the border against the IRA. The Dublin government took the lead in fighting the IRA and resorted to internment, censorship, and police harassment. When large numbers of IRA members were interned the IRA lacked the support for its campaign and had difficulty recruiting new volunteers.[138] Consequently, after many leaders had been imprisoned and a rift appeared in the leadership, the IRA terminated its border campaign and appeared "finished, once and for all."[139] If the IRA had a similarly low level of support during the current conflict, it is likely that the emergency powers would have been effective as well.

In addition to the generally widespread support and sympathy for the IRA, the slow implementation of emergency powers made their use unlikely to be effective. For any terrorist group, the process of recruiting and training volunteers takes time. A quick government response can disrupt a terrorist organization by capturing terrorists faster than they can be trained and deployed. In the case of the IRA, after a potential member volunteered or was recruited, he went through a lengthy training process.[140] Most recruits were initially told to wait and perform peripheral tasks to demonstrate their commitment and motivation. Afterwards, the recruit joined a recruit "class" for weekly lessons that focused on ideology to further test the patience of the recruit. After several months, the recruit was trained to use weapons and conduct operations. Finally, the new member was allowed to engage in terrorist operations. In total, turning a potential recruit into a fully capable IRA member took at least several months.

The security forces, however, were never capable of capturing a large number of IRA members in a short amount of time. While the security forces arrested thousands of suspects and searched tens of thousand of houses a year, only a fraction of the suspects were convicted. The only time that the security forces moved relatively quickly was during the internment raids of 1971, when 342 suspects were detained on the first day and 2,375 people were interned in the first six months. But, as mentioned earlier, the lists for internment were based on outdated intelligence and most people were immediately released from custody. Even if the British could successfully intern hundreds of active terrorists, this would only temporarily diminish the terrorist threat. It would take time, but the IRA could recruit new members from the large numbers of supporters and sympathizers. For example, internment did hinder IRA actions in some areas, but in a matter of weeks, they had replaced and integrated new members into the organization.[141] J. Bowyer Bell argues that even "If all the active [terrorists] had been removed in one sweep, there were ample replacements."[142] Overall, the continued existence of the IRA despite arrests and imprisonment indicates that the speed with which the security forces operated was insufficient relative to the ease with which the IRA recruited new members.

The use of emergency powers in Northern Ireland shows that emergency powers are more likely to be effective if the terrorist group does not have a large base of supporters and sympathizers. If they do, new recruits will join the organization in response to the actions of the security forces. The ineffectiveness of the emergency powers raises an interesting question. If they were as ineffective as I have shown, why did Parliament renew them year after year?

There are several reasons why the emergency powers were retained. One reason is that their ineffectiveness was not immediately obvious; they did, in fact, allow the security forces to arrest thousands of people and search tens of thousands of homes. Also, many people expected the EPA and PTA to be effective because they believed that earlier pieces of emergency legislation were effective.[143] Even as the conflict wore on, the effectiveness of the emergency powers was still in doubt. Lord Jellicoe, in a 1983 report, found no evidence that the emergency powers were effective, but also he could not demonstrate that they were *not* effective.[144] Additionally, the emergency powers had a symbolic effect of showing the British public that the government was strongly opposed to terrorism. If they revoked the emergency powers, it "would have been akin to surrendering to terrorism."[145] Lastly, inertia played an important role in the yearly renewals of the emergency powers. When the emergency powers were first passed, they were justified as being necessary to fight terrorism; however, as the violence continued, members of Parliament had to "prove that [their] withdrawal would have no adverse effect on society."[146] This almost guaranteed that the emergency powers would continue unless there was irrefutable evidence showing that they were ineffective.

Nevertheless, it would probably have been better for Britain if the emergency powers were disbanded entirely. The physical brutality of the army and police in conducting searches and raids as well as the alleged inhumane treatment of prisoners greatly increased the support of the IRA in Catholic communities. In many instances, short-term police successes were more than offset by the increased number of volunteers for IRA. It is likely, then, that the emergency powers actually *decreased* the effectiveness of the anti-terrorism campaign. To many IRA members, the conflict became a fight against the British army, rather than against the Protestant forces. Had the British simply pulled out their troops and policed the province with normal laws and policing methods, much of the support for the IRA probably would have disappeared.[147] Although difficult to know for sure, fighting terrorism in Northern Ireland *without* emergency powers would have been more difficult, but probably more effective.

ABUSES OF EMERGENCY POWERS

While some abuses of emergency powers did occur, Britain mostly avoided any long-term or serious challenges to the constitutional state. The separation of powers—in the form of governmental commissions, debates in Parliament, and independent courts—frequently challenged the army and security forces' use of emergency powers. In addition, the right to free speech, in the form of a free press, publicized any potential abuse. Doctors that examined prisoners after they had been interrogated frequently went to the press to criticize the brutality of the security forces.[148] A free press and the separation of powers were critical, for example, in monitoring and controlling the use of interrogation. Tim Coogan writes, "The use of interrogation techniques has been documented in a variety of ways: reports by Amnesty, Lord Compton, Judge Bennett; the case brought by the Government of the Republic before the Court of Human Rights at Strasbourg ... the accounts given by individuals seeking damages [in court]."[149]

In addition, over time Northern Ireland saw a gradual reduction in the scope of the emergency powers. In each period of emergency powers, their use was criticized, debated, and consequently modified. Internment, the use of interrogations to obtain confessions, Diplock courts, and the use of supergrasses were all abandoned. Gradually, the fight against terrorism in Northern Ireland has returned in many ways to relying on the normal judicial process to try terrorists as criminal, rather than political, suspects.

One type of abuse of emergency powers occurs when they are no longer limited in their duration. In the Northern Ireland case, it is plausible to argue that the powers legislated to fighting terrorism are no longer *emergency* powers, but regular powers. They have been in use for almost three decades; arguably, it is a misnomer for these acts to be called emergency or temporary provisions given their long duration. More worrisome than the length of their use is the fact that they have become accepted as normal law. Paddy Hillyard argues, "It is apparent that successive governments and some independent assessors no longer consider either piece of legislation as temporary."[150]

While these powers have been used for almost thirty years, this does not constitute an abuse of these powers. For an abuse of emergency powers to occur, they must be unlawfully extended in their duration. In Britain, though, the emergency powers were always renewed yearly by Parliament and the legislation expired after a specific length of time;[151] therefore, regardless of how long emergency powers have been used, they are have been effectively limited in their duration to one-year increments. In addition, the lengthy use of emergency powers is consistent with the duration of the emergency situation in Northern Ireland. In other cases, we would expect emergency powers to be used for only a short time, but in Northern Ireland, the violence has continued unabated for thirty years, justifying the use of emergency powers for the duration of the conflict (effectiveness issues aside).[152]

Abuses can also occur in the scope of the emergency powers; that is, when the powers are intentionally used against people not suspected of terrorism or when the powers infringe more liberties than intended. The list of potential abuses along this dimension is long. "There have been repeated allegations of unlawful killings by the security forces, of torture during interrogation, of widespread and random arrests, of 'assembly line' justice and show trials, of mass detention without trial and of systematic ill-treatment of prisoners."[153] For example, the specific power to search and arrest citizens without a warrant was abused by the security forces who treated the whole Catholic population as suspect.[154] Dermot Walsh speculates that the EPA and the PTA have been used to "arrest thousands of people not genuinely suspected of being involved in terrorist activity."[155] Of the 1,200 people detained under the PTA through 1975, only 26 were charged with "serious offences."[156] Laura Donohue estimates that the EPA was applied on average 2,000 times per year, although only one quarter of those arrested were even charged with a crime.[157] By some estimates, 40 percent of the cases in jury-less Diplock courts can be classified as ordinary crimes, unrelated to terrorism.[158] The use of searches and arrests without warrant has also been used for political purposes. "Some of those arrested [under the PTA] appear to have been selected primarily because of involvement in Republican politics rather than suspected terrorism."[159]

Nevertheless, while these abuses clearly occurred, the following sections on the safeguards of the constitutional state will show why these abuses were relatively limited, did not continue, or got worse. In all, some abuses occurred, but democracy, the constitutional state, and (for the most part) individual liberties were preserved and many of the abuses that did occur were limited in their scope and duration.

More serious abuses of emergency powers did not occur because the safe-guards within Britain and Northern Ireland remained intact, despite the emergency powers. While the abuses that did occur were indeed serious, they did not lead to greater abuses because of the independent ability of Parliament, the judiciary, and the press to monitor and check the use of the emergency powers. Each safeguard will be discussed in turn.

The emergency powers restricted a wide range of liberties for citizens of Northern Ireland, but did not affect the separation of powers. Unlike other countries, the prime minister was not given any powers to disband Parliament or allowed to rule by decree, nor was the military given autonomy in conducting the counter-terrorism campaign. Consequently, Parliament—particularly the opposition parties within the House of Commons—continued to function as a monitoring and constraining body against abuses of power. In large part, Parliament devolved these duties to independent committees, which were tasked with reporting on the effectiveness and dangers of the emergency powers before Parliament would debate the re-enactment or renewals of the emergency provisions.[160] The results of these committees were published in reports named after the chair and include: the Cameron Report 1969, the Scarman Inquiry 1969–1972, the Hunt Report 1969, the MacDermott Report 1971, the Compton Report 1971, the Parker Report 1972, the Widgery Inquiry 1972, the Diplock Report 1972, the Gardiner Report 1975, the Shakleton Review 1978, the Bennett Report 1979, the Jellicoe Review 1983, the Baker Review 1984, and the Stalker/Simpson Inquiry 1985–1988.[161]

Many of these reports altered the application of emergency powers in Northern Ireland in important ways. For example, the Diplock Report, as the foundation of the EPA 1973, effectively increased the scope of emergency powers by recommending the continuation of internment while creating the jury-less Diplock courts. After the hostile reaction to internment, the Gardiner report recommended ending the policy of internment, which Britain abolished in 1975 when all internees were released. The Bennett Committee was tasked with investigating complaints of torture of prisoners. In its 1979 report, the committee recommended the introduction of strict controls on interrogation procedures. These controls were implemented in 1979 and led to a "dramatic decline in the number and seriousness of complaints."[162] As a last example, the Baker Report, responding to complaints of unnecessary searches and arrests without warrants, recommended "the introduction of a reasonable suspicion" for searches and arrests.[163]

The yearly debates in Parliament over the renewal of the emergency powers also provided a check on the abuse of these powers. Parliament is not a separate branch of government from the executive like in the United States, but "The House of Commons contains enough enemies of the government of the day to seek to discomfort it at the first sign of any abuse of its power."[164] The renewal debates were not necessarily a "rubber-stamping" exercise, although many sessions were. In many cases, the minority parties opposed the renewal of the emergency powers. In fact, some debates over emergency powers were quite impassioned, such as the debate prior to the enactment of the EPA in 1973.[165] In 1978, Labour refused to approve the renewal of the EPA unless the government incorporated the suggestions of the Baker Report.[166] In 1983, Labour officially opposed the renewal of the PTA on the grounds that it unnecessarily violated civil liberties and its aims could be achieved with normal laws.[167] The lack of vigorous debates in other instances was not an indicator of institutional weakness, but reflective of a general consensus on the value of the emergency powers. In every renewal debate, Parliament always had the opportunity to revoke or modify the emergency powers.

The courts in Britain provide an additional safeguard against abuses of power. In terms of the separation of power, the courts are more independent of the executive than is Parliament. The courts have exercised their power to overturn many of the verdicts in terrorist cases.[168] In one supergrass trial, eighteen of twenty-three suspects convicted on the evidence of the supergrass were set free upon appeal.[169] Despite all the infringements of liberties, any complaint by a citizen in Northern Ireland against a soldier or policeman has to be fully investigated.[170] The courts required that doctors examine suspects before, during, and after interrogations to assess whether any abuses had taken place. Although few personnel from the security forces have been successfully prosecuted for mistreating a prisoner, many prisoners have been acquitted based on doctors' reports stating that the confessions had not been voluntarily given.[171] In sum, the courts have been able to protect individual citizens from being victims of abuses. In this way, the courts have been an important protector of due process rights. However, as mentioned in Chapter 2, the strength of due process rights can limit abuses on a case-by-case basis, but are less valuable for stopping abuses throughout the country. In this way, the courts—as the defenders of due process rights—rectified cases of abuse, but could not stop the security forces from committing additional abuses.

One of the most serious abuses of emergency powers would be if the right to free speech were curtailed. A free press and the right to free speech allow individuals to publicize alleged abuses and force the government to respond to public opinion over the use of emergency powers. For the most part, however, free speech has been guaranteed in Britain and Northern Ireland, with only minor incidents of censorship. Despite public pressure, the British government has, for the most part, resisted the impulse to institute censorship.[172] In one incident of press censorship, the British Broadcast Corporation (BBC) canceled a program in 1985 under pressure from the government; then in 1988, the government imposed a ban that restricted press coverage of individuals supporting terrorism, including the Sinn Fein and Ulster Defence Association.[173] This ban has not been enforced, however, nor has it affected the reporting on terrorism.

Additionally, there have been no prosecutions of the media under the 1989 PTA.[174]

The limits that were placed on the reporting of the conflict came largely from within the media as internal guidelines or as rulings by the Independent Broadcasting Authority. Through 1985, over fifty television programs covering Northern Ireland had been self-censored.[175] Overall, though, the conflict in Northern Ireland has received enormous media attention and public scrutiny. With over 7,000 separate pieces of literature written on Northern Ireland by 1989, and with countless television shows and radio programs, it is clear that the conflict in Northern Ireland has not suffered from any lack of coverage by the press or scholars.[176]

A free and independent press has effectively monitored and publicized abuses in Northern Ireland. The press in Britain and Northern Ireland is "experienced in investigative journalism. The media generally is anxious to publicize any derelictions of duty on the part of the military and civil authorities tasked with enforcing the emergency legislation, and it is equally anxious to criticize those aspects of the legislation which seem unduly oppressive."[177] The press has also acted as a deterrent against even potentially worse abuses.[178] Robin Evelegh contends, "If [the security forces] dealt severely with the [terrorists], the soldiers could be certain of press allegations of military brutality, which would in their turn spark off political inquiries into what they had done, followed by Police inquiries."[179] The civil liberties lobby, in particular, has drawn attention to infringements of liberties in Northern Ireland by conducting detailed and systematic studies of alleged abuses. These studies not only publicized past abuses, but also discouraged possible future abuses. "Without persistent civil libertarian demands ... repression would no doubt have been greater."[180] The right to bring their grievances to the media and publicly debate issues has also allowed citizens to draw attention to particular abuses, such as abusive interrogation techniques, the alleged shoot-to-kill policy, and the supergrass system.[181]

In addition to the previous safeguards, abuses of emergency powers in Northern Ireland were also constrained by several international actors and organizations, including Amnesty International and the European Court of Human Rights.[182] When citizens felt their rights had been abused, they could file complaints with the European Court of Human Rights.[183] After the internment raid of 1971, the European Commission on Human Rights ruled that the "five techniques" of interrogation used during internment constituted torture. This ruling legitimized the complaints of the interned IRA suspects and publicly criticized British actions. Non-governmental organizations, such as Amnesty International, have also investigated allegations of abuse in Northern Ireland. In 1978, Amnesty investigated reports of abuse during the interrogation of suspects. Their report confirmed the abuses and led the government to form the Bennett Committee, whose recommendations led to strict controls on interrogation procedures.[184] In 1988, an Amnesty report criticized the supergrass policy of the early 1980s,[185] while a 1992 report called Britain one of the

worst human rights violators in Europe.[186] The effects of these international institutions on British actions should not be overstated. British sovereignty is
alive and well; Britain can simply ignore the judgments of the European Court
and Amnesty International. These institutions, however, do draw attention to
potential abuses and publicly criticize and humiliate Britain for any unnecessary infringements of liberties. Caroline Kennedy-Pipe observes that, over
time, "The conflict in Ireland, with its repressive legislation, started to appear
increasingly at odds with European opinion and began to draw condemna-
tion."[187]

Overall, the abuses of emergency powers have been constrained by the
watchful eye of a free press and Parliament, independent commissions and
courts, and international political institutions. With these various institutions
monitoring the emergency powers, not only have abuses been minimized but
also the scope of the emergency powers has diminished over time. Internment
without trial was stopped in 1975, interrogation techniques were more closely
monitored after 1979, and the supergrass system was abandoned after many of
the convictions based on supergrasses were overturned. The key to the safe use
of the emergency powers was that the emergency powers themselves did not
weaken any of the safeguards that could check abuses of power. These safeguards ensured that abuses would be both limited and temporary.

THE REVERSE TRADEOFF

The case of Britain's use of emergency powers raises several questions about
the conventional wisdom's assumed tradeoff between fighting terrorism and
protecting democracy. While many scholars assume that emergency powers are
effective but dangerous, this case shows the opposite outcomes for both dimensions. In Northern Ireland, emergency powers were ineffective yet not severely
abused. They were ineffective largely because the IRA enjoyed widespread support among the Catholic community of Northern Ireland. Even when the security forces interned or imprisoned large numbers of IRA members, the
organization continued to operate because new volunteers were readily available to join the cause. Despite some limited and temporary abuses, democracy
and constitutionalism were protected in Britain and Northern Ireland because
an independent Parliament and a free press could investigate, monitor, criticize,
and check any abuse of power.

The implications of this case are several. In deciding whether to use emergency powers, this case reinforces the importance of knowing and appreciating
the degree of support enjoyed by the terrorist group. Also, a government
should be self-conscious of the consequences of using emergency powers and
how they might increase or decrease the support for the terrorists. Several policies, such as internment without trial, indiscriminate searches, and brutal interrogation methods were counterproductive. Also, all aspects of emergency
powers are not equally likely to contribute to abuses of power. The emergency

legislation in Northern Ireland was primarily concerned with suspending many due process rights, but did not give the Prime Minister the right to suspend Parliament and did not seriously undermine the freedom of speech. By maintaining these safeguards, the emergency powers were successfully constrained in their use.

Knowing what we now know about the consequences for Britain of using emergency powers in Northern Ireland, was their implementation a wise decision? In this case the emergency powers were not only ineffective, but counterproductive. As a result, they should not have been used both from an efficacy standpoint and because of the limited dangers to civil liberties from even *using* emergency powers.

NOTES

1. See Caroline Kennedy-Pipe, *The Origins of the Present Troubles in Northern Ireland* (London: Longman, 1997) and Laura Donohue, *Counter-terrorist Law and Emergency Powers in the United Kingdom 1922–2000* (Dublin: Irish Academic Press, 2001), Chapter 1, for good historical overviews of Northern Ireland.

2. Richard Clutterbuck, *Guerrillas and Terrorists* (Chicago: Ohio University Press, 1977), 62–64.

3. J. Bowyer Bell, *The IRA 1968–2000: Analysis of a Secret Army* (London: Frank Cass Publishers, 2000), 58.

4. Thomas Hennessey, *A History of Northern Ireland* (New York: St. Martin's Press, 1997), 11.

5. J. Bowyer Bell, *A Time of Terror: How Democratic Societies Respond to Revolutionary Violence* (New York: Basic Books, 1978), 210–212.

6. Bell, *A Time of Terror*, 214.

7. Tim Pat Coogan, *The IRA: A History* (Niwot, CO: Robert Rinehart Publishers, 1994), 248.

8. Coogan, *The IRA*, 249.

9. Coogan, *The IRA*, 251.

10. Kennedy-Pipe, *Present Troubles in Northern Ireland*, 46.

11. Coogan, *The IRA*, 252.

12. Kennedy-Pipe, *Present Troubles in Northern Ireland*, 52.

13. The Provisionals essentially co-opted the traditional IRA organization, although the Official IRA continued to exist and conducted limited operations. See Bell, *The IRA 1968–2000* for a comprehensive description of the Provisional IRA.

14. Other groups include the Irish National Liberation Army (INLA) and two Loyalist groups, the Ulster Defence Association (UDA) and the Ulster Volunteer Force (UVF).

15. Kennedy-Pipe, *Present Troubles in Northern Ireland*, 48.

16. Kennedy-Pipe, *Present Troubles in Northern Ireland*, 53.

17. Tom Hadden, Kevin Boyle, and Colm Campbell, "Emergency Law in Northern Ireland: The Context," in *Justice under Fire: The Abuse of Civil Liberties in Northern Ireland*, ed. Anthony Jennings (London: Pluto Press, 1990), 7–8.

18. Coogan, *The IRA*, 262; and Martin Dillon, *God and the Gun: The Church and Irish Terrorism* (New York: Routledge, 1999), 7.

19. Dillon, *God and the Gun*, 7.

20. Dillon, *God and the Gun*, 8. See also Kennedy-Pipe, *Present Troubles in Northern Ireland*, 55.

21. Hadden, Boyle, and Campbell, "Emergency Law in Northern Ireland," 6.

22. Hadden, Boyle, and Campbell, "Emergency Law in Northern Ireland," 6.

23. Clutterbuck, *Guerrillas and Terrorists*, 69.

24. Hadden, Boyle, and Campbell, "Emergency Law in Northern Ireland," 6.

25. Clutterbuck, *Guerrillas and Terrorists*, 69; and Donohue, *Counter-terrorist Law*, 122. Prime Minister Faulkner resigned in protest.

26. Christopher Hewitt, *The Effectiveness of Anti-Terrorist Policies* (Lanham, MD: University Press of America, 1984), 15.

27. Clutterbuck, *Guerrillas and Terrorists*, 62.

28. Coogan, *The IRA*, 284, cites five Provisional demands of Britain made in negotiations with the British government in 1971 that serve as useful guidelines to the IRA goals: "1. End its campaign of violence against the Irish people. 2. Abolish Stormont. 3. Hold free elections to establish a regional parliament for the Province of Ulster as a first step towards a new government for the thirty-two counties. 4. Release all Irish political prisoners, tried or untried, in England and Ireland. 5. Compensate all those who had suffered as a result of British violence."

29. In the early years of the Provisional IRA (1971–1972), they instigated riots and gun battles with government forces as a response to the internment operations. Since then, they have focused their efforts on specific targets and have acted more like terrorists and less like urban guerrillas. Coogan, *The IRA*, 285.

30. Coogan, *The IRA*, 287 and 503.

31. See Coogan, *The IRA* for accounts of all these incidents.

32. Clive Walker, *The Prevention of Terrorism in British Law* (Manchester: Manchester University Press, 1986), 2, describes the Provisional IRA as both a terrorist and guerrilla organization. Coogan, *The IRA*, 290 claims that the only time civilians have been deliberately targeted by the IRA is in the British campaign, although many civilians have also died unintentionally in Northern Ireland.

33. Coogan, *The IRA*, 313–326.

34. See Mike Alvarez et al., "Classifying Political Regimes," *Studies in Comparative International Development* 31, no. 2 (summer 1996) and Kenneth Bollen, "Issues in the Comparative Measurement of Political Democracy," *American Sociological Review* 45 (1980).

35. Britain was coded at least a 7 out of 10 on the democracy measure beginning in 1880 in the Polity 98 Dataset. From 1837 until 1879, Britain was coded as a 6.

36. Scott Gordon, *Controlling the State: Constitutionalism from Ancient Athens to Today* (Cambridge, MA: Harvard University Press, 1999), 329.

37. Gordon, *Controlling the State*, 343–348 and 354–357, also considers the bureaucracy and pressure groups as constraints on power.

38. By Parliament, I mean the House of Commons, not both houses.

39. Gordon, *Controlling the State*, 334.

40. Gordon, *Controlling the State*, 336.

41. Although Gordon, *Controlling the State*, 339, points out that there is no legal means or convention to force out a prime minister.

42. Gordon, *Controlling the State*, 340.

43. Gordon, *Controlling the State*, 332.

44. Gordon, *Controlling the State*, 348–353.

45. See Brian Loveman, *The Constitution of Tyranny: Regimes of Exception in Spanish America* (Pittsburgh: University of Pittsburgh Press, 1993), 17 for the history of emergency powers in Britain.

46. J. C. Garnett, "Emergency Powers in Northern Ireland," in *Coping with Crises: How Governments Deal with Emergencies*, ed. Shao-chuan Leng (Lanham, MD: University Press of America, 1990), 54.

47. Donohue, *Counter-terrorist Law*, is an excellent history of emergency powers in Britain and Northern Ireland.

48. Kennedy-Pipe, *Present Troubles in Northern Ireland*, 22; and Donohue, *Counter-terrorist Law*, 16–31.

49. Other notable acts of emergency powers in Ireland and Britain include: Criminal Justice Act 1984, Criminal Law Act 1967, Customs and Excise Management Act 1979, Firearms Act 1968, Offences Against the State Act 1939, Flags and Emblems Act 1954, and Prevention of Violence Act 1939. See Garnett, "Emergency Powers in Northern Ireland," 48; and Anthony Jennings, ed., *Justice under Fire: The Abuse of Civil Liberties in Northern Ireland* (London: Pluto Press, 1990), xi, for a list of emergency legislation.

50. See the Northern Ireland Office's *Guide to the Emergency Powers* (Belfast: HMSO, 1989) for the specific provisions of each act.

51. The Northern Ireland (Emergency Provisions) Act has been passed in 1973, 1975, 1978, 1987, 1991, 1996, and 1998 with yearly renewals in between. The Prevention of Terrorism (Temporary Provisions) Act was first passed in 1974, re-enacted in 1976, 1984, 1989, and 1996 and also renewed yearly. For details on this history, see Donohue, *Counter-terrorist Law*, xi–xvi.

52. Donohue, *Counter-terrorist Law*, 178, calls the supergrass system a complement and result of the emergency powers but not necessarily a part of them.

53. There were also allegations that the security forces had a "shoot-to-kill" policy, especially during the early 1980s. See Anthony Jennings, "Shoot to Kill: The Final Courts of Justice," in *Justice under Fire: The Abuse of Civil Liberties in Northern Ireland*, ed. Anthony Jennings (London: Pluto Press, 1990), 104–130.

54. See Kennedy-Pipe, *Present Troubles in Northern Ireland*, 105, 121–122, and 148 for more on the peace process since 1985.

55. Garnett, "Emergency Powers in Northern Ireland," 47–48.

56. Garnett, "Emergency Powers in Northern Ireland," 51.

57. Hennessey, *A History of Northern Ireland*, 194.

58. One problem with internment is that it is generally used against political prisoners or prisoners of war rather than against ordinary criminals. Consequently,

internment bestowed some degree of legitimacy to the IRA as a political organization and not just a criminal one.

59. Juries were predominantly Protestant. If juries were Catholic, perverse acquittals against Republican suspects would have been a concern as well.

60. Steven Greer and Antony White, "A Return to Trial by Jury," in *Justice under Fire: The Abuse of Civil Liberties in Northern Ireland*, ed. Anthony Jennings (London: Pluto Press, 1990), 47; and Donohue, *Counter-terrorist Law*, 123.

61. For a thorough description of the EPA, see Donohue, *Counter-terrorist Law*, 127–153.

62. Hadden, Boyle, and Campbell, "Emergency Law in Northern Ireland," 7.

63. Walker, *Prevention of Terrorism*, 22.

64. Walker, *Prevention of Terrorism*, 22–23, argues that the Act was *not* just a knee-jerk response by Parliament, but that it was a response to years of bombings and was modeled on earlier, much-debated emergency provisions.

65. Hadden, Boyle, and Campbell, "Emergency Law in Northern Ireland," 8.

66. Walker, *Prevention of Terrorism*, 24–27; and Donohue, *Counter-terrorist Law*, xv-xvi.

67. Peter Taylor, *Beating the Terrorists: Interrogation in Omagh, Gough, and Castlereagh* (New York: Penguin Books, 1980), 70.

68. The impetus for criminalization also came from the Unionists rejection of the Sunningdale Agreement, which was to create a new power-sharing executive in Northern Ireland. With the rejection of this plan, the British were less willing to stay in what they viewed as an interminable conflict. Kennedy-Pipe, *Present Troubles in Northern Ireland*, 75.

69. Greer and White, "Return to Trial by Jury," 48.

70. Hadden, Boyle, and Campbell, "Emergency Law in Northern Ireland," 8.

71. Garnett, "Emergency Powers in Northern Ireland," 75; and Hadden, Boyle, and Campbell, "Emergency Law in Northern Ireland," 8.

72. Taylor, *Beating the Terrorists*, 31.

73. See Eamon Collins and Mick McGovern, *Killing Rage* (London: Granta Books, 1997), Chapter 21, for his account of the psychological and physical pressure put on him during his seven days of interrogation. In the end, he became a supergrass, turning evidence on several other IRA members.

74. Taylor, *Beating the Terrorists*, 147.

75. Taylor, *Beating the Terrorists*, 11.

76. Kennedy-Pipe, *Present Troubles in Northern Ireland*, 88.

77. Taylor, *Beating the Terrorists*, 22 and 25.

78. Hadden, Boyle, and Campbell, "Emergency Law in Northern Ireland," 9.

79. The nickname for these informers, supergrasses, probably originated with the phrase "snake-in-the-grass" while the word supergrass was first used in British press to describe bank robbers who informed on each other and even testified in court, according to Steven Greer, "The Supergrass System," in *Justice under Fire: The Abuse of Civil Liberties in Northern Ireland*, ed. Anthony Jennings (London: Pluto Press, 1990), 74.

80. Hadden, Boyle, and Campbell, "Emergency Law in Northern Ireland," 10.

81. Greer, "Supergrass System," 73.

82. Eamon Collins was the supergrass in 1985. He later withdrew his evidence, was released, and left the IRA. In 1997, he published his story as an IRA member in *Killing Rage*, which offers an insightful look at the daily workings of the IRA.

83. Greer, "Supergrass System," 75, offers a table on the statistics from the supergrass trials.

84. Hewitt, *Effectiveness of Anti-Terrorist Policies*, 64, measures emergency powers on a scale of 1–15, by looking at six components: detention without trial (5 points), increased penalties for terrorism (2 points), special courts (2 points), arrests without charge (2 points), searches without warrants (2 points), and censorship (2 points).

85. Hewitt, *Effectiveness of Anti-Terrorist Policies*, 66–67, 70–74. His five cases include Cyprus and the EOKA, Uruguay and the Tupamaros, Northern Ireland and the IRA, Spain and the Basques, and Italy and the Red Brigade.

86. Garnett, "Emergency Powers in Northern Ireland," 68–69.

87. See Dermont P. J. Walsh, "Arrest and Interrogation," in *Justice under Fire: The Abuse of Civil Liberties in Northern Ireland*, ed. Anthony Jennings (London: Pluto Press, 1990), 36, for a chart of arrests made under the emergency powers.

88. Garnett, "Emergency Powers in Northern Ireland," 50. In 1974, almost 72,000 houses were searched and 26,000 pounds of explosives were found, according to Paul Wilkinson, "British Policy on Terrorism: An Assessment," in *The Threat of Terrorism*, ed. Juliet Lodge (Boulder, CO: Westview Press, 1988), 37.

89. Walker, *Prevention of Terrorism*, 175.

90. Donohue, *Counter-terrorist Law*, 230, points out that members of Parliament actually recognized that the decrease in the level of violence "was due more to a change in PIRA strategy than to British emergency measures."

91. Greer, "Supergrass System," 95.

92. Garnett, "Emergency Powers in Northern Ireland," 69.

93. In the *Handbook for Volunteers of the Irish Republican Army: Notes on Guerrilla Warfare* (Boulder, CO: Paladin Press, 1985), 1 and 17, the importance of popular support is emphasized.

94. Alex P. Schmid et al., *Political Terrorism: A New Guide to Actors, Authors, Concepts, Data Bases, Theories, and Literature* (Amsterdam: North-Holland Publishing Company, 1988), 633, estimate 350 to 400 active members, while Paul Wilkinson, "The Orange and the Green: Extremism in Northern Ireland," in *Terrorism, Legitimacy, and Power: The Consequences of Political Violence*, ed. Martha Crenshaw (Middletown, CT: Wesleyan University Press, 1983), 119, estimates about 300 active members.

95. David Bonner, "United Kingdom: The United Kingdom Response to Terrorism," in *Western Responses to Terrorism*, ed. Alex P. Schmid and Ronald Crelinsten (London: Frank Cass Publishers, 1993), 175, estimates a peak of 1,000 members in the 1970s with 250–300 members in the 1980s.

96. Hewitt, *Effectiveness of Anti-Terrorist Policies*, 12, citing Jack Holland 1981, *Too Long a Sacrifice*, 145.

97. Charles Drake, "The Provisional IRA: Reorganization and the Long War," in *Terrorism's Laboratory: The Case of Northern Ireland*, ed. Alan O'Day (Aldershot, England: Dartmouth Publishing Company, 1995), 94.

98. Coogan, *The IRA*, 286; and Hewitt, *Effectiveness of Anti-Terrorist Policies*, 13. Bell, *The IRA 1968–2000*, 82, writes that they were "young men and women of limited formal education, without property or profession, eager, enthusiastic, determined to serve, to act for the greater good."

99. Bell, *The IRA 1968–2000* makes this point repeatedly.

100. Bell, *The IRA 1968–2000*, 79.

101. John Conroy, *Belfast Diary: War as a Way of Life* (Boston: Beacon Press, 1995), 174.

102. Collins and McGovern, *Killing Rage*, 50–51.

103. Bell, *The IRA 1968–2000*, x and 93.

104. Coogan, *The IRA*, 365.

105. Bell, *The IRA 1968–2000*, 81.

106. Conroy, *Belfast Diary*, 81.

107. Bell, *The IRA 1968–2000*, 85.

108. D. Bonner, "United Kingdom," 178. This is echoed in a report by General Glover: "PIRA will probably continue to recruit the men that it needs. They will still be able to attract enough people with leadership talent, good education, and manual skills to continue to enhance their all round professionalism. The movement will retain popular support sufficient to maintain secure bases in the traditional Republican areas." Quoted in Conroy, *Belfast Diary*, 58.

109. Bell, *The IRA 1968–2000*, 83.

110. Wilkinson, "The Orange and the Green," 119.

111. This is consistent with an estimate cited by Drake, "The Provisional IRA," 94, which says that there were three auxiliaries for each of the 650 gunmen.

112. Hewitt, *Effectiveness of Anti-Terrorist Policies*, 14.

113. Conor Cruise O'Brien, "Terrorism under Democratic Conditions: The Case of the IRA," in *Terrorism, Legitimacy, and Power: The Consequences of Political Violence*, ed. Martha Crenshaw (Middletown, CT: Wesleyan University Press, 1983), 96.

114. Bell, *A Time of Terror*, 228, claims the IRA enjoys more toleration than sympathy from most of the population.

115. Hewitt, *Effectiveness of Anti-Terrorist Policies*, 14.

116. Coogan, *The IRA*, 286–289.

117. D. Bonner, "United Kingdom," 176, claims the IRA had a strong financial support base.

118. Coogan, *The IRA*, 441.

119. Drake, "The Provisional IRA," 96.

120. See Coogan, *The IRA*, 260–263.

121. Bell, *A Time of Terror*, 216.

122. Paddy Hillyard, "Political and Social Dimensions of Emergency Law in Northern Ireland," in *Justice under Fire: The Abuse of Civil Liberties in Northern Ireland*, ed. Anthony Jennings (London: Pluto Press, 1990), 204.

123. Coogan, *The IRA*, 263.

124. Bell, *A Time of Terror*, 217.

125. Garnett, "Emergency Powers in Northern Ireland," 52.

126. Garnett, "Emergency Powers in Northern Ireland," 52.

127. Paul Wilkinson, *Terrorism and the Liberal State* (London: Macmillan Press, 1977), 154–155.

128. Drake, "The Provisional IRA," 89.

129. Coogan, *The IRA*, 356.

130. Coogan, *The IRA*, 356. This report was made public after being seized in an arrest in December 1977.

131. See Coogan, *The IRA*, 427–434, for sections of the *Green Book*.

132. For more on shoot-to-kill see Jennings, *Justice under Fire*, Chapter 5.

133. Coogan, *The IRA*, 439.

134. Martin Dillon, *The Dirty War: Covert Strategies and Tactics Used in Political Conflicts* (New York: Routledge, 1999), xxxiii.

135. Coogan, *The IRA*, 441.

136. Clutterbuck, *Guerrillas and Terrorists*, 70.

137. Bell, *The IRA 1968–2000*, 37.

138. Bell, *A Time of Terror*, 214; Wilkinson, "British Policy on Terrorism," 31; and Bell, *The IRA 1968–2000*, 65.

139. Coogan, *The IRA*, 248.

140. See Bell, *The IRA 1968–2000*, 179–181, for more on the training of IRA members.

141. Hennessey, *A History of Northern Ireland*, 195.

142. Bell, *The IRA 1968–2000*, 133.

143. Donohue, *Counter-terrorist Law*, xxiv.

144. Donohue, *Counter-terrorist Law*, 244.

145. Donohue, *Counter-terrorist Law*, 317.

146. Donohue, *Counter-terrorist Law*, 233.

147. The IRA would still have been motivated by the need to protect Catholic communities from Protestant paramilitary groups.

148. Taylor, *Beating the Terrorists*.

149. Coogan, *The IRA*, 427.

150. Hillyard, "Political and Social Dimensions of Emergency Law in Northern Ireland," 198–200.

151. For example, the PTA of 1984 had to be renewed yearly and expired after five years. In 1989, the PTA was modified and no longer expires after a certain time, but it still has to be renewed yearly by Parliament. Bruce W. Warner, "Great Britain and the Response to International Terrorism," In *The Deadly Sin of Terrorism: Its Effect on Democracy and Civil Liberties in Six Countries,* ed. David Charters (Westport, CT: Greenwood Press, 1994), 19.

152. The fact that the emergency situation continues raises obvious questions about the effectiveness of Britain's use of emergency powers and other terrorist countermeasures.

153. Hadden, Boyle, and Campbell, "Emergency Law in Northern Ireland," 1.

154. Hillyard, "Political and Social Dimensions of Emergency Law in Northern Ireland," 194.

155. Walsh, "Arrest and Interrogation," 37.

156. Donohue, *Counter-terrorist Law,* 231.

157. Donohue, *Counter-terrorist Law,* 240.

158. Walker, *Prevention of Terrorism,* 138. See also Hillyard, "Political and Social Dimensions of Emergency Law in Northern Ireland," 200.

159. Walker, *Prevention of Terrorism,* 138. See also Peter Hall, "The Prevention of Terrorism Acts," in *Justice under Fire: The Abuse of Civil Liberties in Northern Ireland,* ed. Anthony Jennings (London: Pluto Press, 1990), 144; and Hillyard, "Political and Social Dimensions of Emergency Law in Northern Ireland," 183.

160. Garnett, "Emergency Powers in Northern Ireland," 63, also recognizes the importance of these public inquiries as a safeguard of liberty.

161. Hadden, Boyle, and Campbell, "Emergency Law in Northern Ireland," 4–5.

162. See Taylor, *Beating the Terrorists,* 332 and 337; and Hadden, Boyle, and Campbell, "Emergency Law in Northern Ireland," 9.

163. Hadden, Boyle, and Campbell, "Emergency Law in Northern Ireland," 11.

164. Garnett, "Emergency Powers in Northern Ireland," 65.

165. Greer and White, "Return to Trial by Jury," 47–48.

166. Donohue, *Counter-terrorist Law,* 186.

167. Donohue, *Counter-terrorist Law,* 247.

168. Greer, "Supergrass System," 92, cites the instances of the courts overturning verdicts as a sign of the independence of the courts in Northern Ireland. See also Taylor, *Beating the Terrorists,* 66 and 185, for other examples of courts overturning verdicts or acquitting suspects based on unlawfully obtained evidence.

169. Greer, "Supergrass System," 89.

170. Garnett, "Emergency Powers in Northern Ireland," 64.

171. Taylor, *Beating the Terrorists,* 107. The entire book essentially describes the role of the doctors in monitoring abusive interrogation procedures in Northern Ireland.

172. Donohue, *Counter-terrorist Law,* 227.

173. Kennedy-Pipe, *Present Troubles in Northern Ireland,* 139; and Donohue, *Counter-terrorist Law,* 191.

174. Warner, "Great Britain," 21.

175. Conroy, *Belfast Diary,* 38.

176. See Alan O'Day, "The Dilemma of Violence in Northern Ireland," in *Terrorism's Laboratory: The Case of Northern Ireland,* ed. Alan O'Day (Aldershot, England: Dartmouth Publishing Company, 1995), 1, for the number of sources on Northern Ireland and Taylor, *Beating the Terrorists,* 164, 221, 297, and 319, for a sampling of some of the television broadcasts.

177. Garnett, "Emergency Powers in Northern Ireland," 62.

178. Kennedy-Pipe, *Present Troubles in Northern Ireland,* 68, argues that the military initially failed to appreciate the power of the press. They operated in Northern Ireland much as they had while fighting insurgencies in Malaysia and Cyprus, where a free press did not exist that could publicize or criticize the brutality of the security forces.

179. Robin Evelegh, *Peace-Keeping in a Democratic Society: The Lessons of Northern Ireland* (Montreal: McGill-Queen's University Press, 1978), 37.

180. Hillyard, "Political and Social Dimensions of Emergency Law in Northern Ireland," 208.

181. Jennings, "Shoot to Kill,", 122; and Greer, "Supergrass System," 91.

182. Hadden, Boyle, and Campbell, "Emergency Law in Northern Ireland," 22. The British government ratified the United Nations Covenant on Civil and Political Rights in 1976.

183. Garnett, "Emergency Powers in Northern Ireland," 64.

184. Coogan, *The IRA*, 336.

185. Jennings, *Justice under Fire*, xviii.

186. Coogan, *The IRA*, 454.

187. Kennedy-Pipe, *Present Troubles in Northern Ireland*, 113.

Chapter 4

Uruguay and the Tupamaros

When the government of Uruguay used emergency powers to fight the Tupamaros, the emergency powers were effective in eliminating the terrorist threat; however, these powers also led to a military coup and the end of democratic government. The Tupamaros formed in 1962 in response to the economic malaise and hyperinflation that was undermining the Uruguayan welfare state. In 1965, the Tupamaros launched their first operation and subsequently began a series of robberies, political kidnappings, and bombings that led to the imposition of emergency powers in 1968. By 1971, the army had taken over anti-terrorist operations and soon attacked the institutions of constitutional government. In June 1973, the military forced the president to disband the Congress in a coup that turned the country into a military dictatorship. The success of the army in eliminating the Tupamaros was due primarily to the speed with which they arrested actual and suspected Tupamaros in 1972. Furthermore, due to a change in tactics by the Tupamaros, they were no longer widely supported and had difficulty replacing imprisoned members with new recruits. Emergency powers allowed the military to abuse its power because they removed many of the institutional safeguards of the constitutional state. The military arrested political opponents, shut down or censored the media, and seized power in a 1973 coup d'état.

THE BACKGROUND OF THE TUPAMAROS

The Uruguayan state became independent in 1828 when Brazil and Argentina agreed to the creation of a buffer state between their two warring countries.[1] During the latter decades of the nineteenth century, civil war frequently erupted in Uruguay between the liberal, Colorado forces and the more conservative, Blanco forces. These two groups became the basis of Uruguay's two main political parties, with Montevideo supporting the Colorados and landowners in the countryside supporting the Blancos. Under the presidency of José Batlle y Ordóñez (1903–1907, 1911–1915), two significant changes occurred in Uruguayan politics. To dampen the constant political and physical battles between the Colorados and Blancos, Batlle established a collegial executive, known as the Colegiado, in which power was shared between the two parties. Also, Batlle also created the institutional structure that transformed Uruguay into a modern welfare state. An eight-hour workday, a weekly day of rest, minimum wages, social security, labor protection, state participation in industry, universal education, and divorce laws were all legislated under Batlle.[2]

The Uruguayan welfare state depended on good economic conditions to redistribute wealth among its citizens. When the economy (based largely on the raising of sheep and cattle)[3] suffered, the government no longer had the resources to pay the large percentage of citizens who received pensions and unemployment payments. Although Uruguay's exports of beef, wool, and leather increased during World War II and the Korean War, the export boom ended by the mid-1950s.[4] Inefficiencies and technological stagnation in the livestock sector of the economy combined with falling demand to create a situation of low and declining growth rates, rising unemployment, and severe inflation in the late 1950s and 1960s.[5] From June 1967 to June 1968, price levels increased by 170 percent,[6] while the Uruguayan peso dropped from 3.46 pesos to the dollar in 1950 to 1,100 pesos to the dollar in 1973.[7] From 1955 to 1971, the gross national product (GNP) actually declined from $712 million United States dollars to $635 million dollars,[8] while industrial production growth fell from 8.5 percent to only 0.8 percent in the late 1950s.[9]

These economic difficulties put a severe strain on the social welfare system. In 1955, the government employed approximately 166,000 Uruguayans, with another 196,000 receiving government pensions. By 1969, however, 213,000 people were employed by the government and nearly 350,000 citizens received pensions (out of a total population of approximately three million). In fourteen years, the government was paying wages and pensions to an additional 200,000 citizens in a time of decreased tax revenue. In sum, the deteriorating economic situation challenged the ability of the extensive Uruguayan welfare state to provide the full range of social welfare programs.[10] With the welfare state failing, other ideologies became more popular. Marxism, in particular, became a viable alternative after the success of the Cuban revolution and the rise of communist movements across Latin America.

The origins of the Tupamaros can be traced to 1961 when Raúl Sendic, a young Montevideo lawyer, attempted to organize the sugarcane workers in northern Uruguay into the Union of Artigas Sugar-Workers (UTAA). The UTAA marched to Montevideo on May 1, 1961, demanding redistribution of the land, eight-hour working days for workers on the sugar plantations, and minimum wages. The march, however, was violently dispersed by troops from the Republican Guards. Sendic reached two conclusions: His socialist goals would require a clandestine guerrilla movement, and the real battle should take place in Montevideo rather than the countryside.[11] Sendic then disappeared for eight months,[12] during which time he and a few friends were organizing the National Liberation Movement, more commonly called the Tupamaros.[13]

The ideology of the Tupamaros contained elements of both nationalism and socialism, although it was primarily Marxist.[14] The Tupamaros saw the foreign influence of the United States, Britain, Argentina, and Brazil as limitations on Uruguayan development. Consequently, the nationalist aspect of the Tupamaros ideology called for the end of foreign domination of the Uruguayan economy. Similarly, the Tupamaros also saw internal economic oppression by the domestic oligarchy that owned and controlled most of Uruguay's land and businesses. They sought to end their control in typical Marxist fashion: by restoring the means of production to the people of Uruguay.[15]

While these lofty goals were the ultimate objectives of the Tupamaros, the short-term goal was the creation of a situation of "power duality."[16] The Tupamaros hoped to create a parallel, shadow government with its own courts, a "People's Prison," tax collection, and networks for redistributing collected and stolen money.[17] The purpose of power duality was to challenge directly the legitimacy of the state by providing the benefits of citizenship through means other than that of the state. In many regards, the Tupamaros were quite successful in establishing power duality. Their kidnapping victims were held for months in the "People's Prison" and the Tupamaros often acted like modern Robin Hoods by stealing from the rich and distributing money and food to the poor.[18] The Tupamaros would often hijack delivery trucks loaded with food or blankets and deliver the goods to the slums of Montevideo.[19]

The use of violence was very much a part of the Tupamaros' ideology. Not only was the use of violence seen as legitimate, but also the most desirable means to achieve their ends. The Tupamaros believed "The use of violence is an inalienable right of people who wish to revolt against their government ... [and] because their ideological objectives constituted such a radical departure from the beliefs held by Uruguay's ruling oligarchy, the Tupamaros felt that nothing short of revolutionary political, social, and economic changes were required to achieve their objectives."[20] Violence was used with the knowledge and expectation that the government would react with harsh countermeasures. In fact, Robert Moss writes that a key element of the Tupamaros' strategy was "to drive the government towards the use of 'counter-terrorism' in the hope that this would arouse liberal critics at home and abroad and weaken [the government]."[21] Specifically, the Tupamaros hoped that the government would use repressive security measures, which would increase support for the Tupamaros.[22] (In fact, they were successful at this in the early stages of their campaign.)

Membership in the Tupamaros was quite diverse in terms of occupation, gender, and age. By occupation, roughly a third of the Tupamaros were students, a third were middle class professionals, and a third were laborers. The mean age was young (although typical for terrorist groups) at around twenty-six years. About 70 percent of the Tupamaros were male, and 30 percent female.[23] The Tupamaros were organized at the most basic level into cells consisting of four or five members.[24] Cell members did not know the names of others in the cell; each was given a pseudonym to be used at all times. Cells were specialized as either commando units that engaged in military actions and were staffed by the more experienced Tupamaros or service cells who "obtained meeting places, constructed hideouts, purchased food and clothing, gathered intelligence, provided medical treatment, manufactured explosives, obtained and maintained arms and ammunitions, repaired vehicles, and solved transport and communication problems."[25] These cells were then combined into columns that operated in a given geographic area, with several columns in Montevideo alone.[26] Orders were given to the cells or columns by the Executive Committee, which directed the entire organization and created and disbanded cells. Lastly, there was a National Convention that consisted of representatives from every cell and column. The National Convention was to meet every eighteen months, although it probably only met twice, in January 1966 and March 1968.[27]

The first Tupamaro operation was a raid on the Swiss Rifle Club in Montevideo on July 31, 1963, in which twenty-eight World War I and World War II–era guns were stolen.[28] The first time the Tupamaros name was used to claim responsibility for an attack was after an August 8, 1965, bombing of the Bayer chemical plant in Montevideo.[29] In general, in the period from 1963 to 1968, the Tupamaros mostly focused on acquiring money, weapons, and supplies while building up their numbers through recruitment.[30] These formative years of the Tupamaros were marked by both successes and failure. For example, in December 1963, around twenty Tupamaros attacked a delivery truck loaded with food and delivered it to the poor, which gave them a Robin Hood–like following among Uruguay's masses. In raids in January and April 1964, they stole more weapons and explosives from a customs warehouse and a munitions factory.[31] However, they also suffered some losses; in September 1963, Sendic was identified as the leader of the group and captured when some Tupamaros were interrogated after refusing medical care following a routine car accident. In March 1965, three Tupamaros were arrested after a bungled robbery attempt and in December 1966, two terrorists were killed and several more arrested after a failed attempt to steal a car.[32]

Some scholars have argued that the Tupamaros should not be labeled as terrorists during this period; instead, they should be characterized as urban guerrillas or merely organized criminals acting on behalf of the poor of Uruguay.[33] Writing in 1969, Marysa Gerassi claims, "The Tupamaros have achieved the first stages of their strategy without terrorism."[34] She claims that the Tupamaros fought with police only when they were forced to and that they warned civilians before exploding their bombs. Although the Tupamaros may have been "considerate" in their attacks,[35] violence in the form of bombings, kidnappings, and executions intended to frighten a population still constitutes terrorism. Importantly, recall that I do not define terrorism as violence directed only against civilian targets. Terrorists make no distinctions between the military and civilians; attacks on off-duty military personnel can terrorize as much as attacks on civilian targets. For example, the Tupamaros assassinated Ernet Motto, a frigate captain, and Colonel Artigas Alvarez, the brother of the commander of the joint police-army forces. These assassinations created a climate of terror in the security forces and may have led to their desire for a fast and vigorous response to fight terrorism.[36] This climate of fear was also prevalent in the civilian population, according to Alphonse Max, who writes that, while in the early years the Tupamaros

managed to retain an image of well-mannered, considerate, polite, friendly, humane and educated young men and women ... with the robbery at the Casino in Punta del Este ... and the shooting of policemen and innocent bystanders in ever-increasing numbers, the true picture emerged. The public saw the terrorists as cold-blooded, ruthless criminals, determined to achieve their objectives, however vague and contradictory, by means of violence and terror and with utter disregard for the innocent lives they might take.[37]

In sum, the Tupamaros bombed military, police, business, and government buildings, kidnapped a variety of people, shot many policemen, and even searched policemen's homes, taking their weapons and humiliating the officers in front of their families.[38] All of these actions made the Tupamaros terrorists.

After 1968, the Tupamaros were much more aggressive in their attacks on the Uruguayan state, particularly the government of President Pacheco.[39] Arturo Porzecanski writes, after 1968, "The Tupamaros began applying the full range of guerrilla tactics in accordance with their strategic scheme. Robberies of money and arms became a monthly and then a weekly event; political kidnapping was launched and repeatedly applied; propaganda actions were initiated and continued until, by the end of 1969, the existence of the urban guerrilla organization could escape no one and 'Tupamaro' became a household word."[40]

Kidnappings were the most prominent and dramatic tactic used by the Tupamaros,[41] with fourteen people abducted from 1968 to 1972.[42] The first political kidnapping occurred on August 7, 1968, when the Tupamaros abducted Ulises Pereyra Reverbal,[43] the President of the State Electricity and Telephone Services, and close colleague of President Pacheco. Three thousand policemen unsuccessfully searched for him until he was eventually released by the Tupamaros.[44] On September 9, 1969, Gaetano Pellegrini Giampietro, a newspaper director, was abducted by the Tupamaros and later released after seventy-three days in captivity after his family paid $200,000 in ransom money.[45] On July 28, 1970, the Tupamaros captured Judge Pereyra Manelli, who had presided over several trials of arrested Tupamaros.[46] When the Tupamaros' demands for Manelli's release were not met, they kidnapped two more people:

Dan Mitrione, a United States Agency for International Development (AID) official and alleged Central Intelligence Agency (CIA) agent[47] and Aloysio Dias Gomide, the Brazilian consul.[48] A week later, on August 7, Claude Fly, an American agricultural expert, was kidnapped.[49] Tensions mounted after these kidnappings and President Pacheco called for Congress to suspend civil liberties to deal with the Tupamaros.[50] Geoffrey Jackson, the British ambassador to Uruguay, was kidnapped on January 8, 1971. He was held in the "People's Prison" for eight months before he was released.[51] Other kidnapping victims included G. Berro, Uruguay's attorney general in 1971; R. Ferres, a wealthy businessman in 1971; C. Davies, a former Minister of Agriculture in 1971; J. Berembau, a businessman in 1971; H. Farina, a newspaper editor in 1972; N. Bardesio, a police photographer in 1972; and H. Ruiz, President of the House of Representatives in 1972.[52]

Besides kidnappings, the Tupamaros also used assassinations and bombings, and they even held hostage an entire town for a short period of time. On April 3, 1970, the Tupamaros ambushed and killed police inspector Héctor Morán Charquero, the head of the new special police branch charged with combating terrorism.[53] Charquero was targeted because he was believed to be responsible for the police's use of torture on arrested Tupamaros.[54] One of the most daring operations occurred on October 8, 1969, when the Tupamaros held hostage the town of Pando, twenty miles outside of Montevideo. Between thirty-five and fifty Tupamaros converged on the town,[55] captured the police station, cut all telephone lines, and proceeded to rob three banks.[56] The entire operation took about half an hour, although the Tupamaros were delayed slightly when a policeman opened fire at some Tupamaros at one of the banks. The extra delay allowed the police to converge on Pando and capture many of the Tupamaros in their retreat back to Montevideo. Up to twenty-five Tupamaros were arrested,[57] while many others were wounded in gunfights with the police.[58]

In addition to these operations, the Tupamaros gained considerable attention for their break-in of the Financiera Monty, a loan company engaged in illegal and corrupt activities, on February 14, 1969. The Tupamaros stole the account books and forwarded them to a judge. The subsequent investigation into the Monty resulted in a major scandal and the resignation of several government officials with ties to the Monty.[59] The Tupamaros also gained notoriety for the attack on the Naval Training Center on May 29, 1970, in which they successfully held the naval officers hostage and made off with the base's weapons.[60]

THE USE OF EMERGENCY POWERS

Faced with these frequent attacks and kidnappings by the Tupamaros, the Uruguayan government responded repeatedly with emergency powers. Before describing the emergency powers, I will first outline the political context of Uruguay, focusing on the characterization of Uruguay as a democracy, the history of constitutionalism, and the increased power of the presidency resulting from the 1966 constitution.

Uruguay during this period is described by practically every author that writes on Uruguay as a democracy, if not the premier, model democracy of Latin America.[61] Uruguay was commonly called "the Switzerland of America,"[62] or "the Picture of Democracy."[63] Uruguay, until the military coup in 1973, had a free press, regular elections, stable and peaceful transfers of power, a social welfare system, and high literacy rates.[64] Uruguay is also coded as a democracy in the database frequently used by democratic peace scholars.[65] In addition to the positive characteristics of democracy, Uruguay was also known for having good civil-military relations, which was far different from many other Latin American countries. In fact, Uruguay's military was "one of the hemisphere's smallest, most professionalized and least politicized military institutions."[66] It was only with reluctance, and under the initiative of civilians, that the military gradually and increasingly took part in political processes.[67] In the end, though, the military was the most responsible for the abuses of the emergency powers.

Before the military coup, Uruguay had a long history of constitutional government.[68] The government was based on a separation of powers in which power was divided between executive, legislative, and judicial bodies, with each body able to constrain the power of the other bodies, much like in the United States. The role of the executive changed somewhat with revisions in the constitution. The first constitution took effect in 1830, with revisions in 1918, 1933, 1952, and 1966. The different constitutions basically alternated between a collegiate executive and a strong, individual executive.[69] The 1966 constitution restored a strong presidency to Uruguay, after there was growing acceptance that a single, stronger executive would be more capable of dealing with the growing economic troubles facing the country.[70] The president was given the power "to take whatever security measures deemed expedient" when faced with external invasion or internal disorder.[71] According to all five constitutions, the president was elected every five years in an electoral process that simultaneously combined primary and general elections.[72]

The legislature, or General Assembly, was composed of two houses—the Senate and the Chamber of Representatives. The Senate consisted of thirty senators and the vice president and was elected by the country as a whole without electoral districts. The Chamber of Representatives consisted of ninety-nine members elected directly by electoral district. Lastly, the judiciary consisted of multiple layers of court systems, with the Supreme Court of Justice as the highest court. The five judges of the court were appointed for ten-year terms by the National Assembly and had jurisdiction over constitutional issues.[73]

Confronted with declining economic conditions and increasing violence from the Tupamaros, the Uruguayan state responded with various forms of emergency powers from 1968 until 1973, when the military assumed power in Uruguay. In the 1966 election, General Oscar Gestido won the presidency, but died less than a year after taking office. His vice president, Jorge Pacheco Areco became president in 1968.[74] Pacheco's presidency from 1968 to 1972 was marked by the frequent use of emergency powers including, the "suspension of civil liberties, police sweeps, preventive detention and censorship of the news media."[75] President Pacheco often justified his use of emergency powers during his regime as necessary to deal with the threat from the Tupamaros.[76]

Emergency powers were first legislated on June 13, 1968, when, "After the cost of living had increased 160 percent, President Pacheco Areco sought to stop inflation and obtain credits from the International Monetary Fund."[77] In addition, Pacheco wanted to give the police extra powers to put down the frequent protests of students, workers, and civil servants. Pacheco invoked article 168, paragraph 17 of the Uruguayan constitution, which granted him "special powers" in "the case of serious and unforeseen events, foreign attack or internal upheavals."[78] Under these special powers,[79] Pacheco froze prices and wages, closed labor unions, banned public meetings, established limited censorship, and jailed any political agitator.[80] At the end of June, martial law was declared, which put newspapers under official rather than self-censorship and decreed courts martial for anyone demanding wage increases.[81] These measures were ineffective at ending both the economic problems and the protests that arose because of them. It was in the middle of this "state of siege" that the Tupamaros kidnapped Pacheco's colleague and friend, Pereyra Reverbel. The special powers lasted for eight months, until March 15, 1969, when the state of siege was lifted.[82]

The respite from emergency powers was brief. Three months later, on June 24, 1969, a limited state of siege was declared in the face of major strikes protesting wage controls that were enacted when the economy was suffering from high inflation. The government closed several newspapers and arrested labor leaders, but the strikes continued.[83] Soon thereafter, on July 26, the president decreed that he would draft strikers into the army and court martial anyone who resisted.[84]

The next use of emergency powers occurred during the summer of 1970, in response to the increased activity of the Tupamaros. Between July 2 and August 7, four men were kidnapped (Manelli, Mitrione, Gomide, and Fly). On August 10, 1970, after the body of Dan Mitrione was found, the Uruguayan legislature suspended civil liberties for twenty days.[85] The police were permitted to conduct searches without a warrant and could hold suspects indefinitely (suspending habeas corpus).[86]

Following the escape of 38 female Tupamaros and 106 men (including Sendic) in early September 1971, President Pacheco decreed that the army would take over all anti-terrorist operations from the police.[87] This change did not have an immediate impact because the Tupamaros called for a truce during the November elections.[88] The Tupamaros were wary of creating a climate of violence and fear that might have deterred people from turning out to vote for the left wing candidates.[89] Despite the Tupamaros' truce, the Colorado party and their leading presidential candidate, Juan Bordaberry, won the election and formed a coalition government with the Blancos in April 1972.

On April 14, 1972, the Tupamaros violently served notice that their self-imposed truce had ended with assassinations of several officials and skirmishes with army and police officers.[90] Two policemen, a navy officer, and a former deputy minister were all killed by the Tupamaros.[91] The following day, April 15, the legislature granted President Bordaberry emergency powers and declared a "state of internal war."[92] In practice, this meant that the army was given the authority to fight the Tupamaros "without regard for judicial accountability or individual rights."[93] These powers gave the military tremendous powers that they abused (which will be discussed later in this chapter). Most importantly, the military was given complete autonomy in prosecuting the fight against the Tupamaros. Terrorists were tried by military—rather than civilian—courts, which completely undermined the due process rights of anyone arrested by the military. In addition, by removing civilian oversight, the emergency powers eliminated the possibility that the courts or even Congress could check the power of the military. For example, the military arrested members of Congress if they dared to criticize how the military was fighting terrorism. This "state of internal war" was extended for forty-five days on May 15, with a subsequent extension of twenty-two days.[94]

When these emergency powers were set to expire at the end of June, Congress refused Bordaberry's request for an indefinite extension.[95] Instead, Congress renewed the "state of internal war" for just an additional ninety days.[96] At the same time, however, President Bordaberry was urging Congress to pass a new national security law. On July 11, 1972, Congress complied by simultaneously lifting the state of war and passing the State Security Law, which "gave juridical recognition to the suspension of individual liberties and the violent repression that had been conducted by the military under the declaration of a state of internal war."[97] These emergency powers were repeatedly renewed without interruption: Congress renewed them on September 28 and November 30;[98] the President extended the emergency powers for an additional forty-five days on February 15, 1973;[99] Congress renewed them for sixty days on April 1;[100] and President Bordaberry decreed new emergency powers on June 1.[101]

In sum, emergency powers were employed almost continuously from June 1968 until June 27, 1973, when Bordaberry dissolved Congress.[102] Bordaberry, together with the military, used the emergency powers to launch the coup that resulted in Uruguay becoming a military dictatorship. Before discussing the manner in which the emergency powers were abused, the following section will first assess the effectiveness of the emergency powers in fighting the Tupamaros.

EFFECTIVE EMERGENCY POWERS

Emergency powers were initially ineffective at combating the Tupamaros. From 1968 until September 1971 (when the army took over), the Tupamaros continued their kidnappings and attacks with impunity. In the summer of 1968, the Tupamaros kidnapped Pereyra Reverbel in the midst of President Pacheco's use of emergency powers to crack down on strikers. The police launched a counteroffensive aided by emergency powers in an attempt to find Reverbel, but their efforts "only netted a few prisoners, arms, and explosives."[103] In 1969, Marysa Gerassi wrote, "The information obtained by the police [through interrogations] has not led to a major crackdown ... No top-ranking Tupamaro has been caught."[104]

Even when the police had some success during this period, it was not due to the emergency powers. On August 7, 1970, after the Tupamaros had kidnapped four men, the police successfully captured much of the high command of the Tupamaros, including Raul Sendic, their founder and leader;[105] however, the success of this operation was due to standard police work and a bit of luck, and not because of the use of emergency powers.[106] In fact, no emergency powers were even in effect at the time; the Uruguayan government did not pass the emergency powers until August 10, three days after the capture of Sendic. Moreover, even when the emergency powers were in effect, attacks by the Tupamaros continued unabated and the police never found the kidnap victims.[107] In fact, neither the police nor army ever recovered a kidnap victim.[108]

The Tupamaros continued their attacks despite the emergency powers, with the number of terrorist incidents peaking in the summer of 1971.[109] Porzecanski claims that because "the police contributed very little to the long-run defeat of the Tupamaros,"[110] they were soon relieved of their anti-Tupamaros mission. As mentioned earlier, President Pacheco put the army in charge in 1971 after the Tupamaros broke out 144 members from two prisons. The level of violence dropped dramatically, not because of emergency powers, but due to a self-imposed truce by the Tupamaros. The following chart plots the number of attacks per month from 1968 until the end of 1972 (Figure 4.1).

When the Tupamaros ended their truce, the army immediately used the emergency powers to arrest and imprison suspected Tupamaros.

During and after April 14, 1972, the Tupamaros began a series of battles with the armed forces that left 19 dead within 4 days. A state of internal war was declared by Congress, and the final confrontation between the Tupamaros and the security forces was on. By June 2, 30 people (guerrillas, soldiers, policemen, and innocent civilians) had been killed, many more were wounded, and over 500 Tupamaro members and collaborators were detained at military bases.[111]

The armed forces used systematic torture and interrogation "without regard for judicial accountability or individual rights" to coerce information out of prisoners.[112] Torture techniques included two days of continuous standing without food, a week spent blindfolded, dunking prisoners' heads in water almost to the point of drowning, beatings in ways that left no marks, and sleep deprivation.[113]

The use of these techniques aided the army in finally discovering the location of the "People's Prison" and the Tupamaros' printing house for their propa-

Figure 4.1
Terrorist Attacks in Uruguay, 1968–1972

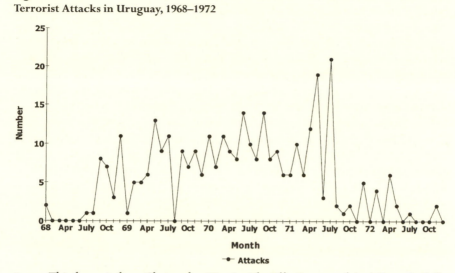

Source: This figure is from Christopher Hewitt, *The Effectiveness of Anti-Terrorist Policies* (Lanham, MD: University Press of America, 1984), 69.

ganda. Moreover, the army began to arrest large numbers of suspected Tupamaros based on the information obtained through interrogation. By September 1972, the army had recaptured Sendic and had imprisoned several thousand suspected Tupamaros.[114] "By the end of 1972, over 5,000 people had been arrested by the military and the Tupamaro organization was virtually destroyed."[115] In terms of measuring the effectiveness of the emergency powers, the destruction of the Tupamaros is a clear indication of success. The success may have been due to other factors or a combination of factors, but the use of emergency powers, specifically, did contribute to the Uruguayan state's success against the Tupamaros.

In general, emergency powers are designed to aid the security forces in capturing terrorists and their affiliates. They will be the most effective when the state can imprison terrorists faster than they can replace imprisoned members with new recruits. The important variables that determine this are the number of active terrorists relative to the level of support and the speed with which the state implements the emergency powers.[116] I will first assess the numbers of active Tupamaros compared to their level of support, showing how the support began to weaken in 1970 and 1971. I will then describe how the army (and not the police) moved quickly and hindered the ability of the Tupamaros to recruit new members to replace those that had been captured.

The estimates on the number of active Tupamaros range anywhere from 50 to 3,000 members. At the low end, some estimates put the number of core Tupamaros at fifty members, but this number is probably too low. During the operation at Pando, around fifty Tupamaros took part and it is unlikely that they would have risked their entire strength for one operation.[117] One author puts the number at 1,000 but with only 50 to 100 as core members who participate in commando operations.[118] At the high end of the estimates, another author claims there were 1,000 core members,[119] while a Uruguayan police chief estimated there were 3,000 militants and 4,000 sympathizers.[120] This estimate by the police chief is almost definitely too high, reflecting his bureaucratic and personal incentives to inflate the threat from the Tupamaros.

An estimate of several hundred active Tupamaros is probably the most accurate for several reasons. Alain Labrousse argues that the Tupamaros must have had at least several hundred "shock troops" based on the ability of the Tupamaros to continue their operations even after thirty members had been arrested in August 1970. However, the estimate of thousands of Tupamaros is probably an overestimate because a newspaper reported that the police had a list with just 428 names of Tupamaros on it.[121] Also, in an interview with Maria Gilio in April 1970, a Tupamaro claims that approximately 150 Tupamaros were in prison with an additional 100 members sought by the police.[122] Lastly, Arturo Porzecanski breaks down the demographic data based on press reports of the 648 Tupamaros arrested from December 12, 1966 to June 22, 1972. He claims that this number (648) excludes some 4,000 suspected Tupamaros held by the military without trial. The larger number (4,000), however, includes active members as well as supporters and collaborators and many innocent Uruguayans wrongly suspected of terrorist activity (see the following section for details on the abuses of emergency powers).[123] Consequently, the number of active members is only a portion of this larger number, in all probability numbering several hundred.[124]

These few hundred Tupamaros were initially well supported by many Uruguayans. Both the Tupamaros and the security forces recognized the importance of public support.[125] Carlos Marighella, the Brazilian guerrilla leader and ideologue of the Tupamaros, wrote in the *Minimanual of the Urban Guerrilla*, "One of the permanent concerns of the urban guerrilla is his identification with popular causes to win public support."[126] In terms of the structure and organization of the support networks, Porzecanski writes:

Each cell, whether commando-type or service-oriented, was encouraged—and, indeed, found it necessary—to establish its own information and propaganda network. In other words, they had to build contacts and to enlist the aid of "peripherics" and "sympathizers." Peripherics were usually those who worked part-time for the Tupamaro organization and did not live clandestinely. They were responsible for distributing propaganda, contacting sympathizers within the population at large, obtaining new supply sources, recruiting, and developing sources of information and intelligence. Sympathizers were those who, in one way or another, aided the Tupamaros by knowingly supplying "inside" information; selling them arms, ammunition, chemicals, and other needed raw materials; suggesting potential recruits; and assisting in the provision of medical and legal aid.[127]

During their early operations in the late 1960s, the Tupamaros were reported to enjoy a high level of support among the general population.[128] Connolly and Druehl write that the Tupamaros "gained an unprecedented following" and that "Few leftist organizations have captured the sympathy of the masses as the Tupamaros have."[129] In 1969, a Gallup poll reported that a majority of Uruguay's citizens held the Tupamaros in high esteem.[130] The Tupamaros were supported by the traditional groups that support radical movements: students, the working class, trade unions, and urban teenagers.[131] In addition, hospital workers frequently treated injured Tupamaros and did not report them to the police.[132] The Tupamaros probably enjoyed their highest level of support in 1968 and 1969, particularly after their kidnapping of Reverbel, who was widely recognized as corrupt, and the operation at Pando, which demonstrated the strength and daring of the Tupamaros.[133] After the Reverbel kidnapping, for example, the Tupamaros enjoyed such widespread support that "new recruits flocked to the movement."[134]

While the level of support enjoyed by the Tupamaros was fairly high in the early years, it started to diminish in 1970 due to the public's reaction to three specific Tupamaro operations. In early July 1970, the Tupamaros simultaneously attacked eight Montevideo policemen in cold blood. Alphonse Max writes that, despite their reputation as "considerate" terrorists, these attacks began to turn public opinion against the Tupamaros. "With the unprovoked attacks on the policemen, the atmosphere changed and became clearly and noticeably hostile to the terrorists."[135] Also, on August 10, 1970, the body of kidnap victim Dan Mitrione was found. He was the only kidnap victim killed by the Tupamaros. According to Robert Moss, "The murder [of Dan Mitrione] lost the Tupamaros some of the popularity they had tried to build up by presenting themselves as Robin Hood figures reluctant to shed blood."[136] Lastly, during the summer of 1970, the Tupamaros used threats of violence in an attempt to disrupt the tourist industry. Operation "Hot Summer," as it was named, was successful, but the workers in the tourism industry suffered as well. Consequently, the Tupamaros lost a great deal of support among the working class.[137] As evidence of this dramatic loss of support, a public opinion poll in September 1972 "showed that only 4 percent of the population thought that the Tupamaros were motivated by a sense of social justice—compared with 59 percent a year before."[138] In the end, "The reasons for the group's brisk demise were closely related to the failure to consolidate support amidst large segments of the Uruguayan urban middle and working class."[139]

Sergio d'Oliveira argues that the Tupamaros were never actually supported by the general population; instead, the people of Uruguay were neutral spectators of the battle between the Tupamaros and the state security forces.[140] In large part, this was because the Tupamaro ideology and propaganda "failed to make any headway among the masses of the population which, according to them, they sought to liberate."[141] Tupamaro ideology was further challenged by the election results in 1971. By calling a truce and supporting the Frente

Amplio (a coalition of leftist parties), the Tupamaros appeared to be abandoning their goal of bringing a revolution through violence. Also, the poor showing of the revolutionary parties in the election undermined the idea that the people of Uruguay truly wanted the revolution described by the Tupamaros.[142] Consequently, when they resumed their attacks in April 1972, the Tupamaros movement "found itself abandoned by the liberal groups that it had surfaced to support in the elections." When the army initiated its campaign against the Tupamaros, the terrorist group "had totally estranged itself from public opinion."[143] By 1972, "The Tupamaros did not represent the will of the people and yet felt they acted in its behalf."[144]

The Tupamaros recruited new members from people who were already supportive of their cause. In general, recruitment into a terrorist organization is a lengthy process, and the Tupamaros were no exception. Potential recruits, inspired by their revolutionary ideology, would either seek out a known member of the Tupamaros or be contacted by one.[145] According to Labrousse, "Each recruit—whether he volunteered or was contacted—was subjected to a long and detailed investigation by his 'sponsors.' After this he had to undergo a whole series of tests to determine his suitability to join."[146] The sponsor would submit a report that contained details on the recruit's "life, habits, political and occupational background, personality, friends, health record, and all other aspects that might be significant."[147] Before becoming a commando in the Tupamaros, the new recruit would have to prove him or herself to be reliable. After the recruit passed the initial security clearance, he was assigned peripheral work—such as intelligence, communications, and repairs—before being given greater responsibility in commando operations.[148] Meanwhile, the new member would go through extensive training in paramilitary skills, such as weapons and explosives training and guerrilla tactics.[149] In all, it would take at least several months for a potential recruit to become a trustworthy and competent commando. In the early years (1962–1970), the Tupamaros had little difficulty in finding recruits. The Tupamaros could take their time and investigate and train the recruits before relying on them in paramilitary operations.[150]

The army was more effective than the police because the Tupamaros began to lose public support and because the army moved more quickly to imprison suspected Tupamaros. The speed of the army's response was due to the information they gained through interrogations.[151] In two and a half months in 1972, according to a report by the joint army-police force for counterinsurgency, 846 Tupamaros had been arrested (out of a total of several hundred active members and a few thousand supporters). In the three months of April, May, and June, 1972, 1,200 suspects were arrested and 30 suspects were killed in street battles.[152] In a four month period in the middle of 1972, 5,600 searches were conducted and almost 2,000 alleged Tupamaros were arrested including most of the Tupamaros that had earlier escaped from prison.[153] By the end of 1972, the security forces held 3,000 suspected Tupamaros in prison and had discovered the location of three "People's Prisons" where kidnap victims had earlier been held.[154] These actions by the security forces were matched briefly by an increase in terrorist activity—including eight kidnappings, and dozens of raids and assaults—but the Tupamaros were unable to continue their pace of operations due to the effectiveness of the armed forces.[155]

The armed forces effectively crushed the Tupamaros within three months of when the Tupamaros resumed their activities in April 1972.[156] In the remaining months of 1972, the army moved to arrest those even peripherally connected to the Tupamaros. At this point, however, with most of the active members in prison, the remaining supporters could do little except hope to avoid arrest. In the end, "Surprised by the speed and strength of the armed forces' counterattack, weakened by information leaks extracted through torture and betrayals, disappointed by the ease with which bases in the countryside collapsed to the military, and plagued by organizational difficulties, the Tupamaros ceased activity and retreated into hiding."[157]

ABUSES OF EMERGENCY POWERS

When the army moved against the Tupamaros in 1972, their operations did not stop with the arrests of suspected terrorists; instead, the military turned its attention to the political opposition and in June 1973, took over the reigns of power in a military coup. Although the coup occurred after the defeat of the Tupamaros, it was still a result of the emergency powers. The military used their additional powers that were granted to them by the emergency powers to undermine the institutions of government in the name of fighting terrorism. By the time the Tupamaros were defeated, the military's power was almost completely unconstrained. Moreover, in fighting the Tupamaros, the quality of civil-military relations changed, with the military desiring an increased role in the political process. According to Edy Kaufman, "The Tupamaros presented Uruguay with a taste of political violence and initiated the chain of events by which military violence was first directed against subversion, but which resulted in the violation of already weakened constitutional principles."[158] In assessing both the effectiveness of emergency powers and whether they will be abused, this is clearly a case where emergency powers posed a dangerous trade-off. While they may have been effective at fighting terrorism, emergency powers also led to the end of the constitutional state. As a result of the conflict with the Tupamaros, "1971 and 1972 saw the definite entrance into Uruguay's political picture of the country's armed forces, as well as a gradual deflation of Presidential power and a definite decay of Uruguay's traditional political institutions."[159]

Emergency powers can be abused, in their scope or their duration. Emergency powers can be extended to result in more severe restrictions of individual liberties and due process rights than originally legislated (torture in this case) and can be used against non-terrorists, such as political opponents of the regime. These abuses in scope are normally committed by the security forces. The right to free speech and the separation of powers are the key safeguards that protect against these abuses. Also, the limits on the duration of emergency powers can be abused. These abuses occur at the hands of the military or the executive. To protect against these types of abuses, the norms of the president (commitment to democratic procedures) and the military (civil-military relations), as well as the continued separation of powers, are the best safeguards. Each type of abuse will be discussed in turn. Afterwards, I will explain why these abuses occurred.

Allegations of torture were widespread against both the police and army.[160] Torture constitutes an abuse of emergency powers because, while the emergency powers curtailed many civil liberties of arrested citizens, the torture of suspects was never permitted. In one case, a suspect testified before the court that he "had been stripped, beaten, burned, and subjected to electric shocks by the police, that his right hand had been smashed and his genitals mutilated."[161] In interviews with Maria Gilio, several Tupamaros reported various experiences of torture at the hands of the security forces, including beatings at the time of arrest, having cigarettes put out in open wounds, running through lines of men who would punch, kick, and beat the prisoners, being dunked in water almost to the point of drowning, and being tied to a metal table, covered in wet rags and then electrocuted (including in the genitals).[162] In addition to these testimonies, independent observers also reported the use of torture by Uruguay's security forces. For example, in 1972 the Roman Catholic Bishops of Uruguay declared that "The Army was guilty of killings, physical oppression, torture, and illegal imprisonment."[163] Amnesty International repeatedly documented the use of torture in Uruguay both before and after the military coup. In 1975, Amnesty reported that around forty people had died while being tortured.[164] Compared to abuses in other countries in this study, Uruguay's security forces were worse than British forces in Northern Ireland, but not as bad as Peru's military against the Shining Path.

A second type of abuse of emergency powers is if they are used to harass, arrest, imprison, or intimidate people unaffiliated with terrorism. In the summer of 1970, the security forces conducted wide-ranging searches for the four men kidnapped by the Tupamaros (Manelli, Gomide, Mitrione, and Fly). In August alone, "The police conducted some 20,000 house searches—trying to find the Tupamaros' kidnap victims. Conducted clumsily, at all hours of the night, and reportedly many times without appropriate warrants, these massive searches created great resentment among Montivideo's population and failed to turn up any Tupamaro."[165] Not only were these searches abuses of the emergency powers by being used against innocent civilians, they were also ineffective and probably counterproductive by turning the citizenry against the government. Earlier, government forces had conducted a similar large-scale and ineffective sweep under the pretext of searching for the kidnapped Reverbel, but really "to show the public that they [the police] could give the Tupamaros 'a taste of their own medicine.'"[166] In many of these and later sweeps, many of those arrested had no connection with the Tupamaros.[167]

In 1972, the security forces began to harass and arrest the political opposition by accusing various individuals of collaborating with the Tupamaros. For example, in June 1972, Luis Batalla, a Christian Democrat labor leader unaffiliated with the Tupamaros, was arrested and later found dead.[168] In November, Jorge Batlle, the grandnephew of Jose Batlle, criticized the armed forces in a radio address. Despite his Congressional immunity, he was arrested and held for twenty-four days.[169] In April 1973, the army accused the left-wing Blanco Senator Erro of protecting terrorists based on a confession obtained by a tortured Tupamaro. Congress's refusal to suspend Erro's immunity so that the army could arrest him eventually led the army to seize power in June 1973.[170] After the coup in 1973, the army turned their attention to those politicians who had opposed them. Several party leaders were forced to flee to Buenos Aires, while numerous Blancos, communists, and members of the Frente Amplio were imprisoned.[171]

The other type of abuse of emergency powers occurs when the emergency powers become permanent. This type of abuse can range from a slight, but permanent change in due process rights to a coup in which the wielder of the emergency powers seizes control of the state. In Uruguay, the latter was the case as the military took power after a coup on June 27, 1973. This section will first describe how the coup occurred and then briefly describe the political situation under the military dictatorship.

Even before the coup in 1973, there was concern that the emergency powers had become normalized. Edgardo Carvalho wrote in *Marcha* in August 1970, "A mechanism provided by the Constitution as a temporary and emergency measure has become the normal means by which our political system functions, and this severely limits the rights and freedoms of the individual."[172] As normal as emergency powers may seem *during* an emergency, however, they are only abused if they become normalized once the emergency, and their justification, passes. In the case of Uruguay, emergency powers were no longer necessary after the Tupamaros had been eliminated in the last half of 1972. Consequently, the abuses of the emergency powers (in terms of their duration) occurred from 1972 until the coup in 1973.

The military coup on June 27, 1973, was a gradual process that can be traced back to Pacheco's decision to put the military in charge of anti-terrorism in the summer of 1971. When the Tupamaros resumed their activity in April 1972, the army moved quickly and effectively to destroy the Tupamaro terrorist organization. In the process of defeating the Tupamaros, the military gradually changed its views on its role in the political process. For most of Uruguay's history, the armed forces were one of the most apolitical in Latin America.[173] However, the military's increasing role in the fight against the Tupamaros politicized the armed forces. In fact, Edy Kaufman claims that the dialogues between captured Tupamaros and their army jailors resulted in "ideological transmission and the political conscience-raising of the military."[174] The possibility of a greater political role drew mixed feelings among Uruguay's officer corps. Some welcomed the new role, while others were troubled by the change in civil-military relations. All officers, though, felt uneasy with the military's "In between role ... Some demanded more responsibility in law enforcement tasks while others wanted the armed forces to be left alone."[175] As the violence from the Tupamaros escalated, however, the military "reached a consensus ... to put an end to the nation's rampant political violence."[176] With greater power, some generals developed contempt for civilian institutions and saw themselves as the only ones capable of solving Uruguay's problems.[177] The use of emergency powers, then, changed the norms of the military in terms of how they understood their relationship with the civilian government. This change within the military was primarily a result of their campaign against the Tupamaros, but was also influenced by "popular disillusion with the existing politician's corruption and failure ... disorders, and leftist ideologies."[178] The lack of civilian oversight of the military (as a result of the emergency powers), coupled with the military's changing views on civil-military relations, gave the military both the means and motive for seizing power. The result was a succession of crises in which the military increased its power vis-à-vis other political institutions.

Following the defeat of the Tupamaros, Uruguay went through three crises in which the military challenged the power of the government.[179] The first crisis occurred in October 1972 when a Frente Amplio senator criticized the army for the arrest and torture of four physicians. The physicians were released but then immediately rearrested and tortured again. In protest, the civilian minister of defense resigned when the lieutenant colonel holding the prisoners refused to release them again.

The second crisis began in January 1973 when a Colorado senator warned in a radio broadcast that the country was entering a "militaristic period." When the army chiefs were refused permission to respond to these accusations, the new, pro-military defense minister resigned and was replaced by a pro-government general. In response, the army and air force seized key strategic positions and access roads to the capital. The navy, however, supported the government and barricaded the harbor and old city of Montevideo. Uruguay was on the brink of civil war, with the army and air force opposed by the navy and government. In mid-February, the chief of the navy resigned and his replacement expressed solidarity with the army and air force, thereby forcing the government to face the combined armed forces alone. On February 23, the military created the Council for National Security (COSENA), composed of the heads of the three military branches, the ministers of defense, interior, foreign affairs, and economics and finance, and the director of planning. Faced with a hostile and united armed forces, Bordaberry was forced to make concessions to the military. Thereafter, President Bordaberry stayed in power, but government policy was controlled by COSENA.[180]

The third and final crisis began in April when the military demanded that Congress lift the immunity of Senator Erro, whom they accused of protecting terrorists. In May, the armed forces began concentrating troops in Montevideo to pressure Congress into lifting Erro's immunity. Erro left for Argentina in early June, at the same time that Bordaberry extended emergency powers without Congressional approval. Frustrated by the actions of Congress, the army decided to seize power completely. On June 27, 1973, the army occupied the Congress buildings while Bordaberry dissolved the Congress, accusing them all of "grave violations of the fundamental principles of the Constitution" for refusing to lift Erro's immunity. In addition, Bordaberry "prohibited the dissemination of any information implying dictatorial motives to the government, and empowered the police and armed forces to take whatever measures were necessary to ensure normal public services."[181] In later years, the military justified the coup and all their actions subsequently as necessitated by the "struggle against subversion."[182]

After the coup in 1973, Uruguay was ruled by a military dictatorship for twelve years; in 1985, the military held elections and withdrew from power.[183] During these twelve years, Uruguay lacked any democratic processes and individual liberties were nonexistent. "With no constitutional safeguards or anything remotely resembling the rule of law, there was only one rule—force—and it was carried out by the military in its paranoid quest for national security."[184] In its quest for security, the military created an authoritarian state. Kaufman characterizes the years of military rule in the following manner:

Guarantees of civil rights have been suspended, and since such an authority which resided in the Congress was dissolved by the executive in 1973, no safeguards whatsoever remain. Not only have basic rights been eliminated (opinion, assembly, speech, etc.), but various new limitations have been added, such as the obligation of all public servants, including teachers, to take the "oath of democratic faith" to demonstrate that they have never belonged to any organization which has attacked the existing system of government ... To an increasing extent, people are being tried [by military tribunals] under charges such as "attack on the morale of the Armed Forces" which in fact means any criticism of the policies of the present de facto regime ... There is, in fact no opposition press ... all media is manipulated by the regime.[185]

The point here is that Uruguay clearly went from a constitutional, democratic state to a military dictatorship with no individual liberties or democratic processes after emergency powers were used to fight the Tupamaros.

The abuse of emergency powers in Uruguay is, at first glance, something of a puzzle. As mentioned earlier in this chapter, Uruguay was known for the strength and duration of its democratic norms and institutions, including a long history of good civil-military relations in which the military was almost completely removed from political life. Yet, despite all this, Uruguay became a military dictatorship after the government empowered the military with emergency powers to fight the Tupamaros. The abuses of the emergency powers were more

likely after the emergency powers removed many of the safeguards that had
protected Uruguay from abuses of power in normal times.

In terms of the abuses of emergency powers, the military was the key actor
responsible for the change in regimes. The military gradually and systematically attacked and weakened the democratic institutions that might have
checked their final abuse of emergency powers in 1973. According to Robert
McDonald, "The growth of military participation was partially sequential, taking on different national institutions in a constantly escalating struggle. The
sequence began with the national police, and expanded to include the press, the
political parties, the broadcast media, the legislature, and the presidency ...
[After the coup, they] continued against the labor unions, the national university, and students."[186]

I will focus on the constitutional constraints that might have protected
Uruguay against abuses of power. First, I will look at how the emergency powers eroded the right to free speech, including a free press and broadcast media.
Next, I will examine how the legislature's power was gradually diminished. I
will then explore how the military eventually turned against the president
himself when these other constraints were no longer effective. Lastly, I will
consider other institutions—such as the judiciary and international actors—
that might have played a role in protecting against abuses of power. In sum, if
the military had tried to seize power while all these institutions were strong,
they probably would have failed. It was only after they used the emergency
powers to successfully diminish the strength of the constitutional safeguards in
a piecemeal fashion that they were able to seize power for themselves.

Using emergency powers to limit free speech—even if not an abuse of the
emergency powers—can *lead* to abuses because a free press can no longer monitor or check against other abuses of power. This case shows that emergency
powers that allow for the curtailment of free speech are more likely to be
abused. The potential for the press to monitor abuses of power in Uruguay was
somewhat mixed, even before emergency powers were used. On one hand, a
Tupamaro captured after the operation at Pando claimed that the police ab-
stained from killing him upon his capture because a journalist was present. A
policeman, who had earlier ordered his subordinate to shoot him, saw a journalist and said, "Leave him be—we can't do it now. We've got the Press here."[187]
On the other hand, the leading newspapers in Uruguay were controlled by the
political parties, such that "practically all ideas expressed followed party lines
with no better chance of influencing the political process and public opinion
than the parties themselves."[188] Despite this, however, the press should not be
viewed as completely incapable of monitoring abuses. Just because people know
the biases of different newspapers does not mean that they discount them entirely; instead they simply assume the truth to be somewhere between the di-
vergent accounts of rival newspapers. Moreover, while newspapers supported
by the political party in government might not have criticized abuses by the
government, rival parties and newspapers could have had some role in moni-

toring abuses, although their accounts may have been somewhat exaggerated or biased.

In an effort to control the media and its portrayal of the government's anti-terrorism campaign, the government gradually shut down the press from 1967 until 1973. The first two newspapers, *El Sol* and *Epoca*, were closed by government decree on December 12, 1967, because they wrote about armed insurgency and published a letter from the Tupamaros.[189] In the next five years, eight newspapers were permanently closed while two radio stations, one television station, and thirty-six newspapers were temporarily closed.

The media outlets were closed because it had become illegal to criticize the government or even write about the Tupamaros or the government's efforts to fight them. In November 1969, President Pacheco tried to "eliminate the word 'Tupamaro' from people's minds"[190] by having the Ministry of the Interior issue the following communiqué: "As from today none of the communications media in the country may use any of the following terms: cell, commandos, extremists, terrorists, subversive, political delinquent or ideological delinquent. Instead, and in pursuance of official regulations, the terms used should be: layabouts, criminals, delinquents, evil-livers, malefactors and other similar definitions contained in the Penal Code."[191] The press resisted such Orwellian efforts at censorship, but many newspapers and radio stations were promptly closed down when they refused to follow these guidelines. Without an independent press free to monitor and report any potential abuse of power, the military could conduct the campaign against the Tupamaros as they wanted without worrying about how the public would react.

The ability of the legislature to check abuses of power was institutionally strong but weakened through the use of emergency powers. The legislature was particularly active in monitoring allegations of torture by the police and army. This role was especially important as press censorship began to weaken the monitoring abilities of the media. In 1970, a Senate Committee investigated allegations of police torture when even pro-government newspapers expressed concern over certain incidents.[192] Moreover, by 1972, accusations of torture "began to be voiced by Congressmen at almost every legislative session."[193]

In addition to investigating allegations of torture, the legislature also acted as a check on abuses of emergency powers because it was constitutionally required to approve all emergency legislation requested by the president. During Pacheco's administration Congress repeatedly refused to renew the emergency legislation requested by the president.[194] These refusals by Congress, however, were ineffective at checking abuses because the president responded by just enacting the special powers by presidential decree. When Congress's Permanent Commission, which legislates during the recess, revoked the emergency powers in March 1970, Pacheco simply ignored Congress.[195] Later, in July 1971, "A joint meeting of Uruguay's Senate and House of Representatives (the General Assembly) voted to lift Mr. Pacheco's security measures—something Congress is entitled to do in accordance with the constitution's article 168/17. President

Pacheco immediately reissued them."[196] Following this, in a moment of potentially effective constitutionalism, the House voted to impeach President Pacheco, but the Senate never completed the procedure. In general, though, the ability of the president to use a presidential decree to invoke emergency powers indicates an already weak separation of powers.

Faced with a legislature unsupportive of the administration, the military—under its authority from the emergency powers—began to arrest members of the legislature who opposed the government and criticized its use of emergency powers. As mentioned earlier in this chapter, several leading opposition leaders were charged with supporting the Tupamaros. According to Kaufman, the military and the president weakened the legislature

through collective accusations against legislators, aimed at reducing the prestige of the Congress in public opinion by exposing the corruption among its members. . . . Simultaneously, the army [accused] their Congressmen of cooperating, negotiating, or protecting the Tupamaros ... [In time] the threat to the Parliament's existence and the army's attack on individual members of the House was finally perceived not as a threat to some partisan groups, but to the system as a whole.[197]

Attacks on politicians weakened the independent role of the legislature both by actually arresting the political opposition and by intimidating those that might oppose the government. In 1972, Ronald McDonald wrote, "Amid an atmosphere of increasing violence, social instability, and censorship, legislative debate became less relevant to national decision-making. Rarely in the past six years has the legislature even raised major policy questions. Legislative debates have been limited to relatively unimportant matters."[198]

In the end, the use of emergency powers enabled the President and the military to turn against their political opposition by charging them with terrorist crimes. Over a short period of time, the legislature lost its ability to check abuses of power. When Congress vainly tried to resist the suspension of Senator Erro's immunity, President Bordaberry simply dissolved Congress and justified it in terms of fighting terrorism.

In any constitutional system—and particularly in Uruguay after a strong presidency was restored in the 1966 constitution—the president has tremendous power and responsibility to protect the constitution. In Uruguay, presidents Pacheco and Bordaberry should shoulder some responsibility for the military's rise to power in 1973. As discussed earlier in this chapter, Pacheco Areco vigorously prosecuted the anti-terrorism campaign when he assumed office in 1968. His use of emergency powers, whether legislated by Congress or by presidential decree, were so frequent that they were in effect for almost his entire term as president. At one point, to avoid having Congress rescind the emergency powers, Pacheco ordered his party supporters not to attend the session, denying Congress the necessary quorum.[199] Similarly, Bordaberry was not an innocent bystander as the Uruguayan regime became more and more oppressive. He never felt closely connected to the traditional democratic parties; earlier in his life, he had been sympathetic toward the Nazis, Franco, and other fascist groups.

Despite the sympathies of Pacheco and Bordaberry toward the military and their methods of fighting the Tupamaros, they clearly had no intention of undermining the power of the presidency and allowing the military to take control of the country. Essentially, the military allied itself with the presidency in its attacks on the police, the media, and the legislature, but after these institutions were weakened, the military turned against the presidency, forcing Bordaberry to cede control in 1973 after three successive crises of power.[200]

In September 1972, Bordaberry extended emergency powers after being pressured by the military. When four doctors were tortured in November (causing the first crisis), Bordaberry initially demanded that the military release them, but later accepted their arrest, essentially allowing the military to dictate their positions to him. In the February 1973 crisis, the military practically took control of the country and allegedly gave Bordaberry an ultimatum to either accept the military coup or be arrested when it occurred anyway.[201] Afterwards, in a public speech, Bordaberry announced that he would "create the appropriate institutional ways for the participation of the Armed Forces in the national task, within the framework of law and the Constitution."[202] In June, the military launched the coup by simply ordering Bordaberry to dissolve Congress when it refused to suspend Senator Erro's immunity from arrest. By this time, "The President and his predecessor, who for years had relied on executive decrees and on the strength of the National Police and the armed forces, could count on help neither from the judicial or legislative branches nor from the population at large."[203]

In a state with a robust set of constitutional constraints on power, other institutions besides the legislature, presidency, and press can monitor and limit abuses of emergency powers. In particular, the judicial branch and international institutions can perform this function, as seen in Chapter 3. In Uruguay, however, the judicial system was simply bypassed in favor of military courts. International organizations can monitor abuses but are limited in their ability to enforce international law within sovereign states.

Until 1970, the courts did constrain the activities of the police at times and with mixed results. For example, when allegations of torture were made against the police in April 1970, the court ordered an inquiry in which Héctor Charquero, the head of the special police, was summoned to answer the allegations. No policemen were found guilty of torture, however, because they had worn hoods and could not be identified.[204] In the summer of 1970, when the security forces were furiously searching for the four kidnap victims, the police asked the courts' permission to use pentothal (a truth drug), but were refused.[205] Although the power of the courts was already limited, they lost all power in 1971 when the military took over anti-terrorist operations. The military "substituted its own procedures and methods for those of the police." The military, for example, was not bound by the rule of habeas corpus, which allowed them to keep prisoners indefinitely in military prisons without having to bring them to trial.[206]

International actors monitored abuses of power in Uruguay, but were unable to stop the abuses.[207] For example, in June 1972, the Roman Catholic Bishops of Uruguay reported that the military was guilty of killings, illegal imprisonment, and torture. A month later, the International Commission of Jurists repeated these allegations in a report in *The Christian Science Monitor.*[208] Even after the military coup, Amnesty International continued to report on allegations of torture.[209] Outside information would have been more important if Uruguayan political institutions and safeguards had been capable of using the information to enforce compliance with the laws. With a weakened legislature and judiciary, though, information about abuses was less valuable.

THE TRADEOFF REALIZED

The conventional wisdom on the use of emergency powers to fight terrorism is that there is a tradeoff—they are effective but dangerous to democracy. While the other case studies show that this tradeoff does not always hold, the case of Uruguay fits the conventional wisdom fairly well. The emergency powers were effective when the military used them to quickly round up most of the suspected Tupamaros and when support for the Tupamaros began to wane following their move toward more violent operations; however, the military and, to a lesser extent, President Bordaberry abused the emergency powers after they weakened the constitutional constraints that might have protected the continuation of a democratic government. The lessons of this case are generalizable to other situations; we should expect similar consequences from using emergency powers if the security forces move quickly against a group with low support and if the emergency powers weaken the constitutional safeguards of the state.

As a policy issue, this case is relatively difficult to resolve. Other cases, such as those where emergency powers are safe and effective or dangerous and ineffective are fairly straightforward. In the former, emergency powers have high benefits and low costs while in the latter, they have high costs and low benefits. In cases such as Uruguay, emergency powers give high benefits (effective), but at high costs (abused). Deciding whether emergency powers should be used hinges on the threat from the terrorist group. If the terrorist group threatens the very existence of the democratic regime or has the capability of inflicting mass casualties, taking a chance that emergency powers may lead to a dictatorship may be worth the costs if the terrorist group can be eliminated. In most cases, however, including Uruguay, terrorism does not pose such a severe threat.[210] In these cases, the costs of fighting terrorism do not justify the benefits. It is better for the citizens of a state to live in a democracy with the fear of terrorism, than in an authoritarian dictatorship with no terrorism except from the state itself.

NOTES

1. Martin Weinstein, *Uruguay: Democracy at the Crossroads* (Boulder: Westview Press, 1988), 18.

2. M. H. J. Finch, "Three Perspectives on the Crisis in Uruguay," *Journal of Latin American Studies* 3, no. 2 (November 1971), 187–189.

3. In 1985, there were nine million head of cattle, twenty-three million sheep, and three million people in Uruguay according to Weinstein, *Democracy at the Crossroads*, 6.

4. Martin Weinstein, *Uruguay: The Politics of Failure* (Westport, CT: Greenwood Press, 1975), 113.

5. Christopher Hewitt, *The Effectiveness of Anti-Terrorist Policies* (Lanham, MD: University Press of America, 1984), 6; and Arturo Porzecanski, *Uruguay's Tupamaros: The Urban Guerrilla* (New York: Praeger Publishers, 1973), 3.

6. Finch, "Crisis in Uruguay," 174. See also Edy Kaufman, *Uruguay in Transition: From Civilian to Military Rule* (New Brunswick, NJ: Transaction Books, 1979), 23, for more figures on inflation.

7. Kaufman, *Uruguay in Transition*, 24.

8. Kaufman, *Uruguay in Transition*, 24.

9. Finch, "Crisis in Uruguay," 175.

10. Kaufman, *Uruguay in Transition*, 25.

11. Robert Moss, *The War for the Cities* (New York: Coward, McCann and Geoghegan, 1972), 215.

12. Alain Labrousse, *The Tupamaros: Urban Guerrillas in Uruguay* (London: Penguin Books, 1973), 35.

13. The name "Tupamaros" comes from the Peruvian Indian leader, Tupac Amaru, who fought against Spanish colonial rule and was executed in 1782. See Porzecanski, *Uruguay's Tupamaros*, 5; and Moss, *War for the Cities*, 215.

14. The Tupamaros have never published a document detailing their ideology; instead, scholars have reconstructed their ideology from various statements, communiqués, and interviews. See Weinstein, *Politics of Failure*, 122.

15. Porzecanski, *Uruguay's Tupamaros*, 6–9.

16. The concept of power duality is similar to the objectives of other guerrilla groups that hope to undermine the power of the government. See Chapter 6 for a similar account of the Shining Path's objectives.

17. Porzecanski, *Uruguay's Tupamaros*, 17.

18. Robert Moss, "Uruguay: Terrorism versus Democracy," *Conflict Studies* no. 14 (August 1971), 7.

19. Porzecanski, *Uruguay's Tupamaros*, 45.

20. Porzecanski, *Uruguay's Tupamaros*, 13–14.

21. Moss, "Terrorism versus Democracy," 3.

22. Anthony Burton, *Urban Terrorism: Theory, Practice and Response* (London: Leo Cooper, 1975), 97.

23. Porzecanski, *Uruguay's Tupamaros*, 28–31. See also Fernando Lopez-Alves, "Political Crises, Strategic Choices, and Terrorism: The Rise and Fall of the Uruguayan

Tupamaros," *Terrorism and Political Violence* 1, no. 2 (April 1989), 219, for demographic data.

24. Moss, *War for the Cities*, 222.

25. Porzecanski, *Uruguay's Tupamaros*, 32.

26. Robert Moss claims the organization of cells into columns probably only existed on paper. Most operations were executed by individual cells or groups of cells working on an ad hoc basis. Moss, *War for the Cities*, 222.

27. Porzecanski, *Uruguay's Tupamaros*, 32–34.

28. Labrousse, *Tupamaros*, 35. See also Moss, *War for the Cities*, 215; and Stephen Connolly and Gregory Druehl, "The Tupamaros—the New Focus in Latin America," *Journal of Contemporary Revolutions* 3, no. 3 (summer 1971), 61.

29. Labrousse, *Tupamaros*, 37; and Moss, *War for the Cities*, 216.

30. Connolly and Druehl, "Tupamaros—the New Focus in Latin America," 62; and Robert Moss, "Urban Guerrillas in Uruguay," *Problems of Communism* 10 (Sept-Oct 1971), 18.

31. Labrousse, *Tupamaros*, 35–36.

32. Moss, *War for the Cities*, 216.

33. Lopez-Alves, "Political Crises, Strategic Choices, and Terrorism," 202, treats the Tupamaros as "guerrillas who adopted terrorism."

34. Marysa Gerassi, "Uruguay's Urban Guerrillas," *The Nation* September 29, 1969, 310.

35. Porzecanski, *Uruguay's Tupamaros*, 48, writes that the Tupamaros were known for their "avoidance of extensive terrorism."

36. Kaufman, *Uruguay in Transition*, 35.

37. Alphonse Max, *Guerrillas in Latin America* (The Hague: International Document and Information Centre, 1971), 84. Max is clearly biased against the Tupamaros.

38. Porzecanski, *Uruguay's Tupamaros*, 46.

39. Moss, "Urban Guerrillas in Uruguay," 18.

40. Porzecanski, *Uruguay's Tupamaros*, 52.

41. Connolly and Druehl, "Tupamaros—the New Focus in Latin America," 60.

42. Ronald McDonald, "Electoral Politics and Uruguayan Political Decay," *Inter-American Economic Affairs* 26, (summer 1972), 29. McDonald begins counting in 1967, but the first kidnapping occurred in 1968. He counts twelve kidnappings by 1971.

43. Reverbel was kidnapped a second time in 1971. Porzecanski, *Uruguay's Tupamaros*, 43.

44. Labrousse, *Tupamaros*, 11.

45. Max, *Guerrillas in Latin America*, 86.

46. Labrousse, *Tupamaros*, 99.

47. See A. J. Langguth, *Hidden Terrors: The Truth about U.S. Police Operations in Latin America* (New York: Pantheon Books, 1978) for an analysis of United States police operations in Latin America, including Dan Mitrione's involvement in Uruguay.

48. Labrousse, *Tupamaros*, 100.

49. Labrousse, *Tupamaros*, 106.

50. Labrousse, *Tupamaros*, 108.

51. Labrousse, *Tupamaros*, 12.

52. Porzecanski, *Uruguay's Tupamaros*, 43–44.

53. Max, *Guerrillas in Latin America*, 90.

54. Labrousse, *Tupamaros*, 78.

55. Moss, *War for the Cities*, 226, estimates thirty-five Tupamaros took part in the operation while Labrousse, *Tupamaros*, 74, puts the number at fifty. Maria Esther Gilio, *The Tupamaros* (London: Secker and Warburg, 1972), 95–117, claims 100 members took part in Operation Pando based on her interviews with Tupamaros.

56. The best accounts of the operation in Pando is Gilio, *Tupamaros*, 95–117; Labrousse, *Tupamaros*, 73–77; Max, *Guerrillas in Latin America*, 85; and Moss, *War for the Cities*, 226.

57. Max, *Guerrillas in Latin America*, 85.

58. Before being arrested, many injured Tupamaros claim to have been beaten and abused by the police. See Labrousse, *Tupamaros*, 76.

59. Porzecanski, *Uruguay's Tupamaros*, 45. See also Labrousse, *Tupamaros*, 46.

60. Labrousse, *Tupamaros*, 80.

61. See Gilio, *Tupamaros*, 7; Weinstein, *Politics of Failure*, xv; Milton Vanger, *The Model Country* (Hanover, NH: University Press of New England, 1980), vii; Samuel Shapiro, "Uruguay's Lost Paradise," *Current History* (February 1972), 98; McDonald, "Electoral Politics and Uruguayan Political Decay," 26; Robert Moss, *The Collapse of Democracy* (London: Abacus, 1975), 197; Kaufman, *Uruguay in Transition*, ix; The Lawyers Committee for International Human Rights, *The Generals Give Back Uruguay* (New York: The Lawyers Committee for International Human Rights, 1985), 3; and Finch, "Crisis in Uruguay," 182.

62. Gilio, *Tupamaros*, 7; Weinstein, *Politics of Failure*, xv; Shapiro, "Uruguay's Lost Paradise," 98; Lawyers Committee for International Human Rights, *The Generals Give Back Uruguay*, 3.

63. Gilio, *Tupamaros*, 7.

64. Finch, "Crisis in Uruguay," 182.

65. Polity 98 Database. From 1951 until 1972, Uruguay is coded by the Polity 98 database as an 8 on the democracy scale and a 0 on the autocracy scale, placing it in the democratic range. Most democratic peace scholars code anything higher than 6 on the democratic measure as democratic. More stringent guidelines require that the democracy score minus the autocracy score be higher than 7. By either criteria, Uruguay is a democracy in the period under consideration.

66. Ronald McDonald, "The Rise of Military Politics in Uruguay," *Inter-American Economic Affairs* 28 (spring 1975), 25. See also Labrousse, *Tupamaros*, 20, for a historical account of the absence of militarism.

67. Porzecanski, *Uruguay's Tupamaros*, 66.

68. Moss, *War for the Cities*, 10.

69. Finch, "Crisis in Uruguay," 181.

70. See Kaufman, *Uruguay in Transition*, 22; Finch, "Crisis in Uruguay," 181; Moss, "Terrorism versus Democracy," 1; Weinstein, *Politics of Failure*, 115; and Thomas

Weil et al., *Area Handbook for Uruguay* (Washington, D.C.: Foreign Areas Studies of the American University, 1971), 195.

71. Brian Loveman, *The Constitution of Tyranny: Regimes of Exception in Spanish America* (Pittsburgh: University of Pittsburgh Press, 1993), 303.

72. The president is the leading vote-getter of the party that receives the most votes. This unique procedure can lead to a president receiving fewer votes than a candidate from a rival party, but winning the election because his *party* won the most votes and he won the most votes *within* his party. Martin Weinstein, "Uruguay: The Legislature and the Reconstitution of Democracy," in *Legislatures and the New Democracies in Latin America,* ed. David Close (Boulder: Lynne Rienner Publishers, 1995), 137–139. See also Kaufman, *Uruguay in Transition,* 21–22.

73. For a general overview of Uruguayan political system, see Weil et al., *Area Handbook for Uruguay,* 196–205.

74. Weinstein, *Politics of Failure,* 117.

75. Connolly and Druehl, "Tupamaros—the New Focus in Latin America," 63. See also Carlos Wilson, *The Tupamaros: The Unmentionables* (Boston: Branden Press, 1974), 32 and 39, for characterizations of Pacheco's presidency as more repressive than others. In 1968, Pacheco set up a special police force, the Metropolitan Guards, to deal with insurgency issues, Moss, *War for the Cities,* 231.

76. Weinstein, *Democracy at the Crossroads,* 38.

77. Gerassi, "Uruguay's Urban Guerrillas," 307. McDonald, "Electoral Politics and Uruguayan Political Decay," 31, writes that the date was June 3, but all other sources put the date as June 13.

78. Labrousse, *Tupamaros,* 53.

79. It is called a "state of siege" by Weinstein, *Politics of Failure,* 117, "special powers" by Labrousse, *Tupamaros,* 53, and "limited martial law" by Gerassi, "Uruguay's Urban Guerrillas," 307.

80. Weinstein, *Politics of Failure,* 117; Gerassi, "Uruguay's Urban Guerrillas," 307; and Labrousse, *Tupamaros,* 9.

81. Labrousse, *Tupamaros,* 10.

82. Gerassi, "Uruguay's Urban Guerrillas," 307; and Labrousse, *Tupamaros,* 54.

83. Weinstein, *Politics of Failure,* 127.

84. McDonald, "Electoral Politics and Uruguayan Political Decay," 31.

85. Labrousse, *Tupamaros,* 108.

86. Max, *Guerrillas in Latin America,* 92.

87. Sergio d'Oliveira, "Uruguay and the Tupamaro Myth," *Military Review* 53, no. 4 (April 1973), 30. McDonald, "Rise of Military Politics in Uruguay," 37, writes the army took over on September 29.

88. Weinstein, *Politics of Failure,* 128.

89. Kaufman, *Uruguay in Transition,* 35.

90. Weinstein, *Democracy at the Crossroads,* 41.

91. d'Oliveira, "Uruguay and the Tupamaro Myth," 30.

92. Gisbert Flanz, "Uruguay Supplement," in *Constitutions of the Countries of the World,* ed. Albert Blaustein and Gisbert Flanz (Dobbs Ferry, NY: Oceana Publications,

1982), 1; Alain Rouquié, *The Military and the State in Latin America*, tr. Paul Sigmund (Berkeley: University of California Press, 1987), 249; and Labrousse, *Tupamaros*, 130.

93. Porzecanski, *Uruguay's Tupamaros*, 68.

94. Flanz, "Uruguay Supplement," 1.

95. Flanz, "Uruguay Supplement," 1.

96. Kaufman, *Uruguay in Transition*, 110; and Labrousse, *Tupamaros*, 131.

97. Weinstein, *Democracy at the Crossroads*, 46.

98. Flanz, "Uruguay Supplement," 1

99. Flanz, "Uruguay Supplement," 1.

100. Kaufman, *Uruguay in Transition*, 30 and 113, and Flanz, "Uruguay Supplement," 1.

101. Flanz, "Uruguay Supplement," 1; and Kaufman, *Uruguay in Transition*, 114.

102. Hewitt, *Effectiveness of Anti-Terrorist Policies*, 69, has a chart measuring the severity of the emergency powers that shows them being fairly constant in their degree of repression as well as nearly continuous from June 1968 to December 1972.

103. d'Oliveira, "Uruguay and the Tupamaro Myth," 27.

104. Gerassi, "Uruguay's Urban Guerrillas," 310.

105. d'Oliveira, "Uruguay and the Tupamaro Myth," 28; and Max, *Guerrillas in Latin America*, 92.

106. Robert Moss, "Urban Guerrillas in Latin America," *Conflict Studies* no. 8 (October 1970), 14.

107. Max, *Guerrillas in Latin America*, 93.

108. Frances Foland, "A New Model for Revolution? Uruguay's Urban Guerrillas," *The New Leader* October 4, 1971, 8.

109. Hewitt, *Effectiveness of Anti-Terrorist Policies*, 69.

110. Porzecanski, *Uruguay's Tupamaros*, 55.

111. Porzecanski, *Uruguay's Tupamaros*, 62.

112. Porzecanski, *Uruguay's Tupamaros*, 68.

113. Porzecanski, *Uruguay's Tupamaros*, 68.

114. Kaufman, *Uruguay in Transition*, 35–36.

115. Porzecanski, *Uruguay's Tupamaros*, 62.

116. Even without emergency powers, the state is more likely to be effective if it moves quickly against a group with low support. Emergency powers are designed to make the security forces *more* effective.

117. Labrousse, *Tupamaros*, 120.

118. Gerassi, "Uruguay's Urban Guerrillas," 309.

119. Foland, "A New Model for Revolution?" 9; and Albert Parry, *Terrorism: From Robespierre to Arafat* (New York: Vanguard Press, 1976), 276.

120. See Labrousse, *Tupamaros*, 120; Moss, "Terrorism versus Democracy," 3; and Moss, *War for the Cities*, 211, for estimates based on an interview with a police superintendent, Otero.

121. Labrousse, *Tupamaros*, 120–121.

122. Gilio, *Tupamaros*, 121.

123. Porzecanski, *Uruguay's Tupamaros*, 28.

124. The estimate of several hundred active members is also supported by other authors, including Max, *Guerrillas in Latin America,* 98; Moss, "Urban Guerrillas in Latin America," 13; and Shapiro, "Uruguay's Lost Paradise," 101. Michael Radu and Vladimir Tismaneanu, *Latin American Revolutionaries: Groups, Goals, Methods* (Washington, D.C.: Pergamon-Brassey's International Defense Publishers, 1990), 348, claim that membership ranged from 200–400 up to as many as 1,500.

125. See Wilson, *Tupamaros: The Unmentionables,* 46, for the Tupamaros' strategies to gain support.

126. Carlos Marighella, "Minimanual of the Urban Guerrilla," in "Urban Guerrilla Warfare," by Robert Moss, *Adelphi Paper* no. 79 (1971), 40.

127. Porzecanski, *Uruguay's Tupamaros,* 33.

128. See Gilio, *Tupamaros,* 4, as an example. Any definitive measure of support is impossible in this case. The following assessment is based on the consensus within the literature on Uruguay and the Tupamaros.

129. Connolly and Druel, "Tupamaros—the New Focus in Latin America," 59 and 67.

130. Foland, "A New Model for Revolution?" 9.

131. Labrousse, *Tupamaros,* 116 and 118; Moss, *War for the Cities,* 220; and Wilson, *Tupamaros: The Unmentionables,* 37.

132. Labrousse, *Tupamaros,* 117.

133. See Labrousse, *Tupamaros,* 65, for an account of the Reverbel kidnapping and Gilio, *Tupamaros,* 123, for a description of the support given to the Tupamaros in the town of Pando.

134. d'Oliveira, "Uruguay and the Tupamaro Myth," 27.

135. Max, *Guerrillas in Latin America,* 91.

136. Moss, "Terrorism versus Democracy," 7. See also Martha Crenshaw, "An Organizational Approach to the Analysis of Political Terrorism," *Orbis* 29, no. 3 (fall 1985), 478, who writes that, "for the Tupamaros ... killing kidnapped hostages when the government refused to comply with demands resulted in popular disaffection."

137. d'Oliveira, "Uruguay and the Tupamaro Myth," 32.

138. Burton, *Urban Terrorism,* 102.

139. Lopez-Alves, "Political Crises, Strategic Choices, and Terrorism," 210.

140. d'Oliveira, "Uruguay and the Tupamaro Myth," 27.

141. d'Oliveira, "Uruguay and the Tupamaro Myth," 32.

142. Weinstein, *Politics of Failure,* 129.

143. Weinstein, *Democracy at the Crossroads,* 41.

144. Lopez-Alves, "Political Crises, Strategic Choices, and Terrorism," 228.

145. Porzecanski, *Uruguay's Tupamaros,* 18 and 34.

146. Labrousse, *Tupamaros,* 43.

147. Porzecanski, *Uruguay's Tupamaros,* 35.

148. Porzecanski, *Uruguay's Tupamaros,* 35.

149. Gerassi, "Uruguay's Urban Guerrillas," 309.

150. As their popularity increased in the late 1960s, the Tupamaros actually ran into problems due to the high numbers of recruits. Many of these new recruits joined the Tu-

pamaros, not because they shared their revolutionary ideology, but merely because it enabled them to live a life of adventure and danger (Max, *Guerrillas in Latin America*, 92). In the end, these types of recruits were less willing to sacrifice their lives for the cause and less likely to continue the fight when operations went poorly. In addition, the secrecy of the cell structure was compromised with the large influx of recruits because they had to be trained in larger groups making it more difficult to limit the number of Tupamaros that any one individual could identify (d'Oliveira, "Uruguay and the Tupamaro Myth," 32). A Tupamaro interviewed by Maria Gilio highlighted the problems faced by a fast-growing movement: "When an organization like ours grows—and ours is growing rapidly—security mechanisms are strained. There is insufficient time to train new cadres. There's another thing too. The same men who catch our eye because we consider them potential militants have also caught the eye of the police for the same reason." Gilio, *Tupamaros*, 135.

151. d'Oliveira, "Uruguay and the Tupamaro Myth," 32.

152. Wilson, *Tupamaros: The Unmentionables*, 73.

153. Parry, *Terrorism*, 279.

154. d'Oliveira, "Uruguay and the Tupamaro Myth," 32.

155. Parry, *Terrorism*, 279.

156. Weinstein, *Democracy at the Crossroads*, 41.

157. Porzecanski, *Uruguay's Tupamaros*, 70.

158. Kaufman, *Uruguay in Transition*, 95.

159. Porzecanski, *Uruguay's Tupamaros*, 51.

160. See, for example, Weinstein, *Politics of Failure*, 118.

161. McDonald, "Electoral Politics and Uruguayan Political Decay," 32.

162. Gilio, *Tupamaros*, 141–172.

163. Wilson, *Tupamaros: The Unmentionables*, 100.

164. Kaufman, *Uruguay in Transition*, 79.

165. Porzecanski, *Uruguay's Tupamaros*, 56.

166. Labrousse, *Tupamaros*, 62.

167. Labrousse, *Tupamaros*, 131.

168. Labrousse, *Tupamaros*, 131.

169. McDonald, "Rise of Military Politics in Uruguay," 34–35.

170. Kaufman, *Uruguay in Transition*, 30, 37, and 113.

171. Kaufman, *Uruguay in Transition*, 30.

172. Quoted in Labrousse, *Tupamaros*, 54.

173. Porzecanski, *Uruguay's Tupamaros*, 66–67, discusses the military's view of its increasing political role.

174. Kaufman, *Uruguay in Transition*, 61.

175. Porzecanski, *Uruguay's Tupamaros*, 67.

176. Porzecanski, *Uruguay's Tupamaros*, 67.

177. Porzecanski, *Uruguay's Tupamaros*, 73.

178. Charlie Gillespie, "The Breakdown of Democracy in Uruguay: Alternative Political Models," *Latin American Program, The Wilson Center, Working Papers* no. 143, (1984), 11.

179. For details and a chronology of these events, see Kaufman, *Uruguay in Transition*, 110–115; and Rouquié, *Military and the State in Latin America*, 250–254.

180. Flanz, "Uruguay Supplement," 1; and Weinstein, *Politics of Failure*, 130.

181. Weinstein, *Democracy at the Crossroads*, 45.

182. Weinstein, *Democracy at the Crossroads*, 108.

183. See Lawyers Committee for International Human Rights, *The Generals Give Back Uruguay*, for detailed descriptions of the political system under the military dictatorship as well as the process by which power was given back to the citizens of Uruguay.

184. Weinstein, *Democracy at the Crossroads*, 45.

185. Kaufman, *Uruguay in Transition*, 77–79 and 82.

186. McDonald, "Rise of Military Politics in Uruguay," 26.

187. As quoted in Gilio, *Tupamaros*, 162.

188. Kaufman, *Uruguay in Transition*, 46.

189. Porzecanski, *Uruguay's Tupamaros*, 57; Wilson, *Tupamaros: The Unmentionables*, 39; Weinstein, *Politics of Failure*, 117; Weinstein, *Democracy at the Crossroads*, 38; and Labrousse, *Tupamaros*, 52.

190. Porzecanski, *Uruguay's Tupamaros*, 59.

191. As quoted in Gilio, *Tupamaros*, 119.

192. McDonald, "Electoral Politics and Uruguayan Political Decay," 32.

193. Porzecanski, *Uruguay's Tupamaros*, 68.

194. See Moss, *War for the Cities*, 232; Robert Moss, "Urban Guerrilla Warfare," *Adelphi Papers* no. 79 (1971), 15; and Moss, "Terrorism versus Democracy," 8.

195. Porzecanski, *Uruguay's Tupamaros*, 59.

196. Porzecanski, *Uruguay's Tupamaros*, 63.

197. Kaufman, *Uruguay in Transition*, 27–30.

198. McDonald, "Electoral Politics and Uruguayan Political Decay," 34.

199. McDonald, "Electoral Politics and Uruguayan Political Decay," 31.

200. See Kaufman, *Uruguay in Transition*, 26, for an account of the military's strategy of allying themselves with the presidency to attack the legislature and then turning on Bordaberry.

201. McDonald, "Rise of Military Politics in Uruguay," 40.

202. Kaufman, *Uruguay in Transition*, 33.

203. Porzecanski, *Uruguay's Tupamaros*, 74.

204. Labrousse, *Tupamaros*, 78.

205. Labrousse, *Tupamaros*, 108.

206. McDonald, "Rise of Military Politics in Uruguay," 37–38.

207. International organizations or institutions have a limited ability to control the behavior of sovereign states. The international political economy literature offers several mechanisms—such as iterated interaction, the provision of information on cheating, and the alteration of norms—as potential ways in which institutions can constrain the behavior of states.

208. Wilson, *Tupamaros: The Unmentionables*, 100.

209. Kaufman, *Uruguay in Transition*, 79.

210. This assumes that the Tupamaros would not have become more dangerous if the emergency powers had not been used to effectively defeat them.

Chapter 5

Canada and the FLQ

In October of 1970, Canada used emergency powers to combat the terrorists of the Front de Libération du Québec (FLQ). The FLQ had kidnapped two men—the British Trade Commissioner and a member of the Quebec provincial government—and held them hostage in exchange for the reading of their manifesto and the release of twenty-two captured FLQ members. In response, the Canadian government invoked the War Measures Act that created a state of emergency in which the army sent troops into Montreal, the police conducted searches and arrests without warrants, suspects were held for up to twenty-one days in jail without being charged, and it was illegal for the media to run stories about the FLQ. These measures were largely successful—no further kidnappings or bombings occurred during the crisis. By the end of 1970, the FLQ kidnappers had been arrested and the FLQ ceased to exist thereafter. In April 1971, the emergency powers ended and were not renewed, restoring all of Canada's liberties. The success of the emergency powers was primarily because they enabled the government to move quickly against a weakly supported FLQ. Without much support, the FLQ could not maintain the pace of their operations in the face of a pervasive presence of police and army forces. Canada's use of emergency powers is also a good example of when emergency powers can be used fairly safely. The powers were not abused because their use was widely debated in the press and in Parliament. These public debates questioned the legitimacy of using the emergency powers as well as monitored their implementation. The role of the press and the Parliament in Canada is in sharp contrast to the capabilities of these institutions in Uruguay, in which the press was unable and Congress unwilling to challenge the Uruguayan military's use of emergency powers.

THE FLQ AND THE OCTOBER CRISIS

Canada was first settled by French fur-traders along the St. Lawrence River valley in the 16th century. In competition with the French, the British also established numerous colonies south of Canada in what became the United States. British and French aspirations frequently came into conflict both in the new world and old. The British and Americans defeated the French in 1763 to end the French and Indian War in North America (the Seven Years War in Europe). As the victors, the British took control of all of France's North America holdings, stretching from Quebec to New Orleans, and ruled Canada as part of the British Empire. In 1867, Britain granted Canada its independence within the British Empire with the British North America Act.[1] Canada became a multi-national confederation of provinces, yet French-speaking citizens remained mostly in the eastern province of Quebec, while British immigrants and English-speaking Canadians expanded westward.[2] The result was that Canada has become a multi-national state but with strong geographic differences. In Quebec, in particular, French Canadians number about 80 percent of the population but only about 30 percent for all of Canada.[3]

In the 1960s, a liberal provincial government in Quebec began to legally recognize a distinct French identity in Quebec. Encouraged by this, several new nationalist movements formed, some of which sought the independence or at least autonomy of Quebec.[4] The most prominent of these was the Parti Québécois (PQ) led by René Lévesque.[5] The FLQ emerged as a radical and violent fringe of this separatist movement. In 1963, about half of Réseau de résistance (Resistance Network—RR), an early separatist movement, split off and formed the FLQ with George Shoeters as their leader.[6]

The FLQ served notice of its existence by throwing Molotov cocktails at three Canadian army barracks on March 7, 1963. Over the next seven years, the FLQ conducted several waves of campaigns consisting of robberies to gain weapons and money as well as numerous bombings of the symbols of English and American nationalism and imperialism. Some of the more notable incidents included the bombing of the Wolfe statue (the British general who defeated the French forces in 1759) in Quebec City in 1963, the bombing of the Montreal Stock Exchange in 1969, the failed kidnapping plots of the Israeli and American consuls in the spring of 1970, and the kidnappings in October 1970 that initiated the October Crisis.[7] In the seven years of terrorism, the FLQ was responsible for approximately 200 bombings and six deaths, although none of the deaths was intentional.[8]

The bombings by the FLQ reflected their motivations and ideology. The FLQ began primarily as a separatist/nationalist organization and many of their targets were English-Canadian businesses that served as symbols of French-Canadian oppression at the hand of the English-Canadians. Over time, however, the FLQ developed a Marxist ideology as well, and consequently targeted some French-Canadian businesses that they believed exploited the working class (which was predominantly French-Canadian).[9] Marcel Rioux posits that, while the FLQ was originally a purely nationalist movement, it "gradually became more aware of the economic stranglehold on Quebec and began to direct its actions as much against North American capitalism as against Ottawa's political control."[10] The ideology of the FLQ was developed primarily by Charles Gagnon and Pierre Vallières, both of whom were arrested in 1966 and spent much of the rest of the decade in court battles and then in prison.[11]

The nationalist and Marxist ideology of the FLQ attracted a fairly young membership base. Most FLQ members came from lower-class backgrounds, with about half having received secondary education, although most had dropped out of school.[12] The average age of those arrested was less than nineteen, although it climbed to the mid-twenties in the later years of FLQ activity. Members commonly were recruited from other separatist groups, although many members were also recruited through friends and family.[13] For example, the cell that kidnapped James Cross was led by Jacques Lanctot, and contained his sister and brother-in-law.[14]

The FLQ was organized into decentralized cells, which usually consisted of five to seven members, with no hierarchy or central command to guide its operations.[15] Ronald Crelinsten describes the FLQ organization as "a centrifugal model minus the hub of the wheel. Successive groups of friends would decide to form a 'cell' and call themselves the FLQ. But there was no central leadership, only a common ideal of a separate Quebec."[16] New members were recruited by the leaders or individuals within particular cells, rather than by a centralized structure that placed them into cells.[17] This method of organization and recruitment made it difficult for the police to combat the FLQ—when one group was captured, a new cell would spring up and resume terrorist activities.[18]

While the FLQ had conducted numerous operations between 1963 and 1970, its most famous operation was the kidnappings of James Cross and Pierre Laporte in October 1970.[19] On Monday, October 5, the "Liberation Cell"[20] of the FLQ drove to the house of James "Jasper" Cross, the British Trade Commissioner in Montreal, and abducted Cross at gunpoint. The cell drove him to a safe-house in northern Montreal, and issued a communiqué demanding the government meet the following seven conditions before Cross would be released: the police were to cease all operations searching for the kidnappers; the manifesto of the FLQ was to be read on the national television network and printed in the major newspapers; twenty political prisoners were to be released; the kidnappers would be allowed to flee Canada to Cuba or Algeria on a waiting airplane; a group of dismissed workers were to be reinstated; a "voluntary" tax of $500,000 would be placed on the airplane; and the name of an FLQ informer was to be made public.[21]

Negotiations for the release of James Cross took place in public—the FLQ issued several communiqués, while the government would respond by having ministers issue counter-demands in public speeches. On October 7, the FLQ issued their fourth communiqué, reducing their demands to only two: the reading of the manifesto by October 8, and the ending of all police searches. On the evening news of October 8, the entire FLQ manifesto was read before a national audience. In response, the FLQ agreed to delay the execution of Cross until October 10 unless the political prisoners were released and the police stopped their searches. On October 10, Justice Minister Choquette announced that the government was dedicated to negotiating with the terrorists and offered safe passage to Cuba in exchange for Cross, but refused the FLQ demand to release the political prisoners. The government essentially called the FLQ bluff. The Liberation Cell, though, was unwilling to go through with the execution and prepared to release Cross in exchange for safe passage and the earlier publication of their manifesto.

A second FLQ group, however, calling themselves the "Chernier cell"[22] watched Choquette's press conference and decided to increase the pressure on the Canadian government by kidnapping a second hostage. Pierre Laporte, the Minister of Labour and Immigration in the Quebec provincial government, was kidnapped forty minutes after Choquette's speech had ended.[23] The Chernier cell threatened to kill Laporte unless the seven original demands of the Liberation cell were met. The two FLQ cells had not coordinated their operations, nor were they in communication with each other during the kidnappings. The result was that all communication between the two cells went through the media.[24]

The kidnapping of Laporte drastically changed the atmosphere in Canada. What was first viewed as an isolated incident by a radical and violent fringe group became, with this second kidnapping, a pattern that might continue unless measures were taken. While the FLQ had been around for nearly eight years before this, these kidnappings were a dramatic escalation in their tactics. During the following week, negotiations took place between appointed mediators for both the FLQ and the Canadian government. At the same time, however, Prime Minister Trudeau, Premier Bourassa of Quebec, and Montreal municipal officials began preparations for a more forceful response.

On Thursday, October 16, army troops began deploying to bases in and around Montreal, Ottawa, and Quebec City. At 4:00 A.M. on Friday, October 16, emergency powers were invoked by the federal government under the auspices of the War Measures Act (WMA). By noon on Friday, 450 people had been arrested without warrant, as allowed by the WMA. The Chernier cell responded by killing Pierre Laporte on October 17. Parliament had been debating the War Measures Act since October 16, but with the murder of Laporte, the debate ended and Parliament overwhelmingly supported the WMA in a vote on Monday, October 19. The security forces, however, were unable to quickly locate the FLQ cells; on November 18, the army troops in Ottawa returned to their barracks with the kidnappers still at large.[25]

The police eventually discovered the location of the Cross kidnappers on December 2. The security forces surrounded the house and negotiated the release of Cross in exchange for the safe passage of his kidnappers and their families to Cuba. Meanwhile, the kidnappers of Laporte had left the city of Montreal and were hiding in a suburb. Their hideout was discovered, and they surrendered to the police on December 28. On January 4, 1971, the troops in Montreal and Quebec City returned to their bases and on April 30, the War Measures Act expired, returning Canada to a state of normalcy.[26]

EMERGENCY POWERS IN CANADA

Before describing the content of the emergency powers, a brief description of Canada's political structure is in order. By every measure, whether objective or subjective, Canada is unquestionably democratic—elections are frequent and regular, power is separated at the federal level between the Prime Minister with the Cabinet and the Parliament, power is divided between national, provincial, and local governments, liberties such as freedoms of speech are protected, and suspected criminals are presumed innocent and are entitled to due process laws.[27]

Similar to other democracies, during times of emergency, the freedoms and rights that are ordinarily protected hinder the ability of the government to deal with the emergency. In Canada, the emergency powers were deemed necessary because the police and judicial system were inadequate in their capacity to effectively combat the FLQ. After the Laporte kidnapping, the police felt overwhelmed and looked for ways to loosen the constraints of due process laws.[28] Mayor Drapeau of Montreal argued that the police forces needed to be "given more extensive investigative powers than we have now. In some European countries, they can pick up 500 people in erratio (random) and keep them in jail for two, or three, or four weeks, as long as they refuse to talk. This is the way we must deal with the situation."[29] These sentiments were echoed in letters from the Montreal police chief and police director. They claimed, "The slow pace of procedures and the restrictions resulting from the legal machinery and means at our disposal do not allow us to meet the situation"[30] and "The incredible amount of checking and searching imposed upon us have taxed and are taxing to the utmost the resources available to our police department."[31]

Emergency powers were first invoked in 1914, when Parliament passed the WMA to assist the Canadian government in preparing for World War I. In 1939, the statute was revived and the War Measures Act was used to intern 22,000 Japanese-Canadians during World War II.[32] The WMA was invoked for only the third time on October 16, 1970.[33] It is important to note that the Prime Minister and the cabinet could enact emergency powers by simply declaring that an emergency existed.[34] Section two of the WMA states, "The issue of a proclamation by Her Majesty, or under the authority of the Governor in Council shall be conclusive evidence that war, invasion, or insurrection, real or apprehended, exists."[35] The approval of the provinces or Parliament was not required.[36] The ability of the prime minister to unilaterally declare emergency powers diminishes the possibility that the separation of powers can constrain their use and abuse. Recall from Chapter 2 that the best situation would be where one branch invokes the emergency powers while a different branch wields those powers.

The War Measures Act gave extensive powers to the federal government. The original legislation specifically listed powers of "censorship, arrest, detention, exclusion and deportation, control of harbours, ports and territorial waters, movement of vessels, all transportation, trading, exports, imports, production and manufacture, and complete power to deal with property, including appropriation, forfeiture and disposition."[37] Under this umbrella of powers, the War Measures Act was used to invoke more specific powers in 1970, called the Public Order Regulations. These regulations outlawed the FLQ and any group advocating violence to change Canada's government, created a five-year prison sentence for any affiliation or support of the FLQ, allowed police officers to arrest suspects and search property without a warrant, hold persons for twenty-one days without charge, and ninety days without a trial, and allowed the courts to deny bail.[38]

In invoking the War Measures Act, the Trudeau government justified the powers by arguing that a situation of "apprehended insurrection" existed. In other words, the FLQ posed a potential or feared threat, rather than a real one. In a nationally televised speech, Prime Minister Trudeau stated, "If a democratic society is to continue to exist it must be able to root out the cancer of an armed, revolutionary movement that is bent on destroying the basis of our freedom."[39] Dan Loomis supports the claim that the FLQ posed a threat to Canadian democratic values. He argues, "The crisis Canada faced in Quebec was indeed a protracted revolutionary war in its early stages, and could have been a long and bloody one had it not been quenched by determined Canadian leaders wholly prepared to meet the challenge."[40] Loomis refutes the notion that the FLQ was just a group of isolated and misguided teenagers by arguing that the FLQ had a "far-flung revolutionary infrastructure across Quebec, [and was] well anchored across Canada."[41] While this seems an exaggeration in hindsight, there were three reasons the FLQ might have been seen as a greater threat than it actually was. The FLQ self-consciously modeled its operations on the Tupamaros of Uruguay who had kidnapped multiple civilians and even held an entire town hostage for a short period. Also, the police believed that 10,000 sticks of dynamite had been stolen in the year before the October Crisis and the FLQ had in their possession 9,000 pounds of this dynamite. Both of these claims are wildly exaggerated, however.[42] Lastly, the Laporte kidnapping changed the perception of the FLQ. After the Cross kidnapping, people could still view the FLQ as a small group of misguided teenagers, but with the Laporte kidnapping, it appeared that the FLQ was larger and capable of even more kidnappings. What was originally viewed as an isolated incident came to be seen as part of a larger pattern.[43]

These claims that Canada was in a state of "apprehended insurrection" and that the police were incapable of dealing with the threat with their existing powers were vigorously contested both during the October Crisis and afterwards. According to George Bain, "What this threat [of apprehended insurrection] consisted of—other than the two kidnappings which, alarming as they were, hardly constituted an insurrection in themselves—has never really been explained."[44] In fact, it was unlikely that the FLQ had the capacity to threaten the security of Canada. Denis Smith writes, "The possibility that there was a serious threat to authority from the FLQ itself is the purest fantasy"[45] while Peter Desbarats argues, "The discussion of a 'parallel power' and 'civil war' seems exaggerated."[46] To many who criticized the government's use of the War Measures Act, the response was out of proportion to the threat.[47]

Despite these objections, the War Measures Act *was* invoked and used to arrest hundreds of people in the early morning of October 16 and keep many of them in jail for the maximum length of time allowed. The police announced that they had made 238 arrests in the early morning hours of October 16.[48] One week after the invocation of the War Measures Act, the police had arrested 379 people, and by the end of the year, 468 people had been arrested and detained by the police under the WMA.[49] Of the total number arrested, 435 were released without being charged.[50] In addition to the arrests, the police also conducted over 3,000 searches of property.[51]

In December 1970, the War Measures Act was lifted and replaced with the Public Order (Temporary Measures) Act, which was almost identical to the original War Measures Regulations, but did not depend on the existence of apprehended insurrection for its justification. On April 30, 1971, this act was allowed to lapse, and Canada's use of emergency powers officially ended.[52]

EFFECTIVE EMERGENCY POWERS

Many opponents of the War Measures Act claimed that the emergency powers were not necessary. In all, they offer four reasons why the War Measures Act was not justified. They argue that the government's claims that the FLQ had hundreds of weapons and thousands of sticks of dynamite exaggerated the threat from the FLQ. Marcel Rioux asks his fellow Canadians, "Did we really need a declaration of 'war,' and the suspension of civil liberties, and a campaign of police raids unprecedented in Quebec's history, all to find these weapons and these dynamite sticks?"[53] The apprehended insurrection that the government used to justify the War Measures Act simply did not exist. This criticism is probably justified; the threat from the FLQ was inflated, although at the time many people thought that the FLQ was more capable than it was.

Also, critics of the emergency powers point out that the police were ultimately successful in finding both FLQ cells through standard police work.[54] Denis Smith claims, "The emergency police sweep [on October 16] failed to locate the two terrorist cells, but normal police activity did so after several weeks."[55] Similarly, Abraham Rotstein argues that it was "conventional if belated police work that discovered the hiding place of the kidnappers of James Cross and turned up the suspected murderers of Pierre Laporte."[56]

The capture of the two cells *was* due, in large part, to standard police work that tracked down the cells through connections to specific members. Jacques Lanctot was a suspect because of his earlier attempted kidnappings, while Marc Carbonneau's fingerprints were identified on the first communiqué. Moreover, a police informer had provided the names of most of those involved in the two kidnappings.[57] The location of the Cross kidnappers was found through routine police work by following a trail from Lanctot's wife to his sister to her husband, who was in the cell that kidnapped Cross. Similarly, the police discovered the hideout of the Laporte murderers from wiretap information.[58] When the police searched the house in which the Rose group was hiding, they found a 30-year-old accountant named Michel Viger whom they had earlier arrested and released. They questioned him intensively until he revealed the kidnappers' hiding place under the basement floor.[59]

All of these arrests used regular police methods and probably could have been achieved without the emergency powers; however, the emergency powers contributed to the police success in an important way. After the Laporte kidnapping, many prominent Montreal officials and businessmen feared that they would be the next kidnap victims. The police, then, were responsible for finding the kidnappers and their victims, protecting the citizens of Montreal from additional kidnappings, as well as doing normal police work. The resources of the Montreal and provincial police forces were insufficient for these tasks. By declaring a state of emergency, the government could, and did, send army troops into Montreal to assist the police. Approximately 12,500 army troops were sent into the province of Quebec, with 7,500 deployed to the city of Montreal. These forces supplemented the 10,000 Montreal policemen.[60] The army took on the task of protecting civilians while the police focused their resources on finding the kidnappers. The critics are right to point out that it was routine police work that eventually discovered the FLQ cells, but should not ignore the fact that it was the emergency powers, and specifically the deployment of army soldiers into Montreal, that allowed the police to track and capture the terrorists. Without the emergency powers, the police would have had to focus on providing physical security instead of focusing on their efforts to find the kidnappers. They might still have been successful, but it would probably have taken them longer or they also might never have found the FLQ kidnappers.

Next, critics of the emergency powers claim they were unnecessary because the police had been successful against the FLQ before emergency powers were ever invoked. From 1963 until 1969, the police responded to every cycle of FLQ terrorism by successfully arresting those involved in terrorist activity.[61] Following the FLQ's first wave of bombings in 1963, the police offered a $60,000 reward for information on the terrorists. Information from an informer helped the police arrest twenty-three people, all but two of which received sentences of up to twelve years in prison.[62] This original FLQ cell was completely defeated; none of its members were involved in later FLQ activities.[63] Likewise, the police stopped the second wave of FLQ attacks when ten FLQ members were captured, including Vallières and Gagnon.[64] In total, 135 people had been sentenced for terrorist offences during the first six years of FLQ operations.[65] If the police had been successful in the past, why did they need new powers in 1970? Additional powers were needed in 1970 because the FLQ had become more threatening in 1970 with its change in tactics from bombings to kidnappings. Their earlier bombings were mostly symbolic; they had done little physical damage and only resulted in accidental human casualties. The kidnappings, in contrast, directly targeted individuals and appeared to be the first stage of a broader campaign. The kidnappings also resulted in much greater attention from the media and from the public. As a result, the government had to not only appear to be doing something (the symbolic value of emergency powers), but also had to take steps to ensure that the FLQ would be defeated (the consequential value of emergency powers).

The final reason given for why emergency powers were not necessary was that the police could already do almost everything that the emergency powers allowed.[66] Even under the normal Criminal Code, if a police officer "reasonably believes that dangerous weapons offences are being committed, he may search *without warrant* persons and places other than dwelling houses. He may enter *without warrant* virtually any place including a dwelling house, which he had reasonable and probable grounds to believe is harbouring a person whom he is entitled to arrest"[67] [italics added]. The WMA, however, gave two additional powers to the police; the ability to keep a prisoner for up to twenty-one days without bringing charges against him and to hold a suspect for up to ninety days before bringing him to trial. These two extra powers allowed the police to hold dozens of suspected and likely FLQ members while they searched for the kidnappers. By holding these suspected FLQ members in jail, the police kept them from forming new cells and launching additional operations. An additional benefit of the WMA, even had it not increased the police's powers in any way, was that it gave legitimacy to the police and the army. Had the army moved into Montreal without the WMA and had the police conducted searches and arrests without warrants, these actions would have been seen as less legitimate. The use of the WMA showed that the government would allow the police to do *only* these things (search and arrest without warrant)—even though they always had these powers—and *only* in times of emergency.

Overall, then, the emergency powers did, in fact, increase the effectiveness of the police and legitimized their actions. In addition, the emergency powers also were effective in ending terrorist violence from the FLQ in both the short term and in the long term. Immediately after the two kidnappings, the arrests of nearly 500 people were intended to detain possible FLQ sympathizers and to assist the security forces in their search for the two kidnapping victims and their captors. Many people feared that after the Laporte kidnapping, more kid-nappings or bombings would occur in support of the first two FLQ kidnappings. It is impossible to prove that more violence would have occurred, but we do know that no more attacks or kidnappings were committed. As Leonard Beaton points out, "Whether as a result of the mass arrests or for other reasons, not a bomb went off. The police action silenced the FLQ completely."[68] The police ac-tion arrested and detained nearly 500 people, 30 of which were eventually brought to trial.[69] It is fair to assume that some of these thirty might have formed a new FLQ cell and carried out a new attack. (Admittedly, it is possi-ble—although unlikely—that the two cells comprised the entirety of the FLQ. If this was the case, then the only contribution of the emergency powers was that they allowed the police to focus on finding the kidnappers.) Furthermore, the response of the government might have deterred other potential terrorists from acting if they viewed their likely arrest and imprisonment as not worth the benefit of continuing the FLQ campaign.

In the long term, the FLQ suffered a rapid decline in power after the October Crisis. The FLQ lost much of its support after the murder of Pierre Laporte;[70] even Pierre Vallières, the ideological theorist of the FLQ, abandoned terrorism and joined the Parti Québécois to pursue Quebec separatism through legitimate political channels. After the October Crisis, the Royal Canadian Mounted Police (RCMP) and the Canadian intelligence service penetrated the FLQ to such an extent that they issued communiqués, stole dynamite, and set off an occasional explosion. By the end of 1972, the last remnant cells of the FLQ, facing relent-less police pressure, were finally dissolved.[71]

In sum, the emergency powers allowed the police to focus on the pursuit of the kidnappers, eliminated any additional violence in the short-term, and led to the extinction of the FLQ within two years. The effectiveness of the emergency powers was a result of two factors: the FLQ had little support, which made it difficult for it to sustain its membership base, and the police moved quickly to arrest suspected terrorists before they could form new cells and launch addi-tional attacks.

In the case of the FLQ, not only did they lack a large support base, they also were relatively small compared to other terrorist groups. The very small size of the FLQ made it easier for any anti-terrorist strategy to work. With only a handful of members, any operation that captured even a few FLQ members was likely to disrupt the organization. The overall size of the FLQ was probably on the order of several dozen to perhaps, at the most, 100 active members. (Recall that the Tupamaros and the IRA probably numbered in the several hundreds.) In a RCMP report, the FLQ was believed to consist of 22 cells, 130 members, and 2,000 sympathizers.[72] Jean Marchand, a Minister in the federal govern-ment, claimed the FLQ numbered between 1,000 and 3,000.[73] Gerard Pelletier gives a lower estimate, while dividing the FLQ into four elements:

first, a nucleus of up to 100 extremists ready to plant bombs, carry out kidnappings, even to commit murders; second, a more limited group, or 'permanent cell,' holding itself apart from violent action, which constituted the editorial and propagandist element of the FLQ; third, a ring of 200 to 300 active sympathizers prepared to support the terrorists by financial aid, concealment, and to otherwise provide a supportive infrastructure; and fourth, a periphery of some 2,000 to 3,000 more or less passive sympathizers who, without formally being members of the FLQ, desired its victory and approved its methods.[74]

In all likelihood, even this estimate was too high. According to the calculations of Peter Janke, only 30 people of the nearly 500 arrested in October 1970 were actually charged with terrorist offences. In addition to the five FLQ members that were exiled to Cuba, this only amounts to a total of thirty-five terrorists.[75] Presumably, there were some FLQ members who escaped the police roundup, but an estimate of several dozen to possibly one hundred is the most substantiated estimate of the number of active FLQ members.

The FLQ was also vulnerable because it lacked a large support base committed to pursuing Quebec separatism *through violent means.* Many Canadians supported the goals of the FLQ, but not their actions. After the manifesto was read on television and radio on October 8, over 50 percent of the callers expressed sympathy for the spirit of the manifesto.[76] Similarly, large numbers of French Canadians expressed support for the manifesto in interviews done after the kidnappings.[77] For many French Canadians listening to the manifesto on the radio, they "could not help recognizing that the injustices listed in the manifesto were very much like those they themselves had suffered, and which, for the most part, were overlooked by the society in which they occurred."[78] In addition to these expressions of sympathy, thousands of students in Montreal held protest rallies to show their support for the FLQ.[79] At one rally with several thousand students, Pierre Vallières read the FLQ manifesto to the crowd, to which the students replied with chants of "FLQ, FLQ, FLQ."[80]

As strong as the support and sympathy may have been for the FLQ manifesto and its demands, there was low support for the FLQ methods of bombings and kidnappings, or any other type of violence. At one radio station allowing listeners to call in, some callers were sympathetic to the FLQ's ideas, but most callers disapproved of their methods.[81] Gustave Morf cites a survey done of 2,000 young French Canadians in which 89 percent of those surveyed were absolutely against the use of violence to solve political problems.[82] Even Pierre Vallières, the FLQ theorist, came to condemn the FLQ's use of violent means during the October Crisis. Writing in 1972, he argued, "Mass armed struggle and mass electoral struggle cannot coexist ... As far as the masses and the present authorities are concerned, the P.Q. is the real alternative—not the unions, the citizens' committees or the F.L.Q ... Is it in the interest of the Quebec people that armed agitation by the F.L.Q. [continue]? The answer is a categorical no."[83]

Even many of the FLQ members lacked a strong commitment to the use of violence. According to Peter Janke, "The 'café revolutionaries' from which the FLQ drew membership and support were playing at revolution rather than pursuing it aggressively."[84] Gustave Morf describes the sympathy for the FLQ among many young French Canadians as "shallow adulation that does not last for long."[85] In the end, the FLQ simply lacked a large support base committed to using violence to achieve their ends. The FLQ also lacked the support from the political parties that also sought Quebec separatism.[86] "No doubt many in the separatist political movement supported the FLQ in spirit, especially in the 1963–69 period of symbolic terrorism which only rarely caused casualties; but the overwhelming majority of French Canadians did not support the actions of the Lanctot group in murdering Laporte. The people of Quebec seemed to be willing to tolerate terrorism as long as no one was hurt."[87]

The low support for the FLQ and its violent methods was further eroded after the murder of Pierre Laporte. Peter Janke describes the effects of the Laporte murder in the following terms: "With the death of Laporte there was an immediate swing of popular opinion behind the government ... a once sympathetic public virtually abandoned the Front ... public sympathy for FLQ actions evaporated overnight."[88] The change in support for the FLQ was largely a result of their change in tactics. This is similar to what happened in Uruguay after the Tupamaros began assassinating policemen on the streets of Montevideo.

The invocation of the War Measures Act also increased support for the government at the expense of the FLQ.[89] A frequent reason that democracies resort to emergency powers to fight terrorists is that they feel pressured to "do something" by a fearful public. For example, an article in the Montreal Star recognized that emergency powers are useful because "They show an anxious public that something's being done."[90] In this way, emergency powers are a weapon in the war for legitimacy that is waged between terrorist groups and governments. By using emergency powers, a government can show that it still controls the state and is the only actor in the state that can legitimately use violence. The decisions to send the army into Quebec, to cut off negotiations with the FLQ, and to invoke the War Measures Act all served to send a clear message: "The State and only the State has the power to determine the political agenda of Quebec."[91] Denis Smith argues that Prime Minister Trudeau, Premier Bourassa, and Mayor Drapeau of Montreal wanted the emergency powers "to shock the Quebec public out of its confusion into support for established authority."[92] Gaining support for the government at the expense of support for the terrorists is especially helpful, as I argue, if the emergency powers are to be effective in reducing terrorism in the long-term. Most importantly, the government was successful in doing so, especially after the invocation of emergency powers, as popular support shifted from the FLQ to the government.[93] A member of Parliament noted during the crisis, "The government has the support of a very, very substantial majority of the Canadian people and the people don't even ask themselves—*they're not interested*—in whether or not the government was justified in any way at all in invoking the War Measures Act, other than that *something* had to be done and they were delighted, for a variety of reasons, that the government had reacted vigorously."[94]

The Canadian government was effective in rallying support to itself in part because the emergency powers allowed it to control the access to the media.[95] Before the emergency powers were invoked, the media was at the center of the crisis. The FLQ sent their communiqués to various media outlets and the government used the media to issue their responses and communicate with the FLQ cells. The media coverage of the two kidnappings helped the FLQ to legitimize their cause and helped them seem more threatening than they really were.[96] The War Measures Act, however, allowed the government to censor media reporting on the FLQ. The difference in the media coverage before and after the invocation of emergency powers was striking. Whereas in the early stages of the crisis, "FLQ communiqués and declarations of support for FLQ goals and/or demands were everywhere to be heard or to be read, once the War Measures Act was invoked and special legislation outlawing the FLQ and forbidding all statements or communications in their favour was passed into law, nothing more was said by or for the FLQ."[97] Moreover, by controlling the media, the government ensured that the FLQ's use of violence and the government's response would be the focus of media coverage, rather than the FLQ's political goals. Ronald Crelinsten argues, "The net result [of the emergency powers] was a switch in the focus of public debate from the legitimacy of the terrorists to that of the governments."[98] This was exactly what the federal and provincial governments wanted; by focusing on the violence of the FLQ (instead of their grievances) and the response of the government, they had completely undermined any support that the FLQ might have enjoyed and put themselves back into the center of popular and media attention.

The War Measures Act was also effective in eliminating the FLQ because the police forces moved extremely quickly to arrest hundreds of suspected FLQ members and sympathizers. In fact, one reason that the emergency powers were invoked was to allow the police to move quickly to surprise potential FLQ cells before they could react. For the police to quickly arrest large numbers of citizens and conduct necessary searches, they needed to be able to act without having to get search warrants and be able to detain people without charging them with a crime.[99] By noon on October 16, eight hours after the invocation of the War Measures Act, around 450 people had already been arrested without a warrant.[100]

The relationship between the speed with which the emergency powers were used and the effectiveness of the government's response to the FLQ is difficult to assess. Essentially, what we know is that the police moved quickly against the FLQ after emergency powers were invoked and thereafter the FLQ did not launch any more kidnappings or plant any bombs. There is no testimony from FLQ members claiming that they were unable to mobilize existing members or recruit new ones after the police imprisoned many FLQ sympathizers and supporters, but the absence of any FLQ operation after the arrests indicate that it is reasonable to argue that this was likely the case. As argued earlier, the FLQ numbered only a few dozen activists, with probably a few hundred supporters.

If we assume that most of these people were on the police's lists of possible FLQ members, it is unlikely that there were many terrorists *not* picked up by the police. In addition, after the FLQ lost almost all popular support following the murder of Laporte, it was unlikely that new recruits would have sought to join the FLQ. One might argue that the small size of the FLQ and their change in tactics (which decreased their support) made the speed of the government's response less important. Even with their small size and low support, though, the FLQ would probably have been able to form a few more cells and possibly kidnap more individuals had the police not been able to quickly capture many suspected FLQ members. In other words, the size and support of the FLQ limited their potential for violence, but the speed of the government's response made sure this potential was not realized.

In addition to using emergency powers, the Canadian government also responded to many of the FLQ's demands with political reforms. By doing so, Canada removed many of the grievances of Quebec separatists and probably diminished the likelihood that Canadian citizens would feel it necessary to resort to terrorism to achieve their ends. In 1972, a language bill made French the official language in Quebec, required immigrants to learn French, required businesses to make French the working language in the workplace, and promoted the use of French in advertising.[101] In addition, the government began to invest more heavily in French-speaking areas and businesses. These measures "helped to deprive those advocating terrorist actions of the support of the moderates among the French community."[102] In 1976, the Parti Québécois (PQ) led by René Lévesque, was elected to power in Quebec, indicating that the issues that motivated the FLQ had resonance within the rest of society.[103]

The point here is that emergency powers by themselves were just one piece of the anti-terrorism response of the Canadian government. The War Measures Act successfully eliminated the FLQ because of the speed with which the police acted, and because of the low support for the terrorists. By accepting and responding to many of the FLQ's grievances, however, the Canadian government also reduced the likelihood that the FLQ would reorganize and renew its campaign on behalf of the French Canadians.

ABUSES OF EMERGENCY POWERS

Emergency powers in Canada were relatively unabused compared to other countries. They were revoked soon after the crisis ended, they were not extended beyond their original scope, and few people were arrested who were not affiliated with terrorism. In large part this was because there was neither the desire nor the opportunity for any individual or organization to abuse their additional powers. The commitment to democracy was strong, and the emergency powers maintained the integrity of the institutional safeguards within Canada: the press was still free to criticize the government's actions, and Parliament was capable of monitoring, debating, and consenting (or not) to Trudeau's use of the War Measures Act.

To review, abuses can occur in two ways: Emergency powers can be extended beyond their initial scope to infringe on liberties or individuals that should have been protected, and they can be extended beyond the time frame dictated by the emergency. In Canada, emergency powers were clearly not abused in terms of their duration or to infringe on more liberties than originally legislated. There is some debate, however, over whether emergency powers were abused to arrest people unaffiliated with the FLQ.

One danger from emergency powers is that they will become permanent. In Canada, however, the use of emergency powers had no long-term consequences for democracy or civil liberties. In fact, the emergency powers were in force for only six months. On April 30, 1971, the Public Order (Temporary Measures) Act, which replaced the War Measures Act, was allowed to lapse, and Canada's use of emergency powers ended.[104] As Cindy Combs puts it, "The crisis had an end point, when civil liberties were restored, the army withdrawn, and local police once again constrained by strict laws on search and seizure operations."[105] This case is in sharp contrast to other cases where emergency powers were abused in terms of their duration. In Uruguay, for example, the emergency powers were in force for a full year after the Tupamaros had been eliminated. During this time, the military used the powers to arrest political opponents to the regime and to eventually launch a coup that put Uruguay under a military dictatorship for twelve years.

Emergency powers may also be abused if they allow the government to extend its powers beyond what is initially legislated. For example, the security forces often use more aggressive interrogation methods (such as torture) or internment beyond the allowed length of time when the emergency powers remove many of the protections that citizens have to due process. In Britain, there were frequent and widespread allegations that emergency powers were abused along this dimension, particularly that the security forces used torture in their interrogations and engaged in unlawful killings.[106]

Canada, however, is remarkable in its difference from the other cases. In fact, Canadians arrested during the October Crisis frequently praised the police for how they were treated. One prisoner claimed, "I expected I was going to be put through all sorts of interrogation. But ... interrogation was only cursory, minimal. Aside from being kept in the cells all the time, everybody was fairly well treated."[107] When the police questioned suspects, it was more like interviews than interrogations, according to Haggart and Golden.[108] Furthermore, the prisoners' rights were not violated beyond what was allowed by the emergency powers. There is no evidence that anyone was held without charge beyond twenty-one days, or held without trial beyond ninety days, or tortured in any way. This is in sharp contrast to the actions of the security forces of the other states in this study. We have already seen that both the British and Uruguayan police and armed forces used abusive interrogation methods on suspected terrorists (although to different degrees). In these countries, the security forces appeared more concerned with defeating terrorism than protecting the liberties of individual citizens. In Canada, though, the police appeared to maintain a strong normative commitment to the rights and freedoms of individuals.

The only dimension of emergency powers in which there is some debate as to how much they were abused is whether the powers were used to arrest and imprison people unaffiliated with terrorism. By some estimates, over 90 percent of those arrested were actually opposed to terrorism.[109] Many of those arrested were members of legal Quebec separatist groups, such as Parti Québécois or the Front d'Action Politique (FRAP). One prisoner recalled that a fellow inmate was an "American girl who answered a little advertisement at the university to get a room. She rented the room from a girl at the university, and that girl's boy friend was in FRAP or the PQ or something, and that caused the room to be raided [and the girl to be taken into custody]."[110] Levin and Sylvester claim, "Most of those arrested were not associated with the FLQ, nor did they have anything to do with the kidnappings."[111]

In defense of the police, these arrests were based on the rationale that these people were the most likely to support, assist, or even join the FLQ. In anticipation of the War Measures Act, the various police forces compiled a list of people to be arrested once the emergency powers were invoked. The list included individuals suspected of being in the FLQ, associated with the FLQ, connected to the Vallières-Gagnon group of the FLQ, as well as individuals who advocated violence or were part of the "extreme left."[112] This list contained 354 names, although close to 500 people were actually arrested. About 435 people, nearly 90 percent of those arrested, however, were released quickly.[113] The average length of time spent in custody for everyone that was arrested was about one week.[114]

Whereas critics of the government will point to the fact nearly 500 people were unnecessarily arrested, they miss the fact that the police released the vast majority of these people after cursory questioning. Another way of looking at this is that *only* 500 people were arrested, and charges were brought against only 65 of them. Compared to other countries, where thousands of people were arrested and imprisoned even though they had no affiliation with terrorism, the use of emergency powers in Canada is a case where few abuses occurred. Of course, unnecessary arrests of hundreds of people are never something to be blindly accepted in a democratic state; however, given the climate of fear in Canada during this crisis, the police acted with a great deal of restraint. By arresting only the people that they plausibly thought were connected to the FLQ and quickly releasing those who clearly had no connections to terrorism, the police minimized the abuses of emergency powers.

Why were emergency powers not abused in Canada? One important reason is that no one *tried* to abuse the emergency powers. This is a reflection that the army, police, and political leaders all held a strong normative commitment to democracy and liberty. The military did not try and seize power for itself, the prime minister did not try and create a police state, and the police were not tempted to use abusive methods in their interrogations.[115] In addition, even if some actor had tried to abuse the emergency powers, there were several institutional constraints that were still strong. In particular, Parliament and a free press monitored, debated, and constrained the use of power such that it would have been difficult for any abuse to occur. The emergency powers did not allow the Prime Minister to rule by decree; instead, the separation of powers between the Parliament and Prime Minister remained strong, with the Parliament maintaining its full capabilities to check the power of Trudeau. In addition, while the emergency powers limited speech about the FLQ, they did not censor the debates over whether the emergency powers themselves were legitimate or necessary. In sum, the emergency powers did not infringe on any of the constitutional actors that constrain power in normal times and allowed them to function even during the emergency. I will discuss each institutional actor in turn.

The ability of Parliament to act as a constraint against abuses of power is somewhat contested. Haggart and Golden contend that the highly charged content of the crisis diminished the independence of Parliament. Trudeau appealed to the people of Canada to support the government during the crisis and the response was overwhelming. Public opinion was firmly behind the government, especially after the Laporte murder. Parliament could still refuse to ratify the War Measures Act, but this would put them firmly on the wrong side of public opinion. Because of Trudeau's successful appeal for public support, Haggart and Golden argue, "The House of Commons lost its leverage; Parliament was largely irrelevant."[116]

This argument about the irrelevance of Parliament is misleading, however. It is true that Parliament was swept up in the overwhelming support for the government's actions, but this did not make them incapable of acting. Nothing about the overwhelming public opinion infringed on Parliament's ability to revoke the use of the War Measures Act. Moreover, the fact that members of Parliament probably agreed with the desirability of using emergency powers and acted and voted as their constituents wanted them to, did not diminish the separation of powers in Canada. In fact, this is how representatives in a representative democracy *should* act.

Parliament might also have been incapable of acting as a constraint against abuses of emergency powers because "The Parliamentary system provides only at election time any real check against arbitrary power."[117] According to this logic, emergencies occur, extra powers are invoked, and these powers are abused before an election can be held to throw the prime minister and his party out of office.[118] In Canada, moreover, the War Measures Act can be invoked by the government (prime minister) without the consent of the Parliament and without judicial review.[119] In general, this argument is correct in recognizing that parliamentary systems have fewer checks against abuses of power than a presidential system where the president has to constantly contend with Congress. In a parliamentary system, if the ruling party has a large majority, it can simply rule as it wants, without having to take the minority parties in Parliament into account. In practice, however, the ruling party does not usually have a large majority and often requires a coalition of parties to stay in power. The prime minister, although clearly the leader of the party, cannot simply command the ministers of Parliament to vote as he wants. If the majority party is dissatisfied with how the prime minister is using or abusing his power, they can replace him with someone from within the party. Parliament, therefore, while not as constraining as an independent legislature, can still check abuses of power by the ruling government.

Although Parliament was not required to approve of the War Measures Act, the fact that they did was still important in legitimizing the original declaration of emergency powers by Trudeau. On October 19, the House of Commons approved the government's actions under the War Measures Act by a vote of 190 to 16.[120] The sixteen members of Parliament that voted against the WMA were all from the New Democratic Party, which had a total of twenty-three members.[121] Support was so overwhelming that every French-speaking member of Parliament approved the WMA.[122] Of course, the approval of Parliament was not necessary for the continuation of emergency powers. Nevertheless, the approval of Parliament was more than a "rubber-stamp" exercise; supporting the WMA legitimized the government's actions by showing that representatives from all parties across Canada agreed with the government's use of emergency powers. Conversely, if Parliament had refused to approve the WMA, it is likely that this would have had the practical effect of revoking the powers, although Trudeau could have reissued them on the same grounds as the initial invocation of the War Measures Act. Also, if Parliament had rejected the WMA, it might have helped deter possible future abuses by showing the government of Trudeau that his actions were not seen as necessary or legitimate. Besides approving of the original invocation of the War Measures Act, Parliament took control of the emergency legislation when they replaced the original Public Order Regulations (under the WMA) with the Public Order (Temporary Measures) Act on December 3, which expired on April 30, 1971.

In addition to its legislative and legitimizing functions, Parliament also served as a forum where the necessity of the emergency powers was openly debated. Between the invocation of the War Measures Act and the passage of the Public Order Act on December 3, Parliament engaged in heated and lengthy debates about what, exactly, constituted the apprehended insurrection that the government used to justify the emergency powers.[123] The opposition parties used the Question Period in Parliament to demand more details on the apprehended insurrection as well as details on those that were already arrested.[124] Even hard-line "law and order" members of Parliament criticized the use of emergency powers at times.[125]

In all, Parliament served as a public forum for debates about whether the emergency powers were justified and necessary. Their approval may have only been a reflection of popular sentiment but had they disapproved, this would have undermined the legitimacy of the government and its use of emergency powers.

In terms of free speech, the War Measures Act censored the media in a way that contributed to the effectiveness of the emergency powers but also protected against any abuse. Specifically, the media was not allowed to print or broadcast anything that mentioned the FLQ or terrorism. As shown earlier, this allowed the government to take public support away from the FLQ by focusing attention on how the government responded to the violence of the FLQ rather than on the FLQ and its demands. Importantly, the press was not censored in its reporting and criticisms of the government's actions. While discussions of anything to do with the FLQ disappeared, debates about the government's use of emergency powers were vigorous and widespread both during and after the crisis.[126] These debates were an additional element in constraining against abuses of power.[127] As Alan Borovy claims, "Unjust governments and unjust policies are not likely to survive in an atmosphere of free public debate."[128]

Criticism of the government's use of emergency powers was widespread throughout the last months of 1970. Many authors argue that this criticism of the government was a result of its corruption and abuse of power. "Very basic questions were raised about the real course of events, the responsibility for those events, the propriety and prudence of suspending civil liberties, and the motives of all the actors engaged in the drama." This criticism of the government, however, also showed that the government was acting with a great deal of restraint (by not censoring the media). Furthermore, it is these public debates that ensured that the government was aware of the limits of what the population would consider legitimate and helped keep the government from using emergency powers unless they were perceived as necessary.

THE BEST POSSIBLE OUTCOME

The use of emergency powers in Canada raises several issues that I have attempted to address. As Haggart and Golden ask, "Were the extraordinary powers assumed by the state necessary and honestly motivated? Were the powers, if necessary, successful? Were they less a threat to the society they sought to serve than the danger they sought to exorcise?"[129]

I have shown that the Canadian government decided to use emergency powers against what they saw as a likelihood of continued FLQ kidnappings. (With hindsight, this threat was probably exaggerated.) The emergency powers contributed to the success of the security forces in eliminating the FLQ because the FLQ did not enjoy widespread support, particularly after the Laporte murder, and because the police moved quickly to arrest potential and suspected FLQ members on October 16. These factors ensured that existing FLQ members would not conduct kidnappings in the short-term and ensured that the FLQ would not be able to continue its operations in the long-term because new recruits would find it difficult and undesirable to join the FLQ. The emergency powers were not abused because there was no desire on the part of the army, police, or political leadership to abuse their power. Even if they had tried, public debates in the press and in Parliament would have monitored abuses, and an independent Parliament could have enforced compliance with the laws.

The use of emergency powers is commonly believed to result in a tradeoff—they are effective against terrorists but dangerous to the democratic character of a state. In Canada, this tradeoff did not materialize. The emergency powers were both effective and safe. To be clear, I do not advocate the use of emergency powers unless they are necessary. Any limitations on the liberties of individual citizens, even if temporary and as limited as possible, are still unwelcome to people who value liberty and democracy; however, the emergency powers used in Canada offer the best possible consequences. If a state deems it necessary to use emergency powers, a situation similar to that of Canada is the best that can be hoped for. With good norms, strong constitutional safeguards that constrain power, and security forces that can move quickly against a poorly supported terrorist group, emergency powers can be both safe and effective.

NOTES

1. Canada became officially and completely independent of Britain in 1982 with the Constitution Act.

2. For basic information on the history of Canada, see the Encyclopedia Britannica.

3. Peter Janke, ed. *Terrorism and Democracy: Some Contemporary Cases* (New York: St. Martin's Press, 1992), 34.

4. For more on Quebec separatism, see Henry Milner and Sheilagh Hodgins Milner, *The Decolonization of Quebec: An Analysis of Left-Wing Nationalism* (Toronto: McClelland and Stewart, 1973); and Lauren McKinsey, "Dimension of National Political Integration and Disintegration: The Case of Quebec Separatism 1960–1975," *Comparative Political Studies* 9 no. 3 (October 1976).

5. Janke, *Terrorism and Democracy*, 37.

6. Gustave Morf, *Terror in Quebec: Case Studies of the FLQ* (Toronto: Clarke, Irwin and Company, 1970), 2; and Malcolm Levin, and Christine Sylvester, *Crisis in Quebec* (Toronto: The Ontario Institute for Studies in Education, 1973), 71.

7. Morf, *Terror in Quebec*, identifies six waves, if one includes the kidnappers of the October Crisis as the sixth and final wave. For a history of FLQ actions, see Anthony Burton, *Urban Terrorism: Theory, Practice and Response* (London: Leo Cooper, 1975), 147–150; Morf, *Terror in Quebec*; Janke, *Terrorism and Democracy*, 37–40; Dan Loomis, *Not Much Glory: Quelling the F.L.Q* (Toronto: Deneau Publishers, 1984), 24–25; and Levin and Sylvester, *Crisis in Quebec*, 71–79.

8. Ron Haggart, and Aubrey Golden, *Rumours of War* (Toronto: new press, 1971), 30.

9. Albert Parry, *Terrorism: From Robespierre to Arafat* (New York: Vanguard Press, 1976), 365.

10. Marcel Rioux, *Quebec in Question,* tr. James Boake (Toronto: James Lewis and Samuel, 1971), 161.

11. Parry, *Terrorism: From Robespierre to Arafat,* 366. For more on Vallières, see Nicholas Regush, *Pierre Vallieres: The Revolutionary Process in Quebec* (New York: Dial Press, 1973).

12. Parry, *Terrorism: From Robespierre to Arafat,* 368.

13. Ronald Crelinsten, "The Internal Dynamics of the FLQ During the October Crisis of 1970," in *Inside Terrorist Organizations,* ed. David Rapoport (New York: Columbia University Press, 1988), 83; and Janke, *Terrorism and Democracy,* 40.

14. See Brian Moore, *The Revolution Script* (Toronto: McClelland and Stewart, 1971); and Janke, *Terrorism and Democracy,* 42.

15. Parry, *Terrorism: From Robespierre to Arafat,* 368; and Denis Smith, *Bleeding Hearts ... Bleeding Country: Canada and the Quebec Crisis* (Edmonton: M. G. Hurtig, 1971), 58.

16. Crelinsten, "Internal Dynamics of the FLQ," 59.

17. Levin and Sylvester, *Crisis in Quebec,* 59, imply the opposite—that a centralized structure organized new recruits into cells; however, all the other evidence on the FLQ points to a completely grass-roots, localized recruitment process.

18. Levin and Sylvester, *Crisis in Quebec,* 78.

19. For more detailed accounts of the kidnappings that led to the October Crisis, the best sources are Moore, *Revolution Script;* John Saywell, *Quebec 70: A Documentary Narrative* (Toronto: University of Toronto Press, 1971); Haggart and Golden, *Rumours of War;* James Stewart, *The FLQ: Seven Years of Terrorism* (Ontario: Simon and Schuster, 1970); and Ronald Crelinsten, "Power and Meaning: Terrorism as a Struggle over Access to the Communication Structure," in *Contemporary Research on Terrorism,* ed. Paul Wilkinson and Alasdair Stewart (Aberdeen: Aberdeen University Press, 1987). The following synopsis is based largely on a synthesis of these sources.

20. The liberation cell was composed of Jacques Lanctot, Marc Carbonneau, Yves Lanlois, Jacques and Louis Cosette-Trudel.

21. See Saywell, *Quebec 70,* for the full text of all the primary documents from this crisis—including all of the FLQ communiqués, the FLQ manifesto, and government documents.

22. The Chernier cell was comprised of Paul Rose, Jacques Rose, Francis Simard, and Bernard Lortie.

23. Laporte was, in fact the acting Premier of Quebec while Premier Bourassa was traveling in the United States. Bourassa returned to Montreal before the Laporte kidnapping after he was unable to fly into Boston because of fog. If he had gone to Boston, Laporte would have been the acting Premier at the time of his kidnapping. See Haggart and Golden, *Rumours of War,* 13–14, for more on this.

24. Janke, *Terrorism and Democracy,* 55–57.

25. Crelinsten, "Power and Meaning," 447.

26. Janke, *Terrorism and Democracy,* 60.

27. The Polity 98 dataset codes Canada as a 10 on the democracy scale (with an autocracy score of 0). For a detailed discussion of civil liberties in Canada, see Schmeiser

1964. For a general overview of Canada's political system, see the Encyclopedia Britannica.

28. Crelinsten, "Power and Meaning," 432.

29. Quoted in Haggart and Golden, *Rumours of War,* 34.

30. Janke, *Terrorism and Democracy,* 56.

31. D. Smith, *Bleeding Hearts ... Bleeding Country,* 45.

32. Levin and Sylvester, *Crisis in Quebec,* 29.

33. Haggart and Golden, *Rumours of War,* 89.

34. W. S. Tarnopolsky, "Emergency Powers and Civil Liberties," *Canadian Public Administration* 15 no. 2 (summer 1972), 209, point out this fact. For Carl Schmitt, the Prime Minister and his cabinet would be the sovereign because they decide on the emergency.

35. Quoted in D. Smith, *Bleeding Hearts ... Bleeding Country,* 39.

36. D. Smith, *Bleeding Hearts ... Bleeding Country,* 38.

37. Haggart and Golden, *Rumours of War,* 90.

38. D. Smith, *Bleeding Hearts ... Bleeding Country,* 40–41. Haggart and Golden, *Rumours of War,* 60, make the point that many of these powers were redundant. The real substantial powers were those of detention for twenty-one days without charge and ninety days without trial.

39. Quoted in Levin and Sylvester, *Crisis in Quebec,* 28.

40. Loomis, *Not Much Glory,* 14. Loomis is clearly a supporter of the government. His book is largely devoted to praising the preparation and operations of the security forces during the October Crisis.

41. Loomis, *Not Much Glory,* 154. Parry, *Terrorism: From Robespierre to Arafat,* 374, similarly overestimates the size and threat of the FLQ.

42. Haggart and Golden, *Rumours of War,* 14, argue that the numbers were too high on all counts. The Cross kidnappers did have some dynamite, but only forty sticks.

43. See Leonard Beaton, "The Crisis in Quebec: Mr. Trudeau Asserts Authority," *The Round Table* no. 241 (January 1971), 149; and Haggart and Golden, *Rumours of War,* 15.

44. George Bain, "The Making of a Crisis," in *Power Corrupted: The October Crisis and the Repression of Quebec,* ed. Abraham Rotstein (Toronto: new press, 1971), 11. See also D. Smith, *Bleeding Hearts ... Bleeding Country,* 46 and 50, for additional skepticism of the government's justification of the emergency powers.

45. D. Smith, *Bleeding Hearts ... Bleeding Country,* 70.

46. Peter Desbarats, *René: A Canadian in Search of a Country* (Toronto: McClelland and Stewart, 1976), 187.

47. Janke, *Terrorism and Democracy,* 70.

48. Crelinsten, "Internal Dynamics of the FLQ," 64.

49. Haggart and Golden, *Rumours of War,* 171 and 70; and Saywell, *Quebec 70,* 125. The total number arrested under the WMA varies slightly between authors but the total number is always close to 500 people.

50. Levin and Sylvester, *Crisis in Quebec,* 14.

51. Parry, *Terrorism: From Robespierre to Arafat,* 374.

52. D. Smith, *Bleeding Hearts ... Bleeding Country,* 38 and 41.

53. Rioux, *Quebec in Question*, 176. See also Beaton, "The Crisis in Quebec," 151, who notes that even in English Canada, there was increasing doubt about the need for emergency powers.

54. See Crelinsten, "Internal Dynamics of the FLQ," 64; Haggart and Golden, *Rumours of War*, introduction; and Janke, *Terrorism and Democracy*, 59–60.

55. D. Smith, *Bleeding Hearts ... Bleeding Country*, xiii.

56. Abraham Rotstein, ed., *Power Corrupted: The October Crisis and the Repression of Quebec* (Toronto: new press, 1971), introduction.

57. Janke, *Terrorism and Democracy*, 48.

58. Janke, *Terrorism and Democracy*, 59.

59. Levin and Sylvester, *Crisis in Quebec*, 35. While Viger had been originally arrested under the auspices of the War Measures Act, he probably would have been arrested regardless of whether emergency powers were used.

60. Loomis, *Not Much Glory*, 144.

61. Janke, *Terrorism and Democracy*, 66.

62. Janke, *Terrorism and Democracy*, 37.

63. Robert Moss, *The War for the Cities* (New York: Coward, McCann and Geoghegan, 1972), 122.

64. Moss, *The War for the Cities*, 123.

65. Haggart and Golden, *Rumours of War*, 253. See also 11 and 129 for descriptions of earlier police successes against the FLQ.

66. Haggart and Golden, *Rumours of War*, 251–252, 261. See also Levin and Sylvester, *Crisis in Quebec*, 25, for a similar argument.

67. Alan Borovy, "Rebuilding a Free Society," in *Power Corrupted: The October Crisis and the Repression of Quebec*, ed. Abraham Rotstein (Toronto: new press, 1971), 101.

68. Beaton, "The Crisis in Quebec," 151.

69. Janke, *Terrorism and Democracy*, 65.

70. Desbarats, *René*, 186, identifies the Laporte murder as the beginning of the end of the FLQ.

71. Janke, *Terrorism and Democracy*, 60–61.

72. See Levin and Sylvester, *Crisis in Quebec*, 78; Loomis, *Not Much Glory*, 28; and Janke, *Terrorism and Democracy*, 63.

73. Rioux, *Quebec in Question*, 176; and Levin and Sylvester, *Crisis in Quebec*, 28.

74. Loomis, *Not Much Glory*, 29. These numbers are consistent with Bain, "The Making of a Crisis," 10, who estimated the FLQ had a maximum membership of 100–150 individuals.

75. Janke, *Terrorism and Democracy*, 65.

76. Crelinsten, "Power and Meaning," 429. Rioux, *Quebec in Question*, 169, also reports that a "high proportion" of radio listeners agreed with the FLQ analysis of the conditions in Quebec.

77. Levin and Sylvester, *Crisis in Quebec*, 59.

78. Ann Charney, "From Redpath Crescent to Rue des Recollets," in *Power Corrupted: The October Crisis and the Repression of Quebec*, ed. Abraham Rotstein (Toronto: new press, 1971), 20.

79. See Burton, *Urban Terrorism*, 150; Crelinsten, "Power and Meaning," 436; Charney, "From Redpath Crescent," 23; Morf, *Terror in Quebec*, 167; and D. Smith, *Bleeding Hearts ... Bleeding Country*, 28.

80. Janke, *Terrorism and Democracy*, 55.

81. Crelinsten, "Power and Meaning," 433.

82. Morf, *Terror in Quebec*, 33.

83. Pierre Vallières, *Choose!*, tr. Penelope Williams (Toronto: new press, 1972), 92–96.

84. Janke, *Terrorism and Democracy*, 61.

85. Morf, *Terror in Quebec*, 95.

86. Martha Crenshaw, "An Organizational Approach to the Analysis of Political Terrorism," *Orbis* 29, no. 3 (fall 1985), 469.

87. Janke, *Terrorism and Democracy*, 70.

88. Janke, *Terrorism and Democracy*, 58–61.

89. See Charney, "From Redpath Crescent," 27; Desbarats, *René*, 190; and Crelinsten, "Internal Dynamics of the FLQ," 64.

90. Quoted in Levin and Sylvester, *Crisis in Quebec*, 32. Abraham Rotstein and Gad Horowitz, "Quebec and Canadian Nationalism: Two Views," in *Power Corrupted: The October Crisis and the Repression of Quebec*, ed. Abraham Rotstein (Toronto: new press, 1971), 124, argue that emergency powers may have *only* symbolic value and even question what exactly the symbolism of the War Measures Act was. For them, it was a symbol of the repression of the state. Haggart and Golden, *Rumours of War*, 42 and 46, argue that the purpose of the emergency powers was to prove that the government was still powerful.

91. Crelinsten, "Power and Meaning," 442.

92. D. Smith, *Bleeding Hearts ... Bleeding Country*, 34.

93. Crelinsten, "Internal Dynamics of the FLQ," 64; and Haggart and Golden, *Rumours of War*, 48.

94. Haggart and Golden, *Rumours of War*, 56.

95. Crelinsten, "Power and Meaning," looks at the role of the media during the October Crisis.

96. Janke, *Terrorism and Democracy*, 62, writes that the media coverage "helped the FLQ create a climate of fear and crisis."

97. Crelinsten, "Power and Meaning," 438.

98. Crelinsten, "Power and Meaning," 442.

99. Haggart and Golden, *Rumours of War*, 101.

100. Janke, *Terrorism and Democracy*, 56. See also Rioux, *Quebec in Question*, 177; and Levin and Sylvester, *Crisis in Quebec*, 6; and Haggart and Golden, *Rumours of War*, 273.

101. Janke, *Terrorism and Democracy*, 68.

102. Cindy C. Combs, *Terrorism in the Twenty-First Century* (Upper Saddle River, NJ: Prentice Hall, 1997), 188.

103. Crelinsten, "Internal Dynamics of the FLQ," 75.

104. D. Smith, *Bleeding Hearts ... Bleeding Country*, 38 and 41.

105. Combs, *Terrorism in the Twenty-First Century,* 187. The limited duration of the emergency powers is supported by the Polity 98 database (www.bsos.umd.edu/cidcm/polity/), in which Canada is coded as a 10 (the highest score) on the democracy variable from 1921 until 1998, showing no evidence that the emergency powers had any long-term consequences for democracy in Canada.

106. Uruguay is also similar in the abuses along this dimension. Torture, in particular, was reported to be a common interrogation technique of the military.

107. Quoted in Levin and Sylvester, *Crisis in Quebec,* 21.

108. Haggart and Golden, *Rumours of War,* 194.

109. Haggart and Golden, *Rumours of War,* 71.

110. Haggart and Golden, *Rumours of War,* 76.

111. Levin and Sylvester, *Crisis in Quebec,* 25.

112. Janke, *Terrorism and Democracy,* 53.

113. Levin and Sylvester, *Crisis in Quebec,* 14.

114. Haggart and Golden, *Rumours of War,* 70.

115. Paul Sniderman et al., *The Clash of Rights: Liberty, Equality, and Legitimacy in Pluralist Democracy* (New Haven: Yale University Press, 1996), 18, contend that the key political actors in Canada shared a strong commitment to democracy.

116. Haggart and Golden, *Rumours of War,* 67.

117. Haggart and Golden, *Rumours of War,* 267.

118. D. Smith, *Bleeding Hearts ... Bleeding Country,* 91, disagrees with this, arguing that in a parliamentary system, "it is to the support of the House, rather than the public that the prime minister should cater from day to day."

119. Tarnopolsky, "Emergency Powers and Civil Liberties," 209.

120. Janke, *Terrorism and Democracy,* 58; Haggart and Golden, *Rumours of War,* 55.

121. Bain, "The Making of a Crisis," 12.

122. Beaton, "The Crisis in Quebec," 150.

123. Saywell, *Quebec 70,* 126.

124. Haggart and Golden, *Rumours of War,* 171.

125. Saywell, *Quebec 70,* 128.

126. Most of the literature on the October Crisis is very critical of the government's actions, particularly the use of emergency powers.

127. No one variable was key to protecting against abuses because the lack of abuses was overdetermined in this case. With strong norms, an independent Parliament, and free speech, any abuse was unlikely.

128. Borovy, "Rebuilding a Free Society," 103.

129. Haggart and Golden, *Rumours of War,* 251.

Chapter 6

Peru and the Shining Path

Beginning in 1980, the Shining Path (Sendero Luminoso) waged one of history's most violent and destructive terrorist campaigns against the government and people of Peru. In response, three different presidential administrations used emergency powers in an attempt to defeat the terrorists. Despite eventually placing close to half of the country under a state of emergency, the state was unable to effectively counter the threat posed by the Shining Path. By the early 1990s, the scope of terrorist violence had grown to such a level that many people feared that Peru was on the brink of civil war. The emergency powers were ineffective because they could not cut into the large base of support that the terrorists could draw on in recruiting new members. Despite substantial losses from deaths and imprisonment, the Shining Path continued to grow and threaten the security of the state. Not only were the emergency powers ineffective, but they also contributed to widespread human rights abuses in the emergency zones. With thousands of civilians killed, tortured, or "disappeared" by the security forces, Peru was annually ranked as the worst human rights abuser in Latin America by international monitoring agencies. These abuses of the emergency powers occurred because the civilian government removed any constraints on the military within the emergency zones. The military used its power to deny access to journalists, Congressional investigators, lawyers, and international human rights agencies. Furthermore, soldiers accused of abuse were tried by sympathetic military courts, rather than by civilian courts. Twelve years of democratic rule came to an end in April 1992, when President Alberto Fujimori, backed by the military, seized power in a "self-coup" in which he disbanded Congress and the Supreme Court to fight the country's growing economic problems and the Shining Path insurgency. In September 1992, the fortunes of the Shining Path turned for the worse when the police captured the leader of the Shining Path, Abimael Gúzman, in a hideout in Lima. Without their leader, the Shining Path quickly dissolved and terrorist violence sharply diminished.

THE SENDERO LUMINOSO

The Sendero Luminoso launched its first operation on May 17, 1980, on the eve of the presidential elections that marked Peru's return to democracy after twelve years of military rule. At first glance, it seems odd that an insurgent group would begin its campaign just as democracy, with all of its mechanisms for legitimizing political opposition, was restored.[1] Cynthia McClintock, in fact, notes, "Peruvian militants rarely mention political exclusion as an explanation for their adherence to the revolutionary organization."[2] The origins of the Shining Path, however, make more sense when placed in the context of Peru's political, economic, and social history.

Modern Peruvian history began in 1824, when Peru became an independent state, ending nearly 300 years of Spanish colonial rule.[3] Since independence, Peru has basically alternated between military and civilian rule, with the longest periods of democracy occurring in 1895–1919, 1963–1968, and 1980–1992.[4] The last military government began its rule in 1968, when the military seized power from President Fernando Belaúnde Terry and ruled for twelve years. The military government, in an unusual twist, was even more reformist than the democratically elected administration of Belaúnde.[5] By 1977, however, many of the military's reforms had failed to revitalize the Peruvian economy, and the military decided to withdraw from power. A Constituent Assembly was called in 1978, which produced the Constitution of 1979 and restored democracy with the elections of May 1980.[6]

Throughout these different regimes, whether civilian or military, certain sociological and economic factors remained constant within Peru. Throughout its history, Peru has faced tension between the urban/center and rural/periphery areas and many "Senderologists" find the origins of the Shining Path in these tensions.[7] Cynthia McClintock, for example, argues, "The correlation between the predominantly rural departments of most severe misery and the emergence of Sendero is clear."[8] Race also continues to be a source of tension in Peru with the population divided into whites, mestizos, and Indians. Simon Strong posits that "Tension between Western [white] and Indian culture is at the heart of Peru's post-conquest history."[9] Lastly, Peru has remained one of the most economically underdeveloped countries in the hemisphere, with the Andean highlands suffering the greatest poverty. Despite the military's efforts at agrarian reform in the 1970s, living standards declined, especially in rural areas.[10] During the 1980s, inflation soared, output declined, and the government was increasingly burdened by international debt.[11] All of these economic failures combined to "exacerbate the already serious plight of Peru's rural highlands."[12]

All of these tensions between white/urban/rich/center and Indian/rural/poor/periphery overlap in Peru and provide a convenient theoretical basis for explaining the rise of the Shining Path insurgency.[13] Looking at economic, political, and social tensions is a common tool for political scientists who are interested in explaining the rise of insurgencies across different countries.[14] Deborah Poole and Gerardo Renique, however, offer a scathing but accurate criticism of much of the literature on the Sendero Luminoso which uncritically accepts these tensions as the source and motivation of the insurgency.[15] They demonstrate that the portrayal of the Shining Path as rural, peasant, Indian revolt misses other and contrasting aspects of the organization.[16] Nevertheless, while the economic and social tensions may not be useful for understanding the *origins* of the Shining Path, they can be understood as factors that the Shining Path took advantage of in its explosive expansion. As Michael Smith contends, "Sendero exploits a host of factors to leverage groups or individuals into revolt. These forces include racial and ethnic hatred, class and generational differences, the lack of employment prospects, ideology, and radicalized political and military practices."[17] The following analysis on the origins of the Shining Path accepts the critiques of Poole and Renique, and shows that the Shining Path was not as completely rural, as Indian, or as peasant-based as many scholars portray them to be; although it did, in fact, originate in the rural, poor, and largely Indian highland province of Ayacucho.

The origins of the Shining Path are inextricably linked to its founder and leader, Abimael Guzmán, who was born in 1934.[18] Guzmán was heavily influenced by the Peruvian Marxist José Carlos Mariátegui, and began teaching communist philosophy at the National University of San Cristóbal de Huamanga in Ayacucho in 1962. The Shining Path began as one of several factions within the Peruvian Communist Party during a turbulent time for the Peruvian left. Peruvian Marxists were swayed by international events, especially the Cuban Revolution and the Sino-Soviet split of 1963.[19] In 1964, the Peruvian Communist Party split into pro-Moscow and pro-Chinese factions (Bandera Roja or Red Flag). Guzmán joined the Chinese faction, and traveled to China to study for several years in the mid-1960s.[20] Following his return to Peru, Guzmán left the Bandero Roja faction in 1970 to establish the "true" Communist Party, whose full name was "The Communist Party of Peru by the Shining Path of José Carlos Mariátegui," which was usually shortened to the Shining Path.[21]

Guzmán cultivated a cult of personality as the leader of the Shining Path, and called himself the "Fourth Sword of Marxism," with Marx, Lenin, and Mao as the first three.[22] Moreover, Guzmán developed an almost religious following and was "regarded like a deity by his followers, who themselves behaved like disciples."[23] In the early years, Guzmán concentrated on building a small and ideologically strong cadre of leadership from within the University. He used his position as Director of Personnel in 1971 and 1972 to hire like-minded professors who spread his brand of communist ideology.[24] In 1973, the Shining Path established front groups and in 1975 established "peoples' schools" that oversaw the political and ideological indoctrination of the peasants.[25] Guzmán used his university position and Sendero's control of the University's education program to send students and teachers into the countryside to train and indoctrinate rural communities.[26] The result was that Sendero was an organization built "from the top down and from the ideology out ... and achieved ideological rigidity and organic cohesiveness."[27] While the Shining Path recruited heavily among the peasants of the Andean highlands, it was founded by "middle-class university intellectuals."[28]

The ability of the university-trained leaders to recruit peasants into the organizations was a reflection of the appeal of the Sendero ideology, which can be summarized as "Maoism tempered by the nationalistic principles of Peruvian Communist party founder José Carlos Mariátegui—all interpreted and dictated by President Gonzalo, a.k.a. Abimael Guzmán Reynoso."[29] Some of the appeal of the Shining Path ideology came from Guzmán's ability to combine and apply the principles of Mao and Mariátegui to the "concrete reality" of Peru.[30] By "designing [the Sendero philosophy] specifically for Peru's rural and urban underclasses, the Indians, and mestizos,"[31] Sendero was able to recruit widely across different social strata. Sendero's ideology was composed of four themes: the primacy of class struggle, the need to combat imperialism, the importance of the vanguard party, and the need for violence.[32] In addition, the Shining Path played on Indian mythical traditions in recruiting members.[33]

The goal of Sendero's campaign was what they called the "New Democratic Republic," which was to be a communist state based on the teachings of Mao and Mariátegui.[34] While never described in much detail, the New Democratic Republic would be a "joint dictatorship of the proletariat, peasantry, and petit bourgeoisie," and would be formed from the existing peoples' committees in areas under Sendero control.[35] To achieve this goal, the Shining Path was willing to use the most extreme violence against the state and anyone who opposed them. Violence was seen as the only way to achieve their ends; struggles through the normal political process were not only doomed to fail but legitimized the existing order. "Armed struggle, in Guzmán's view, is the only means of achieving victory. In the absence of an ability to confront the Peruvian state directly, this has meant a concerted campaign of terror."[36] In fact, the scope of violence caused by the Shining Path has caused some scholars to question whether the Shining Path might have become a "new Khmer Rouge" if it seized power.[37] The Shining Path did not use violence as a *last* resort; rather, violence was an end in itself,[38] extolled as both a strategy for revolution and a means to socialize the people under Sendero control.[39] Members of the Shining Path were expected to willingly give up their own lives in what was called "the quota."[40] Gustavo Gorriti writes, "Preparing for death became a central precon-

ception for each militant as well as a way to indoctrinate cadres. After agreeing
to the quota, militants no longer owned their lives. Manuscripts read and mem-
orized in meetings, the notes taken in the margins, began to repeat and hammer
home this idea. To be prepared for death, to renounce life."[41]

With the dedication of its cadres willing and eager to die for the cause, the
Sendero Luminoso was prepared to launch its campaign of violence on the Peruvian state. Before describing Sendero's strategy and operations, a brief discussion of whether they should be classified as terrorists groups is in order. Of
course, labeling a group a terrorist organization carries with it moral, political,
and legal ramifications.[42] Insurgent groups often reject the terrorist label because it erodes whatever legitimacy they may have. Similar to many other
groups, the Sendero Luminoso has rejected the terrorist label. Hazleton and
Woy-Hazleton argue, "In Sendero's eyes, the 'terrorist' label, applied by the Peruvian government, the United States and the Peruvian Left, seeks to discredit
and isolate its genuine revolution, to hide the people's war."[43] David Scott
Palmer claims that the "Shining Path uses terror to further its revolutionary
ends but is not a terrorist movement."[44] Palmer, Hazleton, and Woy-Hazleton
do not label the Shining Path as a terrorist group because the Senderos do not
engage in "indiscriminate violence"[45] "with no political focus."[46] They want to
argue that the Shining Path was not some irrational group that killed people for
no reason. Terrorist groups, however, should not be defined by whether they
practice indiscriminate or unfocused violence. In fact, the opposite is the case.
Recall that in Chapter 1, terrorism was defined as the use of violence to cause
fear and *lead* to a political change. The fact that the Sendero Luminoso discrim-
inated in its targets and chose them for political purposes does not remove
them from the category of terrorists, even if some of their targets were military
personnel.

For my purposes, I am less concerned with labeling a group as a guerrilla versus a terrorist organization and instead focus on whether they conducted terrorist operations or used terrorist tactics. By these criteria, even the authors
cited in the previous paragraph recognize that the Shining Path used terrorism
to achieve their ends. As Carlos Iglesias notes, "To achieve its goals, the Shining
Path would not hesitate to attack the civilian population and to use varied
methods of terror against persons uninvolved in the conflict."[47] In fact, the
Senderos targeted civilians in greater numbers than military personnel. Mc-
Clintock reports that "only 17 percent of Shining Path's victims were members
of the military or police; most victims were unarmed civilians ... nuns, priests,
journalists, agronomists, food aid workers, and even human rights activists
were directly targeted and killed."[48] The Shining Path did use guerrilla tactics
in engaging isolated units of the police and military, causing many people to
label them as a guerrilla group as well.[49] Nevertheless, whatever type of group
they might be labeled, Sendero Luminoso clearly engaged in frequent and
deadly terrorist operations against both civilians and the military to achieve
their goals.

The overarching strategy of the Shining Path was to gain control of the countryside and then strangle Lima by cutting off its access to the periphery. Guzmán borrowed and then expanded Mao's three stages of protracted struggle into five stages. For Mao, the movement first goes through a period of strategic defensive where the insurgents lay the groundwork for armed struggle. When the power of the guerrilla forces come into equilibrium with those of the state, the struggle is in its second stage, the war of movements, where rebel forces directly confront the state's forces. The final stage, the strategic offensive, occurs when the rebels take the military initiative and cause the collapse of the government.[50] In Guzmán conception, the struggle would start with agitation and propaganda, followed by sabotage and guerrilla action, which would lead to more generalized and larger scale violence. As the insurgency gained more territory, the rebels would then consolidate and expand their territory, eventually leading to the fall of the cities and the total collapse of the state.[51]

To gain control of territory, Sendero provided services for the rural communities that the government was unable to provide and thereby became a shadow government that replaced the Peruvian state.[52] Sendero hoped to create liberated zones in which "popular committees" would create a "new power" that would establish Sendero as the de facto government in those areas.[53] (This concept is analogous to the strategy of "power duality" espoused by the Tupamaros of Uruguay.) The task of the Senderos in establishing this "new power" was made easier by the weakness of the state in many of the rural areas. Raymond Bonner argues that Sendero was able to expand in rural communities "because the Peruvian state has done so little for the people in the remote regions."[54] The Peruvian state was highly centralized and weak in the periphery, relying on local power brokers to control the rural population.[55] The result was "a state unable to process effectively and respond appropriately to the demands of the population."[56] The Shining Path took advantage of this power vacuum by offering solutions to concrete problems, including "economic needs, safety concerns, problems of corruption, [and] immorality."[57] Sendero successfully implemented this strategy in many communities in which they "systematically eliminated government authority."[58]

Sendero often instigated spirals of violence in which peasant communities were the primary victims. Sendero actions were frequently calculated to provoke violent reactions by the security forces.[59] Sendero would then exploit the vindictive reaction of the security forces by offering protection for villages that had been or were likely to be attacked by the army or police. As Gustavo Gorriti puts it, "The goal was to provoke blind, excessive reactions from the state ... Blows laid on indiscriminately would also provoke among those unjustly or disproportionately affected an intense resentment of the government."[60]

Over the course of their struggle, Guzmán declared five strategic plans that roughly correspond to the five stages of revolutionary war discussed earlier in this chapter. The implementation of these plans would "create an axis of Shining Path-controlled or influenced areas up and down the Andes Mountains" from which Sendero could strangle Lima and the coastal cities.[61] The first plan was the "Starting Plan," which began in 1980 and consisted of initiating the armed struggle, accumulating supplies, and spreading propaganda. In January 1981, Guzmán initiated the second plan, the "Plan to Develop the Guerrilla War," which organized and expanded the operation zones and people's committees. The third plan, the "Plan to Conquer Support Bases" was initiated in early 1983 and lasted until 1986. Its objectives were the creation of the People's Guerrilla Army, support bases, and widespread violence. In the fourth plan, "To Develop the Support Bases," the goal was to consolidate and strengthen the areas under Sendero control. The fifth and final plan, "Developing Bases in Order to Conquer Power," was launched in 1989 and was designed to expand people's committees and increase the size of the guerrilla army to create a situation of strategic equilibrium.[62]

Such grandiose plans for seizing political power required an organization that could translate the objectives into reality. Sendero's organizational structure is commonly portrayed as a hierarchical pyramid with five levels.[63] Guzmán was at the apex of the organizational pyramid along with a small group of individuals who were recruited at the university in Ayacucho.[64] This top level of leadership comprised the Central Committee (or "cupola"). Below them, in the second tier, were the commanders who were assigned to specific regions and were responsible for all military and political activity in their region. In the middle level were the militants who were the rank and file members of the Popular Guerrilla Army and conducted the majority of operations. Militants were organized into cells, much like other terrorist organizations. Each cell was usually composed of five individuals, which limited the number of contacts any one Sendero would have within the organization and made infiltration difficult.[65] The fourth tier was composed of activists. They were students and workers who educated the masses through propaganda. The final level was composed of sympathizers who provided logistical, military, financial, and medical support and also took part in demonstrations. Along with this hierarchical structure, Sendero divided Peru into six geographic regions, including one specifically for Lima. Each region was then further divided into zones, sectors, and cells.[66] Lastly, Sendero controlled several legal organizations that participated in propaganda efforts and provided Sendero with support and recruits.[67]

Sendero Luminoso conducted its revolutionary struggle through assassinations, bombings, and power blackouts. Assassinations were the most common tactic used by the Shining Path in its campaign to control the rural areas of Peru. According to an Amnesty International report from 1989, "On entering a new area Shining Path typically rounds up the inhabitants and kills government officials, landowners and traders, and threatens to kill those who do not support the movement ... Killings are often carried out in public after mock trials, sometimes after torture and mutilation."[68] Mayors and other government officials were often the primary targets of the Shining Path. For example, in 1983 the Shining Path killed the deputy mayor of Ayacucho in front of his family.[69] Through assassinations and intimidation, David Scott Palmer estimates that "At least one-third of Peru's four-thousand odd honorific justice of the peace positions, long a mark of some status in the local community, remained unfulfilled [in 1989] due to a lack of candidates."[70] Sendero also targeted other symbols of state authority, such as policemen, soldiers, and community leaders. For example, the first military installation was attacked in 1983, and a vice admiral in the navy was assassinated in 1986.[71] Also, Sendero killed more than fifty union leaders and more than forty leaders of grass-roots organizations in the 1980s.[72] Politicians were often the targets of Sendero attacks, too. After the prison massacres in 1986, Sendero threatened to kill ten American Popular Revolutionary Alliance (APRA, the political party in power) politicians for every dead Sendero.[73] By 1988, more than 250 APRA leaders were killed and 2 former cabinet ministers were assassinated in 1990.[74] This tactic of assassination was effective in terrorizing the population and disrupting the political process. "Frightened local officials resigned en masse, and teachers, parish priests and persons whose names appeared on SL [Shining Path] death lists fled the region."[75] In 1989 alone, Sendero killed over one hundred candidates for municipal offices and intimidated countless others into resigning. The result was that "Twenty-five percent of Peru's district and provincial councils could not carry out their elections at all."[76]

In addition to assassinations, Sendero set off bombs in Lima and other large cities, targeting what they saw as symbols of foreign imperialism and domestic, exploitive capitalism. Targets included oil pipelines, tourist attractions, businesses, farming cooperatives, and foreign embassies (including the American, Chinese and Soviet embassies).[77] The most frequent targets for Sendero's bombs were the electricity pylons that carried power into Lima. These attacks were designed to black out the city of Lima and serve as unavoidable symbols of Sendero's power. From 1980 until 1990, over 1,200 electrical towers were bombed, with a repair cost of $600 million U.S. dollars.[78] Often while the city was blacked out, the Senderos would light a giant hammer and sickle that would burn on the hillsides above Lima for everyone to see. In 1985, for example, Sendero cut power to Lima's airport and burned a hammer and sickle just as the Pope was about to land.[79] These burning hammer and sickles also appeared on Guzmán's birthday (December 4) and other Sendero holidays.

In total, Sendero's attacks were aimed at a wide variety of targets, including civilians, security forces, property, and infrastructure. Philip Mauceri breaks down the terrorist attacks by target between 1980 and 1988 and finds the following distribution: electrical towers (939), police stations (866), banks (464), private homes (411), government buildings (335), political groups (306), population centers (213), and bridges (165).[80] As these figures show, the Shining Path was both an active and violent insurgency group. These figures justify characterizing Sendero as a terrorist group.

Sendero used these tactics and strategies to attack the Peruvian state beginning in 1980 in a campaign that turned out to be tremendously costly to the Peruvian state. With attacks eventually covering the entire state of Peru, violence related to the Shining Path was responsible for close to 30,000 deaths (which includes terrorists, civilians, and security forces) and over $20 billion dollars in damages.[81]

The Shining Path's first attack occurred on May 17, 1980, on the eve of the national elections that restored democracy to Peru. On the morning of May 17, five hooded youths entered the voter registration office in the town of Chuschi and burned the registry and ballot box. This incident, however, went largely unnoticed throughout Peru.[82] For most of the early 1980s, the Shining Path concentrated its operations in the highland areas in and around Ayacucho. This early phase was highlighted by the Sendero attack on the Ayacucho prison in March 1982, when 50 Senderos freed 247 prisoners, including many Sendero leaders.[83] The government of President Belaúnde took an increasingly harder line in the early 1980s by placing ever greater areas of the Andean region under military control. Over several years, the military was effective in diminishing Sendero activity in the Andean highlands (more on this in the Ineffective Emergency Powers section). The Shining Path, however, responded by shifting and expanding its operations to other areas of Peru.[84]

One area in which Sendero increased its operations was the Upper Huallaga Valley, in which much of the world's coca (which is later processed into cocaine) is grown.[85] Sendero had been conducting sporadic operations in this region in the early 1980s, but entered in force in the mid-1980s. In the fourth plenary session of the Central Committee in 1986, Sendero developed a plan to take control of the region. Their strategy was predicated on "an alliance with the peasants and a *modus vivendi* with the coca lords."[86] The coca farmers benefited because the Shining Path offered protection from the government and from the cocaine traffickers. To the drug traffickers, Sendero offered disciplined farmers, protection from the government forces, and potentially even greater government destabilization.[87] For the Shining Path, control of the Upper Huallaga Valley provided the organization with millions of dollars of revenue. By some estimates, Sendero received approximately $30 million a year, which they acquired through a 5 percent tax on the coca paste sold by the farmers to the traffickers as well as from fees levied on the traffickers for using the airstrips in the region.[88]

The final region of Sendero operations was the city of Lima. As mentioned earlier in this chapter, the overall strategy of the Shining Path was to control the countryside and then strangle the cities and ultimately topple the government. Consistent with this plan, Sendero began operations in Lima in 1987 and increased the tempo of their operations following the 1988 meeting of the Sendero leadership.[89] Sendero began its penetration into Lima by first controlling the small towns outside of Lima and then moved into the slums or shantytowns on the outskirts of Lima.[90] From there, Sendero recruited and trained members, and launched attacks on targets within the heart of Lima.[91] By 1992, Sendero had effectively expanded its operations into much of Peru, bringing with them their campaign of violence and terror.

EMERGENCY POWERS IN PERU

The government of Peru responded to the violence of the Shining Path by declaring states of emergency in particular departments (states) and provinces (counties). The emergency powers restricted civil liberties and gave the military a free reign in emergency areas. Before analyzing the content of the emergency powers, I will first discuss the constitutional structure and democratic norms and procedures in Peru.

After twelve years of military rule, democracy was restored to Peru with the 1979 constitution and the elections of 1980. The new constitution created a separation of powers between the executive, legislative, and judicial branches, although the executive held the most power. The president was elected every five years by a direct popular vote and could not serve two consecutive terms. Besides being the commander in chief, the president "had the power to appoint members of the Council of Ministers and the Supreme Court of Justice, submit and review legislation enacted by Congress, rule by decree if so delegated by Congress, declare states of siege and emergency, and dissolve the Chamber of deputies."[92] With such wide-ranging powers, especially the ability to rule by decree, the executive was the strongest branch of government. The legislature, however, was not powerless. The Congress, which was composed of two houses and elected for five-year terms that ran concurrently with the presidential terms, "had the power to initiate and pass legislation; interpret, amend, and repeal existing legislation; draft sanctions for violations of legislations; approve treaties; approve the budget and general accounts; authorize borrowing; exercise the right of amnesty; and delegate the legislative function to the president [allow the president to rule by decree]."[93] Furthermore, the legislature also could monitor and check the power of the executive through its right to investigate any matter and compel the resignation of any minister or the entire cabinet.[94] Also, the president did not have veto power over any legislation passed by the congress. The judiciary was widely regarded as the weakest of the three branches.[95] The Supreme Court of Justice was the highest judicial body, and its members were nominated by the president from a list of candidates submitted by an independent council and then approved by the Senate. While the Supreme Court had the power to interpret the constitution, in practice, the judiciary was ineffective because it "has been hampered by scarce resources, a tradition of executive manipulation, and inadequate protection of officials in the face of threats from insurgents and drug traffickers."[96]

Individual liberties protected by the Peruvian constitution included "freedom of expression and association and the right to life, physical integrity, and 'the unrestricted development of one's personality.'" In addition, freedom of religion, collective bargaining rights for workers, and the right to strike were all protected.[97] Peru's freedom of the press was not only protected, but also "vigorously exercised by many newspapers, magazines, radio and television. The media represented as wide a spectrum of political thought as in any Western country."[98] Peruvian citizens also enjoyed a wide range of protected due process rights, including:

The right to habeas corpus; the right not to be convicted under ex post facto laws; the right to be presumed innocent until proven guilty in judicial proceedings; the right not to be arrested except pursuant to a judicial warrant or during the commission of an offense; the right to be brought before a judge within twenty-four hours of arrest (with exceptions for crimes involving terrorism, espionage, and unlawful drug trafficking); the right to be informed immediately and in writing for the reason for detention; the right to communicate with an attorney from the time of arrest; the duty of authorities to report location of the detainee; the inadmissibility of forced statements; the right not to be held in incommunicado detention; the right not to be transferred to a jurisdiction not provided for by law; and the right not to be tried under procedures other than those established by law. Additionally, the constitution prohibits the practice of torture or inhumane treatment and abolishes the death penalty except for treason during foreign war, an exception that does not encompass a domestic state of emergency.[99]

Beyond the constitutional separation of powers and the protection of rights, Peru also *acted* like a democracy with frequent, contested, and open elections.[100] Competition for political offices was open to all parties, including Marxist groups, and public participation was heavy in all elections.[101] In addition, a democratic civil society was strong in Peru. According to Philip Mauceri, "Civil society was highly organized via dynamic popular-sector organizations that included unions, peasant federations, and neighborhood associations."[102]

Civil-military relations were also relatively good, especially considering the record of intermittent military rule throughout Peru's history. When the military returned power to the democratic government in 1980, they distanced themselves from political decision-making. In fact, the military's decision to step down in 1980 was largely due to a frustration and inability to solve many of the country's economic and political problems.[103] Moreover, the election of Fernando Belaúnde as president in 1980 served to repudiate the military's twelve years rule because Belaúnde had been president in 1968 when the military had seized power. Civil-military relations in Peru, however, were not ideal. The military retained a great deal of autonomy over many military issues, although not an exceptional amount compared to other South American countries. David Pion-Berlin evaluates the autonomy of the militaries in Argentina, Brazil, Uruguay, Peru, and Chile and gives Peru a score of moderate for its level of military autonomy, with low levels of autonomy over senior personnel decisions and questions over force levels, but high autonomy in decisions about junior personnel, military reform, intelligence gatherings, and human rights issues.[104] While there was always some concern that the military might seize power in another coup, this threat was only taken seriously in the late 1980s when the economy was in ruins and the Shining Path was commonly believed to be on the verge of coming to power.[105]

Within this political context, three successive presidential administrations responded to the violence of the Shining Path. In addition to resorting to emergency powers, however, the government also enacted normal laws that were aimed against terrorism. The first anti-terrorism law was passed by decree by President Belaúnde on March 10, 1981. This law, Legislative Decree 46, defined terrorism and characterized it as a criminal act.[106] This decree also allowed the police to detain suspects for up to fifteen days and enacted stricter penalties for terrorist offenses.[107] Decree 46 was replaced by Law 24651, which was enacted by Congress on March 19, 1987, and essentially eliminated the definition of terrorism as a criminal act. Congress then enacted Law 24700 in June 1987. This law provided protection for people detained on terrorist charges. Law 24953 was enacted by Congress on December 7, 1988, and reinstated the earlier definitions and categories of terrorist offenses.[108] Although some of these laws eroded civil liberties in Peru, these laws are not part of the analysis of emergency powers because they were designed to be permanent. As such, they constitute a danger to the democratic values and procedures of Peru, but are not theoretically problematic in the ways that emergency powers can be. The danger and problem of emergency powers is in knowing when they might be used in ways that are unintended whereas we can assume that normal laws will be used as intended, even if the intent is to permanently erode civil liberties in the name of fighting terrorism.

As the violence from the Shining Path began to increase, the government soon resorted to using emergency powers in addition to these permanent anti-terrorism laws. Emergency powers could have taken two forms in Peru: a state of emergency, or a state of siege, although the latter has never been used. The legal basis for the state of emergency came from Article 231 of the 1979 Constitution, which allowed "the president ... to decree both states of exception unilaterally, upon notification of the congress."[109] The states of emergency lasted for sixty days, but could be renewed by presidential decree. The president was also allowed to give responsibility to the armed forces for maintaining public order. The emergency powers were limited in their scope by the Constitution and consisted of the suspension of only four rights: the freedoms of assembly and movement, and the freedoms from arbitrary arrest and unwarranted search and seizure.[110] These are the only rights that could be suspended by the emergency powers; any other abrogation of rights would have constituted an abuse of the emergency powers. Amnesty International notes that "Certain fundamental rights are non-derogable: No exceptional circumstances whatsoever may be invoked to suspend them. These include the right to life and freedom from torture and the right to freedom of conscious."[111] In addition, the right to habeas corpus, by which individuals are protected from indefinite internment, could not be suspended by states of emergency.[112] This right was especially important given South America's history of "disappearances."

States of emergency were declared repeatedly in Peru in ever-increasing numbers of departments and provinces. According to a wide variety of sources, states of emergency were first declared in nine provinces around Ayacucho in 1982. In 1984, thirteen provinces were declared emergency zones and the number of provinces under a state of emergency rose to twenty-eight in 1986, thirty-six in 1988, and fifty-six in 1989. By 1991, 47 percent of Peru's population lived under a state of emergency, including the citizens of Lima, which had been declared an emergency zone in 1986.[113]

The increase in the number of provinces under emergency powers reflected the increasing strength of the Sendero Luminoso. To counter the threat from the Shining Path, all three presidential administrations—Belaúnde (1980–1985), García (1985–1990), and Fujimori (1990–1992)—used emergency powers as part of their counterinsurgency campaign.[114] In the early 1980s the Shining Path was largely ignored by the government for two reasons. Sendero was still engaged in its propaganda and recruitment phase and was not responsible for much violence. Also, President Belaúnde had just replaced the military government that had earlier ousted him from power. Consequently, he was reluctant to use the military to fight the growing insurgency because he wanted to show that democratic political processes could counter the Shining Path and that a repressive military response was not necessary.[115] By 1982, however, the Shining Path could no longer be ignored, especially after their daring attack on the Ayacucho prison. President Belaúnde reversed course and declared a state of emergency in several provinces around Ayacucho and allowed the military to assume full responsibility for the counterinsurgency campaign. This strategy was all "sticks" and no "carrots"—no socioeconomic reforms were enacted that might have undercut support for the Shining Path.[116]

This "exclusively repressive strategy" was maintained until the election of President García in 1985. Responding to allegations of widespread human rights violations, García developed a counterinsurgency strategy that would respect human rights as well as reduce the poverty of Peru's Andean highland regions.[117] "Ultimately, however, the economic aid effort failed to stop Sendero's expansion. Already entrenched in many of these provinces, Sendero attacked development workers … Also, especially in later years, resources for development programs were scant and embezzlement common."[118] García's commitment to human rights resulted in a temporary reduction in the level of abuses in the first few years of his administration; however, following growing economic troubles and increasing violence from the Shining Path, García gradually acquiesced to the military's demands for greater autonomy in conducting the counterinsurgency campaign. By the end of García's term, human rights abuses had returned to the levels of 1983–1985.[119]

President Fujimori came to power in 1990 and gave even greater control to the military in fighting the Shining Path. Faced with growing violence from the Shining Path and continued economic contraction, Fujimori seized power in a "self-coup" on April 5, 1992. Shortly thereafter, the police captured Abimael

Guzmán on September 12, 1992. The capture of Guzmán was not a result in changes in the counterinsurgency strategy, but rather a result of standard police work.[120] After 1992, the Shining Path quickly dissolved as a terrorist or guerrilla movement.

INEFFECTIVE EMERGENCY POWERS

The government of Peru used emergency powers for ten years in its effort to combat the Sendero Luminoso. Despite the added powers that the emergency powers gave to the security forces, however, the Shining Path was not defeated. As Michael Smith points out in 1991, Sendero has "consistently maintained the political and military initiative, deciding when, where, and how it strikes."[121] Looking back in 1995, Philip Mauceri observes, "The armed force made little headway in stopping Sendero's growth ... Sendero's influence had spread throughout Peru, into urban as well as rural areas."[122] While the emergency powers were not only ineffective, they may have also led to an *increase* in violence. According to an Americas Watch report, "There is no direct relationship between the areas under a state of emergency and any reduction in the number or severity of terrorist acts or any increase in the success of the struggle against terrorism. On the contrary, a case can be made that in some places terrorist activity has actually increased once a state of emergency has been imposed."[123]

The ineffectiveness of the emergency powers is demonstrated by the common perception in the early 1990s that the Shining Path was pushing the Peruvian state to the brink of total collapse. In 1988, 4 percent of the Peruvian public believed that Sendero would eventually be victorious in seizing power from the government. In 1989, this number rose to 15 percent and in 1991, 32 percent of Lima residents believed Sendero would win.[124] The possibility of a Sendero victory was also contemplated by many outside observers.[125] Many political analysts predicted that Peru would be plunged into anarchy, with neither the government nor the Shining Path capable of defeating the other. There was a real possibility "of the country being torn apart in bloody civil conflict, or atomized into a collection of violent local and regional struggles akin to those of the Lebanon."[126]

Looking at the graph (Figure 6.1) for the number of attacks and deaths highlights the ineffectiveness of the emergency powers. The number of attacks is only for four departments around and including Ayacucho (the total number of attacks is probably on average twice as high), while the number of deaths (civilian, military, and terrorists) is for the entire country. The line for emergency powers is based on the number of provinces placed in a state of emergency modified by a multiplier, which puts these numbers on a similar scale as the other figures.

Several facts are highlighted by this graph. The level of emergency powers, measured by the number of provinces placed under a state of emergency, in-

Figure 6.1
Statistics for Peru, 1980–1994

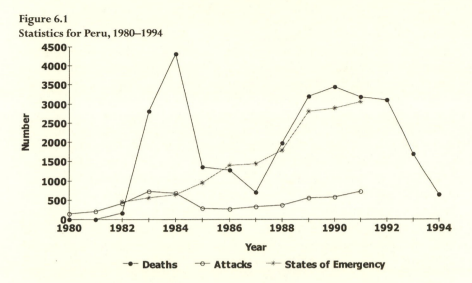

Source: The statistics on this graph come from a variety of sources. For the number of attacks in the departments of Ayacucho, Huancavelica, Junín, and Pasco see Nelson Manrique, "The War for the Central Sierra," in *Shining and Other Paths: War and Society in Peru, 1980–1995*, ed. Steve Stern (Durham, NC: Duke University Press, 1998), 195; Gordon McCormick, "The Shining Path and Peruvian Terrorism," in *Inside Terrorist Organizations*, ed. David Rapoport (New York: Columbia University Press, 1988), 118 provides statistics for nationwide Sendero attacks but only between 1980 and 1985. For the number of deaths attributable to terrorism, the figures come primarily from Cynthia McClintock, *Revolutionary Movements in Latin America: El Salvador's FMLN and Peru's Shining Path* (Washington, D.C.: United States Institute of Peace Press, 1998), 117 and are supplemented by Richard Clutterbuck, "Peru: Cocaine, Terrorism and Corruption," *International Relations* 12, no 5. (August 1995), 79; Philip Mauceri, "Military Politics and Counter-Insurgency in Peru," *Journal of Interamerican Studies and World Affairs* 33, no. 4 (winter 1991), 97; and Manrique, "The War for the Central Sierra," 194.

creased steadily between 1982 and 1992, yet the level of violence did not diminish in ways that correlate with the geographic extent of the emergency powers. If emergency powers were effective, we should expect some inverse relationship where the introduction and expansion of emergency zones would lead to a decrease in violence. This is not reflected in the graph shown in Figure 6.1. The reasons for the ineffectiveness of the emergency powers will be discussed in the following section.

The second fact highlighted by this graph is that the violence related to the Sendero Luminoso peaked in 1984, diminished for the next several years and then peaked again in the early 1990s. The lower levels of violence in the mid-1980s raise the possibility that the emergency powers might have been successful. If the graph in Figure 6.1 is cut off in 1987, it appears that violence decreased as increasing numbers of provinces were placed under a state of emergency. In some respects, the emergency powers *were* temporarily effective. Violence in the southern highlands region declined after the Peruvian military took over counterinsurgency operations with the declaration of states of emergency. The military conducted a brutal counterinsurgency campaign that generated numerous human rights abuses, including widespread allegations of torture, "disappearances," and extra-judicial killings (more on this in the following section). The presence of the military in the emergency zones made it extremely difficult for the Shining Path militants to conduct operations. Consequently, Sendero activity declined and the military could claim some success against the insurgents.[127]

While it may have appeared that the government was winning the war against the Shining Path, the increase in violence beginning in 1987 raises doubts as to whether the government's strategies were really effective. What happened in the mid-1980s is that the armed forces defeated the Sendero Luminoso in a classical military sense. That is, the military seized and held territory and denied the Shining Path the initiative within that territory. In traditional military logic, this outcome would be deemed a success, but for counterinsurgency operations, the criteria for success are different. For guerrillas, and especially terrorists, the control of territory is largely meaningless. The strength of their organization lies in the commitment of its members and their ability to move through a supportive population to conduct operations at their initiative. Consequently, despite the ability of the Peruvian military to deny the Shining Path the initiative in the southern highlands, they did not defeat the militants of the Sendero Luminoso. In fact, Gustavo Gorriti writes that the security forces began to realize in the mid-1980s that "They had only begun to glimpse the tip of the iceberg of insurrection."[128] The Shining Path responded to the military's control of the southern highlands by redeploying their militants and expanding their operations to other areas of the country, particularly the Upper Huallaga Valley and in Lima. As mentioned earlier, these operational areas were already part of Guzmán's grand strategy. The state's use of emergency powers in the southern highlands temporarily diminished the level of violence because the military had forced the Senderos to retreat; however, the Shining Path had not been defeated and in a few years, resumed its activities across all of Peru.

A third fact highlighted by the graph in Figure 6.1 is that there was a dramatic and permanent drop-off in the level of violence beginning in 1992, which coincided with Fujimori's coup and the capture of Guzmán. Like the earlier drop in violence in the mid-1980s, this raises the question of whether the emergency powers were actually effective. Several possible factors might explain why the Shining Path was defeated after 1992. The emergency powers might have actually been effective; it just took them several years before their effects were felt. Also, the capture of Guzmán might have been a devastating blow to the Shining Path organization, which was extremely centralized and in which Guzmán was worshiped almost like a religious figure. Lastly, other government policies, such as the establishment of armed peasant communities, called rondas, might have shifted support from the Shining Path to the government of Peru. This puzzle will not be addressed immediately because assessing the efficacy of the emergency powers involves a detailed and lengthy analysis. Instead, I will first discuss why the emergency powers were not effective throughout the 1980s and 1990s. After this, I will then return to the other possible explanations for Sendero's ultimate collapse, namely the capture of Guzmán and the spread and strengthening of the rondas.

When emergency powers were declared, they were expected to aid the state in the defeat of the Shining Path. Despite the restrictions on civil liberties and the military's control over the emergency zones, however, the Shining Path continued to thrive. The reason that the emergency powers were ineffective is that they were unable to capture, arrest, and imprison members of Sendero Luminoso faster than they could be replaced by new recruits. This section will first look at the recruitment process into the Shining Path, followed by a description of the size of the active militants and the supporters of the Shining Path. These numbers will show that the level of support for the Shining Path was high enough that, even when the security forces imprisoned or killed large numbers of terrorists, there were always sufficient numbers of new recruits willing to replace them. Moreover, given the large size of the Sendero Luminoso, the government forces were never able to move quickly against the terrorists. Even when large numbers were quickly arrested or killed, their numbers were insignificant to the overall strength of the Sendero organization.

How did the Sendero recruit new members? Who were the people that joined, why did they join, and how did the recruitment and training process work? The people who joined the Shining Path came from two different backgrounds.[129] In the upper levels of the organization, members were predominantly university students and teachers.[130] At the lower levels, most members were Quechua-speaking Indians from small villages in the rural highlands,[131] although they tended to be from the lower-middle-class rather than peasants.[132] It was "rural youth with secondary-school education ... who swelled the party ranks and constituted the most active sector of Shining Path."[133] After the prison massacres in 1986, Sendero also found it easier to recruit among the sympathetic "revolutionary left" in Lima.[134] Similar to other insurgent movements, Sendero recruits tended to be in their twenties or even teens.[135] According to Tom Marks, "The heart and soul of the movement remains youth from the disenfranchised, landless, former middle class. Frequently, the youth who join Sendero will have university training and be twenty to twenty-five years old."[136] One study found that at least 60 percent of those convicted of terrorism were younger than twenty-five.[137] Women also played a dominant role throughout the organization.[138]

People joined the Sendero Luminoso for a variety of reasons. Many joined because they were supportive of Sendero's Marxist ideology: "Sendero's ideological message presented these students with the possibility of radical changes in their social situations."[139] The recruits that joined for ideological reasons exhibited "extraordinarily high morale."[140] Many others were coerced into joining the Shining Path because of threats to themselves and their families. People who opposed the Shining Path were often publicly beaten or killed.[141] As the insurgency dragged on, Sendero increasingly began to rely on coercion for new recruits. "To maintain bases and control territories, Sendero would recruit additional youth, more by coercive than voluntary means. The guerrillas carried out forced recruitment in both the sierra [mountain] and selva [jungle] communities ... In contrast to the cadres and militants of the first generation ... many of these new militants participated under pressure and out of fear of retaliation."[142] Still others joined out of strategic or material interests. They believed that Sendero would provide them with benefits that the state was incapable of providing. These recruits "had little hope of achieving progress by way of the market, migration, or more education. Suddenly, they were presented with the concrete possibility of social ascent through the new *senderista* state."[143]

The process by which a new recruit would join the Shining Path was a lengthy one. In the early years of the campaign, the Shining Path sent teachers into town squares to hold meetings and spread the Sendero ideology to potential recruits.[144] In addition, as the movement expanded and consolidated its control, it established youth organizations from which it could draw new recruits.[145] After a recruit decided to join the Sendero Luminoso, he or she went through a period of training and indoctrination: "Before an individual can achieve militant status ... he must prove his worth and commitment to the movement by serving first as a sympathizer and then as an activist. At each of these stages, every recruit must undergo rigorous indoctrinational training, which gives all Senderistas valuable hands-on experience and a more profound understanding of the movement itself."[146]

Estimates of the size of the Sendero Luminoso (leaders, commanders, and militants) vary somewhat between analysts. At the start of the 1980s, estimates of the number of Senderos range from 100 to 500 members.[147] As the organization grew throughout the 1980s, most observers estimated that the Sendero Luminoso had a strength of between 3,000 and 6,000 members.[148] At the high end, some scholars estimate the Shining Path had a strength of 10,000,[149] 15,000,[150] or even 23,000 combatants.[151] If we assume that the Shining Path had somewhere close to 5,000 members, however, they would still rank as one of the largest terrorist groups in history. In comparison, the IRA and Tupamaros probably numbered only in the hundreds of active members.

To replace senderistas that had been killed or imprisoned, the Shining Path needed a large support base (what they called activists and sympathizers) from which they could draw new recruits. Several scholars estimate that the Shining Path had between 20,000 and 100,000 supporters.[152] Other scholars more loosely label the level of support for the Shining Path as "considerable,"[153] "significant,"[154] "far-reaching,"[155] and a "substantial reservoir."[156] In the southern highlands where the Shining Path originated and was the most active, support was even higher. Cynthia McClintock quotes an Ayacucho policeman who claimed, "Eighty percent of the townspeople of Ayacucho sympathize with Sendero."[157] In other towns, support for the Sendero was estimated as 25 percent of the population.[158] For all of Peru, one scholar estimates that 15 percent of the population supported the Senderos;[159] however, these numbers (50,000 versus 15 percent) do not add up. Fifteen percent of Peru's population would equal three million people, which is several orders of magnitude larger than the other figures. The reason for this discrepancy is that different scholars mean different things when they use the term support. The tens of thousands of Sendero supporters probably refers to those people that provided concrete support to the organization, by distributing propaganda, attending demonstrations, donating money, and offering medical or logistical assistance. These people are what I called supporters in Chapter 2, but would include what the Senderos themselves called activists and sympathizers. The 15 percent of the population that supported the Sendero is probably referring to people who sympathized with the Sendero's goals, strategies, and methods but did not offer them any assistance. I refer to these people as sympathizers (but they are not the same as the Sendero's label of sympathizers) and are an important element of the overall level of support for any terrorist group, especially as the security forces start to imprison active members of the organization. In sum, the 5,000 or so active members of Sendero probably relied on the support of 20,000 to 30,000 supporters, and the sympathy of perhaps millions of Peru's citizens.

To add greater confusion to the question of Sendero support, however, many other scholars argue that the Senderos were not, in fact, well supported, particularly among peasants and in the cities.[160] For example, Ronald Berg writes that, "Sendero exploits popular resentment against merchants, cooperatives, and the state, but it has not succeeded in rallying the peasants under the banner of Mao ... there is sympathy for the movement among young adults, but this reflects neither revolutionary sentiment nor active support."[161] Along similar lines, Henry Dietz argues, "[Sendero] has not been able to mobilize the peasantry on a large scale into people's armies, nor has it been able to win over the 'hearts and minds' of the peasantry on a long-term basis."[162] (In contrast, Cynthia McClintock's early work on the Sendero Luminoso focused on the peasant base of the organization and labeled it a "peasant rebellion."[163])

Clearly there is some disagreement over the degree and strength of support for the Shining Path. While some scholars claim tens of thousands (if not millions!) supported or sympathized with the Senderos, others claim that it was not well supported by the peasantry or the people in the cities. These different descriptions of Sendero support are probably a result of what the scholars are using as a basis for comparison. For those that see Sendero as an insurgency taking over the apparatus of government, widespread support is indispensable. For Sendero to succeed at its own strategy, it must be able to win over the peasants and workers of Peru, just as Mao did in China. For the scholars that see the Shining Path as a guerrilla or terrorist group (albeit a quite large one) capable of inflicting violence on the state, the level of support that is needed is considerably less. For my purposes, I am concerned with the latter scenario. In asking whether emergency powers can be effective, the key variable here is whether the terrorist group has enough support to sustain itself against a concerted government response. According to this criteria, Sendero enjoyed a large support base, with five to ten times as many supporters as active members.

There is also some debate as to whether the support for Sendero was given voluntarily or coerced. In the early 1980s, supporters, like many activists, were attracted to Sendero because of their ideology and promise of a better future. Many supporters joined a host of organizations run by the Senderos as a seedbed for recruitment.[164] As the insurgency continued, however, the Shining Path increasingly relied on force or coercion to gain support.[165] Consequently, the support for Sendero was often "tentative."[166] Because "Sendero generally imposed itself by force, it commanded respect for that reason. It did not necessarily command much loyalty. Sendero thus found it difficult to build up a real and durable political support which went beyond obedience for fear of reprisals."[167]

The level of support for the Shining Path also declined as the conflict wore on.[168] Initially, however, Sendero enjoyed a high level of support as it expanded to different villages. Billie Jean Isbell writes that several communities "supported Sendero for the first two years because SL's short-term goals corresponded with their own: first, get rid of enemies ... then set up better schools, and finally ... organize committees to govern without corruption."[169] Over time, though, Sendero lost some support for three reasons. The violence and terror of the Shining Path cost them considerable support. In one village, Sendero "met with resistance when its cadres attempted to assassinate people whose infractions were deemed minor."[170] Also, Sendero lost support because of its economic policies, especially when Sendero closed down markets and forced peasants to practice subsistence farming.[171] Lastly, Sendero frequently ignored or disrespected local traditions. Peter Stern contends that Sendero lost support from "its contempt for 'traditional' systems of community authority [and] its neglect of local bonds and social dynamics."[172] Despite the loss of some support, though, overall support for the Shining Path remained fairly high throughout the 1980s and early 1990s.

The ability of the Shining Path to replace the large numbers of arrested and killed members is testament that the level of support they enjoyed was high enough to sustain the organization. Throughout the insurgency, the Shining Path suffered large numbers of losses. In 1983, the government claimed over 2,000 Senderos had already been captured and over 1,000 killed.[173] Between 1980 and 1985, a government intelligence report claimed that 4,700 senderistas had been killed and over 3,000 arrested,[174] while other official estimates claimed 8,000 Senderos had been killed in the same time frame.[175] By 1991, 11,000 suspected terrorists had been killed, nearly 5,000 were in jail, 4,000 had repented of terrorism, and many others had left the organization.[176] (Note that the government claimed that all of those killed were Senderos, but many were actually innocent civilians.) With such high rates of attrition, especially for a group that numbered between 5,000 and 10,000 members, it would seem unlikely that the Shining Path could have continued to exist. The Sendero Luminoso not only survived, however, but actually grew during the 1980s despite the government's efforts. The reason the Shining Path was able to grow was because of the large number of supporters who were willing to join the organization to replace those killed or arrested. The result was that "During the mid-1980s, the Shining Path's recruitments were higher than the losses they suffered."[177] The Shining Path found replacements for killed or imprisoned cadres at all levels of the organization, from the new recruit to the top leadership positions. "Despite the Peruvian government's claims that it has captured or killed many top Sendero leaders ... Shining Path's expansion suggests that the system is reinforced by a standing cadre of militants able to step up into leadership positions as needed."[178]

A second factor that influences whether emergency powers will be effective is how quickly the government moves to arrest and imprison suspected terrorists. Even if the terrorists have a large support network, if the security forces move quickly to arrest large numbers of terrorists, there will be too few remaining members to train new recruits. In most cases the speed of the government's response does not depend on the size of the terrorist group; recall that in Uruguay, the army and police arrested thousands of suspected Tupamaros in a matter of months. In Peru, however, the Shining Path had thousands, if not tens of thousands of armed militants who were spread out across the whole country, including many remote regions in the Andes and the Amazon. Consequently, the Peruvian security forces were incapable of moving quickly against the entire Sendero organization.

During most of the 1980s and 1990s, the security forces rarely acted with sufficient speed to disrupt the Shining Path. Even when large numbers of suspected terrorists were arrested, these counterinsurgency operations were carried out in localized areas of Peru, and were not nationwide operations.[179] Because of Sendero's large size, the government forces had difficulty seizing the initiative against the Senderos. The army could seize towns or occupy provinces, but Sendero would just shift its forces and re-deploy its combatants to other areas. Had Sendero had only a few hundred members, it is more likely that the government forces would have been able to deliver a quick strike in which they might have captured a large portion of the organization. Faced with a large and dispersed enemy, however, the security forces were unable to move quickly against Sendero.

The only evidence of the security forces moving quickly to round up suspected Senderos occurred after the capture of Guzmán in September 1992. When the police found Guzmán, they also found information on the entire membership of the Senderos.[180] Within a few days of Guzmán's arrest, 200 senderistas were arrested, and within a few weeks, more than a 1,000 had been captured.[181] By the end of 1992, twelve out of nineteen central committee members had been arrested; of the rank and file militants, 3,600 were arrested within eighteen months and 7,000 were arrested within two years of Guzmán's arrest.[182]

With the capture of most of the Sendero leadership, thousands of militants, and Guzmán himself, the Shining Path was eventually defeated. The preceding analysis, however, shows that the eventual success of the state was *not* a result of the emergency powers. Despite the arrests and killings of thousands of suspected senderistas, the Shining Path took advantage of a large support base to recruit and train new members in greater numbers than those that had been arrested or killed. Moreover, the state was incapable of moving quickly against large numbers of Senderos throughout the 1980s and early 1990s. Consequently, up until Guzmán's capture, the violence of the Shining Path had pushed Peru to the brink of anarchy.

Returning to the question of the eventual success of the Peruvian state against the Sendero Luminoso, the success might be explained by several factors. The most important cause of Sendero's demise was the capture of Guzmán on September 12, 1992. The capture of Guzmán was particularly damaging to Sendero because "The loyalty of the movement's membership appears to be to the man and his image rather than to the organization."[183] With his capture, "Guzmán's heroic, mythical image was virtually destroyed."[184] Captured along with Guzmán were several high-ranking leaders of Sendero as well as computer records that allegedly contained information on Sendero's organization and membership.[185] In addition, Guzmán called for a period of peace while in prison; this led to the surrender of over 3,000 Senderos under a new Repentance Law.[186] In sum, the capture of Guzmán was a devastating blow to the Shining Path. Morale and support plummeted, while the organizational records found with Guzmán allowed the police and army to capture thousands of members. In other cases, specifically Uruguay and Canada, the security forces used emergency powers to exploit similar drops in support. In this case, though, Sendero was so dependent on the leadership and spiritual guidance of one man, that emergency powers were not necessary to defeat the terrorists; therefore, even with the defeat of the Shining Path after the capture of Guzmán, the emergency powers should not be classified as effective.

Another factor that contributed to the Sendero's defeat, albeit less important than the capture of Guzmán, was the development of armed peasant communities, called rondas. Security forces first tried to establish these civil defense patrols in the early 1980s and President García reinvigorated this strategy in 1989.[187] Under Fujimori, the strategy of arming peasants in rondas became a focal point of the counterinsurgency campaign.[188] As a result, the war with Sendero became, in some areas, a peasant war between Sendero forces and armed villagers that supported the government.[189] It is not clear, however, exactly how much the rondas contributed to the eventual defeat. They probably made Sendero operations increasingly more difficult in Andean regions where the rondas were most prevalent and where Sendero did not have much peasant support to begin with. In any case, by 1992, Sendero had already shifted its attention to the Upper Huallaga Valley and to Lima, where rondas were not present.[190]

ABUSES OF EMERGENCY POWERS

In assessing what counts as an abuse of the emergency powers, we must look at the content of those powers. As described earlier in this chapter, the emergency powers in Peru suspended four rights ordinarily guaranteed by the constitution: the freedoms of assembly and movement, and the freedoms from arbitrary arrest and unwarranted search and seizure. The violation or suspension of any other rights would constitute an abuse of the powers because they were not authorized under the state of emergency.

The use of torture by Peru's police and military was first reported by Amnesty International in 1983,[191] and continued through the duration of the government's counter-terrorism campaign.[192] Numerous Amnesty International and Americas Watch reports found the use of torture to be "the norm"[193] in the emergency zones and "the method habitually used by police bodies to interrogate those suspected of both common and security offenses."[194] Particular methods of torture included near drowning, electric shocks, burnings, beatings, and sexual abuse of women.[195] Prisoners also were subject to various techniques designed to inflict tremendous amounts of pain. One prisoner recounted his experience as, "The marines kept me blindfolded without food and water for fourteen days, hanging me up by my hands tied behind my back until my eyes were popping out ... I was punched and half drowned ... I was lucky—a prisoner accused of blowing up a bridge had his hand cut off with an ax in front of me. He confessed."[196] Prisoners were also subjected to the "application of electric shocks to the genitals; burning with cigarettes, insertion of bottles into the anus; stabbing with knives; and tying of people to metal sheets before leaving them to toast in the sun."[197]

The security forces also resorted to the tactic of "the deliberate arbitrary arrest of persons who were later made to 'disappear.'"[198] Those that were disappeared were denied all due process rights, from the right to a trial to the protection from torture. Frequently, the disappeared later turned up dead after having been tortured and killed by the security forces. Peru was not the first Latin American country to resort to disappearing its citizens, although it was one of the worst violators. There were more disappearances in 1983 and 1984 in Peru, for example, than in the first six years of Pinochet's regime in Chile.[199] According to a variety of sources, nearly 3,500 disappearances were reported over a twelve-year span.[200] The actual number of disappearances is probably even higher, however, as relatives of those disappeared were reluctant to report the disappearances and because human rights organizations were often denied access to emergency zones by the military.

In addition to torture and disappearances, the Peruvian security forces also resorted to extra-judicial killings. Instead of arresting suspected terrorists and allowing the legal system to work, army and police units often killed those they suspected were Senderos.[201] The military would often respond to Sendero attacks by "laying waste to whole communities where it believed the guerrillas lived or were helped and protected."[202] In 1983, the first year under a state of emergency, 2,223 unnatural civilian deaths were reported.[203] By 1989, the number of extra-judicial killings probably exceeded the estimated 3,000 "disappearances."[204] In addition to attacking entire villages, many cases of extra-judicial killings "involved individuals who were seized at their homes, during community assemblies or at roadblocks, and were taken away by troops and later found dead."[205] Most of these killings occurred in the emergency zones in the Andean highlands, with numerous reports of mass graves within a short radius of Ayacucho.[206] In comparison to these thousands of people killed by the security forces in Peru, recall the outrage in Britain over the government's alleged "shoot-to-kill" policy, which may have led to a few *dozen* deaths of IRA members.

The most notorious incident of extra-judicial killings occurred following the prison riots in 1986. On June 18, 1986, the Sendero inmates of the El Frontón, Lurigancho, and Santa Bárbara prisons in Lima simultaneously took over all three facilities.[207] President García authorized the military to retake all three prisons. At El Frontón, the navy destroyed the building that the inmates had seized, killing 123 people. At Lurigancho, at least 100 of the 124 inmates killed were shot in cold blood after surrendering and two prisoners were killed at Callao.[208] In all, at least 249 prisoners were killed with another 50 or so unaccounted for.[209]

Possibly the greatest abuse of emergency powers occurs when they are used to end democratic rule in a state. This type of abuse is at least plausible in light of Fujimori's "self-coup" on April 5, 1992.[210] Increasingly frustrated with an obstructive Congress, the country's economic decline, and the inability to defeat the Shining Path, Fujimori disbanded Congress, purged the judiciary, suspended the constitution, and ruled by decree.[211] This coup, while clearly an abuse of power, was *not*, however, a result of the emergency powers. Hypothetically, emergency powers might contribute to a coup in several ways. They might remove some of the constraints on the executive branch of the government making it easier for a president to seize power in a coup. For example, a president might be granted the right to rule by decree by the emergency powers. He might then use these powers to alter the constitution. Also, emergency powers might give the military a greater role in political decisions. The military might get frustrated by the restrictions posed by a democratic system on its counterinsurgency campaign. Frustrated by these constraints, the military might use its new powers granted to it during the emergency to seize more power for itself. (This is what occurred in Uruguay.) Lastly, a continued state of emergency might erode the norms of constitutional rule such that people become accustomed of the restrictions imposed by emergency powers. As a result, an actor within the government might seize ever greater powers to fight the continued emergency until eventually the constitutional state no longer exists.

In Peru, however, emergency powers had none of these effects. Fujimori was not granted extra powers by the declaration of the state of emergency. He could already pass legislation by presidential decree and did so frequently.[212] Conversely, under no circumstances was he permitted by law to disband Congress or the judiciary.[213] Also, the emergency powers did give greater prominence and authority to the armed forces. Even though Fujimori seized power with the support of the military, he was not their puppet, as Bordaberry was in Uruguay. Lastly, it might be argued that the continued use of emergency powers created a situation where the people of Peru came to accept restrictions on civil liberties as normal and even welcome in the war against the Shining Path. In fact, Fujimori's popularity soared after the coup,[214] which gives credence to the possibility that the emergency powers had eroded the commitment to democracy and civil liberties. Fujimori's popularity, however, was due more to a shared perception that Congress was corrupt and inefficient and the expectation that he would solve the country's economic problems. His popularity, therefore, did not indicate that the people of Peru had become less concerned with their democratic rights.

In sum, Fujimori did not take advantage of any aspect of the emergency powers when he undertook the coup. Instead, the coup would probably have happened even had emergency powers never been used, given the country's economic problems, history of short-lived democratic governments, an authoritarian personality in Fujimori, and a twelve-year campaign of violence from Sendero. (Note that this case poses some problems for constitutional theory. Peru had strong democratic institutions in areas not put under a state of emergency, yet the coup still occurred. Consequently, this case should be seen as an indication of the limits of constitutionalism and the ability of institutions to check power when a coup is so likely.) Even if Fujimori's coup does not by itself constitute an abuse of emergency powers, the thousands of cases of torture, killings, and disappearances clearly make the case of Peru one in which emergency powers were abused.

Why were the emergency powers abused by the security forces in the emergency zones? Recall that abuses of emergency powers are most likely to occur when some actor desires to abuse power and when the constitutional safeguards in a country are weak. In Peru, the military clearly was not strongly committed to upholding democratic norms or human rights.[215] Had they been, abuses would have been much less likely. Nevertheless, even if a military lacks a strong normative commitment to human rights, other political institutions might still be able to check abuses of power. In particular, a free press and strong separation of powers are key if abuses are to be monitored and checked. In Peru, numerous possible actors—including the press, the judiciary, the legislature, the president, and international actors—were incapable of constraining the actions of the military in the provinces placed under a state of emergency. Without the constraints of these actors, the military conducted its counterinsurgency campaign without concern for basic human rights.

When states of emergency were declared, some liberties were suspended in the emergency zones. More importantly, however, the military was given total autonomy within the emergency zones and became unaccountable for its actions.[216] Because of the "abdication of civilian political, administrative, and juridical authority over the military," the constitutional safeguards in Peru were unable to operate in the emergency zones.[217] Without any civilian or legal oversight, the "Peruvian military forces acted with the knowledge that they were virtually immune from prosecution."[218] In fact, not one member of Peru's military forces was convicted of human rights abuses during the 1980s.[219] Only a few policemen were convicted of human rights abuses and most of these occurred following the prison riots of 1986.[220]

In a country with a free press, we should expect the press to monitor and publicize potential abuses of power.[221] The ability to monitor and publicize abuses is particularly valuable when information on possible abuses is scarce. In Peru, the press was one actor with the potential of reporting on human rights abuses in the Andean regions. In general, the press was relatively free and debated a range of policy issues; while many publications were biased or sensationalistic, others were objective and informative.[222] In fact, at the beginning of the military's campaign against Sendero, the press functioned as an effective safeguard in publicizing abuses of power. In 1983, the military's use of "dirty war" tactics was discussed in the national media.[223] In Peru's emergency zones, however, the military quickly denied or limited access to Peru's journalists.[224] "Both local and foreign journalists who have traveled [to the emergency zones] report that the military denies access to certain zones and witnesses."[225] In 1983, at the start of the counterinsurgency campaign, Amnesty International expressed concern over the limited press access in a letter to the president. "[Amnesty International] is concerned at evidence that independent monitoring, reporting or inquiry into abuses by new media and Peruvian human rights organizations have been obstructed by intimidation of their representatives through arrests, threats and acts of violence by forces of the Ayacucho political-military command."[226] In one of the most deadly attacks against the press, eight journalists were killed outside the small town of Uchuraccay on January 26, 1983. In response to the widespread outrage, President Belaúnde created a commission to investigate the murders. The commission found that the journalists had been killed by local villagers who had believed them to be senderistas based on information given to them by the security forces.[227] Afterwards, "Journalists were reluctant to enter the remote and dangerous combat zones, and the military authorities discouraged them from doing so."[228]

By giving the military complete authority in the emergency zones, the emergency powers also undermined the judicial system.[229] Civilian courts no longer had jurisdiction in the emergency zones, thereby denying citizens the protection of due process rights. For example, the large number of disappearance was possible because judges and prosecutors could not file writs of habeas corpus or gain access to military detention centers.[230] Judges and lawyers who tried to investigate abuses were threatened and intimidated, just as reporters were.[231] As a result, in Ayacucho, only fourteen writs of habeas corpus were filed in 1983 and 1984, even though several thousand citizens were disappeared by the military.[232] The civilian courts were also unable to try soldiers for human rights abuses within the emergency zones.[233] Unless the alleged abuse occurred while the soldier was off duty, the civilian courts ceded jurisdiction to the military tribunals.[234] The result was a complete abdication of civilian judicial oversight of the military and its methods in the emergency zones.

Affiliated with the judicial branch, but technically independent, was the Public Ministry. This institution was designed to protect the rights of individual citizens from abuses of power and was headed by the Attorney General with representatives at the departmental and provincial level.[235] Victims of human rights abuses could take their cases to representatives of the Public Ministry who were then empowered to undertake legal matters to remedy the abuse.[236] In several instances, Public Ministry representatives attempted to monitor allegations of disappearances; however, the military obstructed their investigations in the emergency zones.[237] Representatives of the public Ministry were also intimidated by "anonymous threats, bombings, harassment and warnings to halt investigations into armed forces' abuses."[238]

In a constitutional system, the independent power of the legislature is often valuable in protecting against abuses of power. Recall the importance of the British Parliament in establishing numerous commissions that investigated the security forces' implementation of the emergency powers. Under Peru's constitution, Congress "had wide-ranging investigative powers that enabled special commissions to visit the sites of alleged human-rights abuses, take testimony from witnesses, and solicit evidence from military officials ... [and] issue reports that would serve as the basis for judicial investigations and subsequent criminal proceedings."[239] In practice, however, Congressional commissions were often unable to effectively monitor or constrain human rights abuses.[240] The commissions were frequently unable to produce unanimous conclusions, with opinions split along party lines. In addition, the commissions often came to conclusions that defended the government and military in spite of evidence of abuses. Americas Watch describes the outcomes of these commissions as "a serious evasion of public responsibility."[241] Even when the commissions recommended that charges be brought against human rights abusers, no trials occurred. For example, following an army massacre in Accomarca that left sixty-nine peasants dead, a Congressional commission forwarded its findings to the Public Ministry, who took the case to the Supreme Court.[242] The case was

dismissed, however, because the Supreme Court ruled that the incident occurred in an emergency zone and should therefore be tried in a military
court.[243] In sum, although Congress was capable of monitoring abuses, it was
incapable of stopping abuses or punishing those responsible.[244] These limitations were due to the politicized nature of the Congressional commissions as
well as the inability of the civilian courts to bring cases to trial if they involved
military personnel in emergency zones. The weakness of Congress was, in part,
a result of the emergency powers, but also a consequence of its history of corruption and politicization.

Because abuses of power were mostly perpetrated by the Peruvian military
and not the executive, there was at least the potential for the executive branch,
particularly the president, to provide a check on the power of the military. The
three presidents of Peru during the Sendero insurgency (Belaúnde, García, and
Fujimori) each provided different degrees of oversight to the military and its
counterinsurgency campaign.[245] Belaúnde ignored the initial attacks by
Sendero, and then unleashed the military, giving them free reign to conduct a
"dirty war." By 1985, the military and government were coming under increasing domestic and international pressure to better protect human rights.
García was elected, in part because he promised in his election campaign to fight
Sendero while respecting human rights.[246] Soon after the 1985 election, García
made good on his promise in his response to the discovery of mass graves. García responded by relieving some top military commanders and firing over 1,700
corrupt policemen.[247] As a result of García's commitment to human rights, reports of abuses began to decline in 1985.[248] Over time, however, García's concern for human rights began to diminish as he was faced with escalating
violence from Sendero, a worsening economic situation, and a sharp drop in his
personal popularity.[249] Human rights violations soon returned to the levels of
the Belaúnde administration. When Fujimori took power in 1990, his commitment to human rights was practically non-existent. He passed numerous executive decrees that gave the military even greater authority with fewer
constraints in its fight against the Shining Path.[250] Overall, abuses of power
roughly corresponded to each president's commitment to human rights.

International organizations often have the ability to monitor and publicize
human rights abuses. For example, recall the role of the European institutions
in publicizing allegations of brutal interrogation methods in Northern Ireland.
Likewise in Peru, human rights organizations—particularly Amnesty International and Americas Watch—tried to closely document many of the abuses
committed by Peru's security forces. While these organizations can monitor
abuses, they cannot compel the state to take action based on their findings. Even
their ability to monitor abuses was limited in Peru. The military denied access,
threatened, and intimidated human rights observers, just as they did to reporters and Congressional investigators.[251] According to Amnesty International, "Independent human rights monitors and investigators have been
forced out of the emergency zones by threats and the savage example of the

death or 'disappearances' of their colleagues."[252] The safety of human rights observers only worsened in the early 1990s as "A wave of threats and attacks took place ... including a grenade attack on the headquarters of the Andean Commission of Jurists, the bombings of the local office of Amnesty International, [and] the detention and disappearance of a human rights director in Huancavelica."[253] Despite these dangers, many human rights observers continued to report abuses at tremendous danger to their own lives.

THE WORST POSSIBLE RESULTS

This case highlights the difficulty and danger of combating terrorism with emergency powers.[254] As Cynthia McClintock concludes, "The Peruvian regime was unable to develop a counterinsurgency strategy that was both effective and respectful of human rights."[255] The use of emergency powers in Peru provides us with a worst-case scenario: Not only were the emergency powers ineffective at eliminating or even reducing the level of violence, they also contributed to widespread human rights abuses including torture, extrajudicial killings, and disappearances.

This case also raises several policy issues relating to the design and use of emergency powers. How could the emergency powers been safer for democracy and human rights? The one aspect of the emergency powers that most contributed to their abuse was the abdication of civil authority to the military in the emergency zones. This allowed the military to abuse their power mostly unwatched and unconstrained by the state institutions that would normally protect against abuses of power. Conversely, the content of the emergency powers was fairly limited and did not seem to contribute to the human rights abuses. The emergency powers, remember, only suspended four liberties, and left the separation of powers and a free press unaffected, *except in the emergency zones.* In the emergency zones all constitutional safeguards were compromised. Had the emergency powers left out the provision granting the military total authority, the abuses of power would probably not have occurred.

Also, how might the emergency powers have been designed to be more effective against the Sendero Luminoso? This is a more difficult task because of the strength and size of the Shining Path. In fighting a group as powerful as the Senderos, there is little that emergency powers can provide that will be of much assistance. Extra powers of interrogation or the suspension of habeas corpus would probably have done little to change the conduct or outcome of Peru's struggle against the Senderos. Instead, the government should probably have implemented economic and political strategies that would have undermined Sendero's support base before turning to emergency powers. Unfortunately, the case of Peru shows that with a terrorist group as large and powerful as the Shining Path, emergency powers, however designed, are unlikely to be effective.

NOTES

1. In fact, the Shining Path grew during the 1970s when the military government instituted wide-ranging land reforms and expanded education. See David Scott Palmer, "Introduction: History, Politics, and Shining Path in Peru," in *The Shining Path of Peru*, ed. David Scott Palmer (New York: St. Martin's Press, 1994), 2.

2. Cynthia McClintock, *Revolutionary Movements in Latin America: El Salvador's FMLN and Peru's Shining Path* (Washington, D.C.: United States Institute of Peace Press, 1998), 16.

3. See Daniel Masterson, *Militarism and Politics in Latin America: Peru from Sánchez Cerro to Sendero Luminoso* (New York: Greenwood Press, 1991), 299–302, for a good chronology of Peruvian political history.

4. See Peter Klarén, "Historical Setting," in *Peru: A Country Study*, ed. Rex Hudson (Washington, D.C.: Federal Research Division, Library of Congress, 1993) for a history of Peru from Andean society before the Incas to the 1980s; and James Rudolph, *Peru: The Evolution of a Crisis* (Westport, CT: Praeger Publishers, 1992), for a history of modern Peru.

5. Palmer, "Introduction: History, Politics, and Shining Path in Peru," 11.

6. Palmer, "Introduction: History, Politics, and Shining Path in Peru," 13.

7. Ton de Wit and Vera Gianotten, "The Center's Multiple Failures," in *The Shining Path of Peru*, ed. David Scott Palmer (New York: St. Martin's Press, 1994), 68.

8. McClintock, *Revolutionary Movements in Latin America*, 160.

9. Simon Strong, *Shining Path: Terror and Revolution in Peru* (New York: Random House, 1992), 35.

10. McClintock, *Revolutionary Movements in Latin America*, 159.

11. David Werlich, "Debt, Democracy and Terrorism in Peru," *Current History* 86, no. 516 (January 1987), 29.

12. McClintock, *Revolutionary Movements in Latin America*, 14.

13. Orin Starn, "New Literature on Peru's Sendero Luminoso," *Latin American Research Review* 27, no. 2 (1992), 213, shows that "Sendero was depicted as, among other things, a peasant rebellion, an ethnic-based Indian uprising, and an insurrection of Peru's Andean periphery against the coastal center."

14. David Scott Palmer, "Rebellion in Rural Peru: The Origins and Evolution of Sendero Luminoso," *Comparative Politics* 18, no. 2 (January 1986), 127, however, argues that Sendero was unique in its combination of these factors: "Sendero Luminoso is fundamentally a *sui generis* phenomenon. If indeed the context is familiar and replicable in some other Third World settings, the specific circumstances in the local environment out of which Sendero eventually emerged as a radical guerrilla movement are, for all intents and purposes, unique."

15. Deborah Poole, and Gerardo Renique, "The New Chronicles of Peru: US Scholars and their 'Shining Path' of Peasant Rebellion," *Bulletin of Latin American Research* 10, no. 2 (1991).

16. This argument is also made by Starn, "New Literature on Peru's Sendero Luminoso."

17. Michael Smith, "Taking the High Ground: Shining Path and the Andes," *Terrorism, Violence, and Insurgency Report* 10, no. 3 (1991), 3.

18. Peter Stern, *Sendero Luminoso: An Annotated Bibliography of the Shining Path Guerrilla Movement, 1980–1993* (Austin, TX: SALALM, 1995), xxiii.

19. David Werlich, "Peru: The Shadow of the Shining Path," *Current History* 83, no. 490 (February 1984), 80.

20. William Hazleton and Sandra Woy-Hazleton, "Sendero Luminoso: A Communist Party Crosses a River of Blood," *Terrorism and Political Violence* 4, no. 2 (summer 1992), 63–68.

21. Strong, *Shining Path*, 19.

22. M. Smith, "Taking the High Ground," 7.

23. McClintock, *Revolutionary Movements in Latin America*, 63.

24. Hazleton and Woy-Hazleton, "Sendero Luminoso," 67.

25. P. Stern, *Sendero Luminoso*, xxiii.

26. Hazleton and Woy-Hazleton, "Sendero Luminoso," 67.

27. Carlos Ivan Degregori, "Return to the Past," in *The Shining Path of Peru*, ed. David Scott Palmer (New York: St. Martin's Press, 1994), 53.

28. Orin Starn, "Maoism in the Andes: The Communist Party of Peru—Shining Path and the Refusal of History," *Journal of Latin American Studies* 27, no. 2 (May 1995), 403.

29. David Scott Palmer, "Peru's Persistent Problems," *Current History* 89, no. 543 (January 1990), 8.

30. Hazleton and Woy-Hazleton, "Sendero Luminoso," 69.

31. Gabriela Tarazona-Sevillano and John Reuter, *Sendero Luminoso and the Threat of Narcoterrorism* (New York: Praeger Publishers, 1990), 17.

32. Starn, "Maoism in the Andes," 407–509.

33. Strong, *Shining Path*, 57.

34. Tarazona-Sevillano and Reuter, *Sendero Luminoso and the Threat of Narcoterrorism*, 24.

35. Hazleton and Woy-Hazleton, "Sendero Luminoso," 69.

36. Gordon McCormick, "The Shining Path and Peruvian Terrorism," in *Inside Terrorist Organizations*, ed. David Rapoport (New York: Columbia University Press, 1988), 114.

37. See William Rosenau, "Is the Shining Path the 'New Khmer Rouge'?" *Studies in Conflict and Terrorism* 17, no. 4 (1994).

38. Henry Dietz, "Peru's Sendero Luminoso as a Revolutionary Movement." *Journal of Political and Military Sociology* 18 (summer 1990), 132.

39. McClintock, *Revolutionary Movements in Latin America*, 67. Degregori, "Return to the Past," 55, writes that Sendero "rejected the primacy of politics in favor of the primacy of violence."

40. Gustavo Gorriti, *The Shining Path: A History of the Millenarian War in Peru*, tr. Robin Kirk (Chapel Hill, NC: University of North Carolina Press, 1999), 99.

41. Gorriti, *Shining Path*, 105.

42. David Scott Palmer, "The Revolutionary Terrorism of Peru's Shining Path," in *Terrorism in Context*, ed. Martha Crenshaw (University Park, PA: The Pennsylvania

State University Press, 1995), 250, recognizes that governments label a group as terrorists to discredit them.

43. Hazleton and Woy-Hazleton, "Sendero Luminoso," 63.

44. David Scott Palmer, "Conclusion: The View from the Windows," in *The Shining Path of Peru*, ed. David Scott Palmer (New York: St. Martin's Press, 1994), 265.

45. Palmer, "Conclusion: The View from the Windows," 265.

46. Hazleton and Woy-Hazleton, "Sendero Luminoso," 63.

47. Carlos Basombrío Iglesias, "Sendero Luminoso and Human Rights: A Perverse Logic That Captured the Country," in *Shining and Other Paths: War and Society in Peru, 1980–1995*, ed. Steve Stern (Durham, NC: Duke University Press, 1998), 431.

48. McClintock, *Revolutionary Movements in Latin America*, 68.

49. See Tarazona-Sevillano and Reuter, *Sendero Luminoso and the Threat of Narcoterrorism*, vii; and Palmer, "Peru's Persistent Problems," 7, for examples.

50. Strong, *Shining Path*, 89.

51. Dietz, "Peru's Sendero Luminoso," 131; and Tarazona-Sevillano and Reuter, *Sendero Luminoso and the Threat of Narcoterrorism*, 29–30, both have similarly labeled stages. David Scott Palmer, "Revolutionary Terrorism of Peru's Shining Path," 264, cites an earlier, 1974 Sendero document which laid out five slightly different stages. They are: development and infiltration, building the party in rural areas, undertaking the Prolonged People's War, creating liberated zones, and total Prolonged People's War.

52. Gustavo Gorriti, "Peru's Prophet of Terror," *Reader's Digest*, September 1992, 95. See also Strong, *Shining Path*, 87.

53. Philip Mauceri, *State under Siege: Development and Policy Making in Peru* (Boulder, CO: Westview Press, 1996), 122.

54. Raymond Bonner, "Peru's War," *The New Yorker*, January 4, 1988, 39.

55. Mauceri, *State under Siege*, 124.

56. de Wit and Gianotten, "The Center's Multiple Failures," 73.

57. Ponciano del Pino, "Family, Culture, and the 'Revolution': Everyday Life with Sendero Luminoso," in *Shining and Other Paths: War and Society in Peru, 1980–1995*, ed. Steve Stern (Durham, NC: Duke University Press, 1998), 179.

58. Sandra Woy-Hazleton and William Hazleton, "Sendero Luminoso and the Future of Peruvian Democracy," *Third World Quarterly* (April 1990), 22.

59. Juan Méndez, *Human Rights in Peru after Garcia's First Year* (New York: Americas Watch Committee, 1986), 37.

60. Gorriti, *Shining Path*, 104.

61. Gustavo Gorriti, "Shining Path's Stalin and Trotsky," in *The Shining Path of Peru*, ed. David Scott Palmer (New York: St. Martin's Press, 1994), 186.

62. Strong, *Shining Path*, 90–95 and 216.

63. For similar descriptions of Sendero's organization, see Tarazano-Sevillano and Reuter, *Sendero Luminoso and the Threat of Narcoterrorism*, 68; Hazleton and Woy-Hazleton, "Sendero Luminoso," 72; Dietz, "Peru's Sendero Luminoso," 134; and McClintock, *Revolutionary Movements in Latin America*, 72.

64. Palmer, "Revolutionary Terrorism of Peru's Shining Path," 260.

65. Mauceri, *State Under Siege*, 122; and Cynthia McClintock, "Why Peasants Rebel: The Case of Peru's Sendero Luminoso," *World Politics* 37, no. 1 (October 1984), 81.

66. Tarazona-Sevillano and Reuter, *Sendero Luminoso and the Threat of Narcoterrorism*, 57; and Palmer, "Revolutionary Terrorism of Peru's Shining Path," 269.

67. Gabriela Tarazona-Sevillano, "The Organization of Shining Path," in *The Shining Path of Peru*, ed. David Scott Palmer (New York: St. Martin's Press, 1994), 194.

68. Amnesty International, *Caught between Two Fires* (New York: Amnesty International, 1989), 5.

69. Rudolph, *Peru: The Evolution of a Crisis*, 89.

70. Palmer, "Revolutionary Terrorism of Peru's Shining Path," 266.

71. McCormick, "Shining Path and Peruvian Terrorism," 116; and Méndez, *Human Rights in Peru*, 36. See also Tarazona-Sevillano and Reuter, *Sendero Luminoso and the Threat of Narcoterrorism*, 41, for more on the assassination of the vice admiral.

72. McClintock, *Revolutionary Movements in Latin America*, 294.

73. Susan Bourque and Kay Warren, "Democracy without Peace: The Cultural Politics of Terror in Peru," *Latin American Research Review* 24, no. 1 (1989), 17.

74. David Werlich, "Peru: García Loses His Charm," *Current History* 87, no. 525 (January 1988), 15; and Timothy Stater, "Sendero Luminoso's Relentless War," *Terrorism, Violence, and Insurgency* 10, no. 3 (1991), 19.

75. Werlich, "Peru: The Shadow of the Shining Path," 82.

76. Palmer, "Introduction: History, Politics, and Shining Path in Peru," 16.

77. Tarazona-Sevillano and Reuter, *Sendero Luminoso and the Threat of Narcoterrorism*, 38, 39, and 43.

78. Rudolph, *Peru: The Evolution of a Crisis*, 114; and Tarazona-Sevillano and Reuter, *Sendero Luminoso and the Threat of Narcoterrorism*, 39.

79. Tarazona-Sevillano and Reuter, *Sendero Luminoso and the Threat of Narcoterrorism*, 39.

80. Mauceri, *State under Siege*, 118.

81. Estimates for the costs of Sendero violence vary slightly but generally converge at 30,000 deaths and $20 billion. The following sources provide the following figures for total costs in billions of dollars and deaths: Palmer, "Introduction: History, Politics, and Shining Path in Peru," 2 ($24, 30,000); Palmer, "Revolutionary Terrorism of Peru's Shining Path," 251 ($24, 26,000); P. Stern, *Sendero Luminoso*, xviii ($22, 27,000); Stater, "Sendero Luminoso's Relentless War," 18 ($12, 23,000); Daniel Fitz-Simons, "Sendero Luminoso: Case Study in Insurgency," *Parameters* 23, no. 2 (summer 1993), 64 ($22, 24,000); Eduardo Ferrero Costa, "Peru's Presidential Coup," *Journal of Democracy* 3, no. 1 (January 1993), 29 ($20, 17,000); and Philip Mauceri, "Military Politics and Counter-Insurgency in Peru," *Journal of Interamerican Studies and World Affairs* 33, no. 4 (winter 1991), 84 ($10, 20,000).

82. Gorriti, *Shining Path*, 17.

83. Rudolph, *Peru: The Evolution of a Crisis*, 89; Werlich, "Peru: The Shadow of the Shining Path," 82; and Cynthia McClintock, "Sendero Luminoso: Peru's Maoist Guerrillas," in *Problems of Communism* 32 (September-October 1983), 30.

84. Rudolph, *Peru: The Evolution of a Crisis*, 91; and Nelson Manrique, "The War for the Central Sierra," in *Shining and Other Paths: War and Society in Peru, 1980–1995*, ed. Steve Stern (Durham, NC: Duke University Press, 1998), 201.

85. The most comprehensive sources on Sendero's operations in the Huallaga Valley include Tarazona-Sevillano and Reuter, *Sendero Luminoso and the Threat of Narcoterrorism*, chapter 6; and José Gonzales, "Guerrillas and Coca in the Upper Huallaga Valley," in *The Shining Path of Peru*, ed. David Scott Palmer (New York: St. Martin's Press, 1994).

86. Gonzales, "Guerrillas and Coca in the Upper Huallaga Valley," 127.

87. Tarazona-Sevillano and Reuter, *Sendero Luminoso and the Threat of Narcoterrorism*, 116 and 118.

88. Richard Clutterbuck, "Peru: Cocaine, Terrorism and Corruption," *International Relations* 12, no. 5 (August 1995), 80.

89. Tarazona-Sevillano and Reuter, *Sendero Luminoso and the Threat of Narcoterrorism*, 53.

90. McClintock, *Revolutionary Movements in Latin America*, 87. For more on Sendero's operations in Lima's shantytowns, see Jo-Marie Burt, "Shining Path and the 'Decisive Battle' in Lima's *Barriadas*: The Case of Villa El Salvador," in *Shining and Other Paths: War and Society in Peru, 1980–1995*, ed. Steve Stern (Durham, NC: Duke University Press, 1998).

91. Alma Guillermoprieto, "Down the Shining Path," *The New Yorker*, February 8, 1993, 64.

92. Carol Graham, "Government and Politics," in *Peru: A Country Study*, ed. Rex Hudson (Washington, D.C.: Federal Research Division, Library of Congress, 1993), 213.

93. Graham, "Government and Politics," 214.

94. Cynthia McClintock, "Peru: Precarious Regimes, Authoritarian and Democratic," in *Democracy in Developing Countries: Latin America*, ed. Larry Diamond, Juan Linz and Seymour Martin Lipset (Boulder, CO: Lynne Rienner Publishers, 1989), 361.

95. See Rudolph, *Peru: The Evolution of a Crisis*, 79; McClintock, "Peru: Precarious Regimes, Authoritarian and Democratic," 361; and Graham, "Government and Politics," 217.

96. Graham, "Government and Politics," 217–218; and McClintock, "Peru: Precarious Regimes, Authoritarian and Democratic," 361.

97. Graham, "Government and Politics," 212.

98. Juan Méndez, *A Certain Passivity: Failing to Curb Human Rights Abuses in Peru* (New York: Americas Watch Committee, 1987), 41. See also Americas Watch, *Peru under Fire: Human Rights since the Return to Democracy* (New Haven: Yale University Press, 1992), xxiii.

99. Angela Cornell and Kenneth Roberts, "Democracy, Counterinsurgency, and Human Rights: The Case of Peru," *Human Rights Quarterly* 12 (1990), 542.

100. McClintock, *Revolutionary Movements in Latin America*, 13.

101. Philip Mauceri, "State Reform, Coalitions, and the Neoliberal *Autogolpe* in Peru," *Latin American Research Review* 30, no. 1 (1995), 8; and Cynthia McClintock, "Theories of Revolution and the Case of Peru," in *The Shining Path of Peru*, ed. David

Scott Palmer (New York: St. Martin's Press, 1994), 250. High voter participation was a result of mandatory voting laws.

102. Mauceri, "State Reform, Coalitions, and the Neoliberal *Autogolpe* in Peru," 8.

103. Bourque and Warren, "Democracy without Peace," 9.

104. David Pion-Berlin, "Military Autonomy and Emerging Democracies in South America," *Comparative Politics* 25, no. 1 (October 1992), 91.

105. McClintock, *Revolutionary Movements in Latin America*, 130.

106. Gorriti, *Shining Path*, 90.

107. Cornell and Roberts, "Democracy, Counterinsurgency, and Human Rights," 535; and Rudolph, *Peru: The Evolution of a Crisis*, 88.

108. Tarazona-Sevillano and Reuter, *Sendero Luminoso and the Threat of Narcoterrorism*, 79–83.

109. Cornell and Roberts, "Democracy, Counterinsurgency, and Human Rights," 543.

110. Cornell and Roberts, "Democracy, Counterinsurgency, and Human Rights," 543; Méndez, A *Certain Passivity*, 5; and Tarazona-Sevillano and Reuter, *Sendero Luminoso and the Threat of Narcoterrorism*, 89 and 90.

111. Amnesty International, *Peru: Human Rights in a Climate of Terror* (New York: Amnesty International, 1991), 16.

112. Amnesty International, *Peru* (London: Amnesty International, 1985), 9.

113. For various accounts of the number of provinces under a state of emergency, see the following sources: McClintock, *Revolutionary Movements in Latin America*, 81; Amnesty International, *Peru*, 1; Rudolph, *Peru: The Evolution of a Crisis*, 114; Tarazona-Sevillano and Reuter, *Sendero Luminoso and the Threat of Narcoterrorism*, 94; Méndez, A *Certain Passivity*, 5; Méndez, *Human Rights in Peru*, 39; Juan Méndez, *Tolerating Abuses: Violations of Human Rights in Peru* (New York: Americas Watch Committee, 1988), 23; Amnesty International, *Caught between Two Fires*, 1; John Crabtree, *Peru under García: An Opportunity Lost* (Hong Kong: University of Pittsburgh Press, 1992), 203; McClintock, "Why Peasants Rebel," 52; Palmer, "Peru's Persistent Problems," 8; and Bourque and Warren, "Democracy without Peace," 18. These sources do not give identical figures, although most are quite close to each other. Palmer, "Revolutionary Terrorism of Peru's Shining Path," 298, offers a table on the number of provinces put under states of emergency and his numbers are somewhat higher for each year. He finds the following number of provinces declared in states of emergency: five in 1981, fourteen in 1982, twenty-four in 1983, twenty-six in 1984, twenty in 1985, twenty-four in 1986, thirty-six in 1987, forty-four in 1988, seventy-one in 1989, ninety in 1990, sixty-one in 1991, and sixty-two in 1992.

114. For an analysis of the role of the military in fighting the Sendero Luminoso, see Mauceri, "Military Politics and Counter-Insurgency in Peru."

115. Palmer, "Revolutionary Terrorism of Peru's Shining Path," 293.

116. McClintock, *Revolutionary Movements in Latin America*, 140–141.

117. Palmer, "Revolutionary Terrorism of Peru's Shining Path," 295; and Michael Reid, "Building Bridges? Garcia Confronts Sendero," *NACLA Report on the Americas* 20, no. 3 (June 1986), 44 and 45.

118. McClintock, *Revolutionary Movements in Latin America,* 142.

119. McClintock, *Revolutionary Movements in Latin America,* 144.

120. McClintock, *Revolutionary Movements in Latin America,* 147–148.

121. M. Smith, "Taking the High Ground," 1.

122. Mauceri, "State Reform, Coalitions, and the Neoliberal *Autogolpe* in Peru," 25.

123. Méndez, *Tolerating Abuses,* 24.

124. Woy-Hazleton and Hazleton, "Sendero Luminoso and the Future of Peruvian Democracy," 21; and McClintock, *Revolutionary Movements in Latin America,* 10.

125. Carlos Ivan Degregori, "After the Fall of Abimael Guzmán: The Limits of Sendero Luminoso," in *The Peruvian Labyrinth: Polity, Society, Economy,* ed. Maxwell Cameron and Philip Mauceri (University Park, PA: The Pennsylvania State University Press, 1997), 188. See also Clutterbuck, "Peru: Cocaine, Terrorism and Corruption," 77.

126. Crabtree, *Peru under García,* 185.

127. See Gorriti, *Shining Path,* 139 and 144; and Americas Watch, *A New Opportunity for Democratic Authority* (New York: Americas Watch Committee, 1985), 26.

128. Gorriti, *Shining Path,* 160.

129. Starn, "Villagers at Arms: War and Counterrevolution in the Central-South Andes" 1998, 229, claims "dark-skinned kids born in poverty filled the bottom ranks under a leadership composed of mostly light-skinned elites."

130. Starn, "Maoism in the Andes," 405; McClintock, *Revolutionary Movements in Latin America,* 271; and Cornell and Roberts, "Democracy, Counterinsurgency, and Human Rights," 534.

131. Strong, *Shining Path,* 60.

132. Hazleton and Woy-Hazleton, "Sendero Luminoso," 73. Palmer, "Peru's Persistent Problems," 8, argues that the peasantry formed the backbone of the organization, in contrast to the other sources.

133. Carlos Ivan Degregori, "Harvesting Storms: Peasant *Rondas* and the Defeat of Sendero Luminoso in Ayacucho," in *Shining and Other Paths: War and Society in Peru, 1980–1995,* ed. Steve Stern (Durham, NC: Duke University Press, 1998), 128.

134. Woy-Hazleton and Hazleton, "Sendero Luminoso and the Future of Peruvian Democracy," 23.

135. R. Bonner, "Peru's War," 36, argues that Sendero targets 13–15-year-olds because they are easier to indoctrinate.

136. Tom Marks, "Making Revolution with Shining Path," in *The Shining Path of Peru,* ed. David Scott Palmer (New York: St. Martin's Press, 1994), 213.

137. Mauceri, *State under Siege,* 126.

138. See Isabel Coral Cordero, "Women in War: Impact and Responses," in *Shining and Other Paths: War and Society in Peru, 1980–1995,* ed. Steve Stern (Durham, NC: Duke University Press, 1998), 349–353.

139. Mauceri, *State under Siege,* 127.

140. Tarazona-Sevillano and Reuter, *Sendero Luminoso and the Threat of Narcoterrorism,* 45.

141. Gorriti, "Peru's Prophet of Terror," 96.

142. del Pino, "Family, Culture, and the 'Revolution'," 164, as well as 166, 171, and 178.

143. Degregori, "Harvesting Storms," 130. Strong, *Shining Path*, 60, writes that "The movement offers hope, identity, and self-advancement as well as a chance to unleash historic ethnic and social vengeance."

144. McClintock, *Revolutionary Movements in Latin America*, 277.

145. Degregori, "Harvesting Storms," 145.

146. Tarazona-Sevillano and Reuter, *Sendero Luminoso and the Threat of Narcoterrorism*, 74.

147. Rudolph, *Peru: The Evolution of a Crisis*, 87; McClintock, "Why Peasants Rebel," 52; Fitz-Simons, "Sendero Luminoso," 64; and Palmer, "Revolutionary Terrorism of Peru's Shining Path," 270.

148. Palmer, "Introduction: History, Politics, and Shining Path in Peru," 34; Eugenio Chang-Rodríguez, "Origin and Diffusion of the Shining Path in Peru," in *APRA and the Democratic Challenge in Peru*, ed. Eugenio Chang-Rodríguez and Ronald Hellman (New York: Bildner Center for Western Hemisphere Studies, 1988), 81; Strong, *Shining Path*, 217; M. Smith, "Taking the High Ground," 1; Stater, "Sendero Luminoso's Relentless War," 19; David Scott Palmer, "Peru, the Drug Business and Shining Path: Between Scylla and Charybdis?" *Journal of Interamerican Studies and World Affairs* 34, no. 3 (autumn 1992), 76; Starn, "Maoism in the Andes," 411; R. Bonner, "Peru's War," 39; Robert Davis, "Sendero Luminoso and Peru's Struggle for Survival," *Military Review* 70, no. 1 (January 1990), 79; Dietz, "Peru's Sendero Luminoso," 136; Peter Gaupp, "Peru on the Downslide," *Swiss Review of World Affairs* 39, no. 4 (July 1989), 24; Guillermoprieto, "Down the Shining Path," 64; Hazleton and Woy-Hazleton, "Sendero Luminoso," 73; McClintock, "Sendero Luminoso: Peru's Maoist Guerrillas," 19; Cynthia McClintock, "The Prospects for Democratic Consolidation in a 'Least Likely' Case," *Comparative Politics* 21, no. 2 (1989), 130; Palmer, "Peru's Persistent Problems," 8; Linda Seligman, *Between Reform and Revolution: Political Struggles in the Peruvian Andes, 1969–1991* (Stanford: Stanford University Press, 1995), 195.

149. McClintock, *Revolutionary Movements in Latin America*, 73; Michael Radu and Vladimir Tismaneanu, *Latin American Revolutionaries: Groups, Goals, Methods* (Washington, D.C.: Pergamon-Brassey's International Defense Publishers, 1990), 325; Andrew Wheat, "Shining Path's 'Fourth Sword' Ideology," *Journal of Political and Military Sociology* 18, no. 1 (summer 1990), 48; Palmer, "Revolutionary Terrorism of Peru's Shining Path," 270.

150. Fitz-Simons, "Sendero Luminoso," 64.

151. McClintock, *Revolutionary Movements in Latin America*, 74.

152. R. Bonner, "Peru's War," 39; and Chang-Rodríguez, "Origin and Diffusion of the Shining Path in Peru," 82, both estimate they had 20,000 supporters. Gaupp, "Peru on the Downslide," 24, puts the number of supporters at 30,000. Strong, *Shining Path*, 217, cites a police report which estimates the Senderos had the support of 22,000 people but other security forces put the number at twice that. Palmer, "Revolutionary Terrorism of Peru's Shining Path," 270, estimates 50,000 supported the Senderos, while McClintock, *Revolutionary Movements in Latin America*, 75, puts the number of supporters at between 50,000 and 100,000.

153. McClintock, "Sendero Luminoso: Peru's Maoist Guerrillas," 30; and McClintock, "Why Peasants Rebel," 48.

154. Nelson Manrique, "Time of Fear," *NACLA Report on the Americas* 24, no. 4 (December/January 1990/1991), 29.

155. Tarazona-Sevillano and Reuter, *Sendero Luminoso and the Threat of Narcoterrorism*, xvi.

156. Palmer, "Rebellion in Rural Peru," 129.

157. McClintock, "Why Peasants Rebel," 55.

158. Strong, *Shining Path*, 137.

159. McClintock, *Revolutionary Movements in Latin America*, 78.

160. Hazleton and Woy-Hazleton, "Sendero Luminoso and the Future of Peruvian Democracy," 76; and McClintock, "Why Peasants Rebel," 50, both argue for Sendero's lack of support in Lima and other coastal cities.

161. Ronald Berg, "Peasant Responses to Shining Path in Andahuaylas," in *The Shining Path of Peru*, ed. David Scott Palmer (New York: St. Martin's Press, 1994), 103 and 117.

162. Dietz, "Peru's Sendero Luminoso," 142.

163. See McClintock, "Why Peasants Rebel."

164. Tarazona-Sevillano and Reuter, *Sendero Luminoso and the Threat of Narcoterrorism*, 62

165. See Strong, *Shining Path*, 137; and Berg, "Peasant Responses to Shining Path," 110.

166. Fitz-Simons, "Sendero Luminoso," 68.

167. Crabtree, *Peru under García*, 208.

168. McClintock, *Revolutionary Movements in Latin America*, 291.

169. Billie Jean Isbell, "Shining Path and Peasant Rebellion in Rural Ayacucho," in *The Shining Path of Peru*, ed. David Scott Palmer (New York: St. Martin's Press, 1994), 89.

170. Isbell, "Shining Path and Peasant Rebellion," 79. McCormick, "Shining Path and Peruvian Terrorism," 121, writes, "Sendero's early base of support has not survived its liberal use of terror to enforce obedience and unpopular 'revolutionary reforms.'"

171. Colin Harding, "The Rise of Sendero Luminoso," in *Region and Class in Modern Peruvian History*, ed. Rory Miller (Liverpool: Institute of Latin American Studies, 1987), 192; and McClintock, "Why Peasants Rebel," 82.

172. Steve Stern, ed., *Shining and Other Paths: War and Society in Peru, 1980–1995* (Durham, NC: Duke University Press, 1998), 122.

173. Radu and Tismaneanu, *Latin American Revolutionaries*, 325.

174. Harding, "Rise of Sendero Luminoso," 180.

175. Sandra Woy-Hazleton and William Hazleton, "Sustaining Democracy in Peru: Dealing with Parliamentary and Revolutionary Changes," in *Liberalization and Redemocratization in Latin America*, ed. George Lopez and Michael Stohl (New York: Greenwood Press, 1987), 119.

176. McClintock, *Revolutionary Movements in Latin America*, 75.

177. Gorriti, "Peru's Prophet of Terror," 96.

178. Tarazona-Sevillano, "Organization of Shining Path," 201.

179. Werlich, "Peru: The Shadow of the Shining Path," 90, claims that the police arrested 15,000 people following the initial declaration of a state of emergency in 1983. It is not clear, however, who these 15,000 people were. Undoubtedly, most were not senderistas.

180. Clutterbuck, "Peru: Cocaine, Terrorism and Corruption," 85.

181. Cynthia McClintock, "Peru's Fujimori: A Caudillo Derails Democracy," *Current History* 92, no. 572 (March 1993), 117; and Palmer, "Revolutionary Terrorism of Peru's Shining Path," 301.

182. Palmer, "Introduction: History, Politics, and Shining Path in Peru," 3; and P. Stern, *Sendero Luminoso*, xvii.

183. McCormick, "Shining Path and Peruvian Terrorism," 123.

184. McClintock, *Revolutionary Movements in Latin America*, 92.

185. Carlos Ivan Degregori, "Shining Path and Counterinsurgency Strategy since the Arrest of Abimael Guzmán," in *Peru in Crisis: Dictatorship or Democracy?* ed. Joseph Tulchin and Gary Bland (Boulder, CO: Lynne Rienner Publishers, 1994), 95.

186. Clutterbuck, "Peru: Cocaine, Terrorism and Corruption," 86 and 87.

187. McClintock, *Revolutionary Movements in Latin America*, 148.

188. Mauceri, *State under Siege*, 143; and Clutterbuck, "Peru: Cocaine, Terrorism and Corruption," 86.

189. Mauceri, "Military Politics and Counter-Insurgency in Peru," 98.

190. Gorriti, *Shining Path*, xiv, disagrees with this conclusion. He claims, "The Shining Path was finally defeated not by the army and its blind blows, but the police and the people themselves, who rebelled against the rebels and made the countryside, Mao's launch pad of revolt, hostile to them."

191. Amnesty International, *Peru: Torture and Extrajudicial Executions* (New York: Amnesty International, 1983), 2.

192. Guillermoprieto, "Down the Shining Path," 64, claims that torture is "routine" in Peru.

193. Amnesty International, *Caught between Two Fires*, 24.

194. Méndez, *Tolerating Abuses*, 44.

195. See Americas Watch, *Peru under Fire*, 85; Amnesty International, *Caught between Two Fires*, 24; and Amnesty International, *Peru: Torture and Extrajudicial Executions*, 2.

196. Strong, *Shining Path*, 138.

197. Strong, *Shining Path*, 138.

198. Méndez, *Human Rights in Peru*, 16.

199. R. Bonner, "Peru's War," 57.

200. These figures are from Kenneth Roberts and Mark Peceny, "Human Rights and United States Policy toward Peru," in *The Peruvian Labyrinth: Polity, Society, Economy*, ed. Maxwell Cameron and Philip Mauceri (University Park, PA: The Pennsylvania State University Press, 1997), 198; Cynthia Brown, *In Desperate Straights: Human Rights in Peru after a Decade of Democracy and Insurgency* (New York: Human Rights Watch, 1990), 24 and 25; and Americas Watch, *Peru under Fire*, 19.

201. Tarazona-Sevillano and Reuter, *Sendero Luminoso and the Threat of Narcoterrorism*, 93.

202. Strong, *Shining Path*, 134.

203. Tarazona-Sevillano and Reuter, *Sendero Luminoso and the Threat of Narcoterrorism*, 91.

204. Amnesty International, *Caught between Two Fires*, 14.

205. Amnesty International, *Caught between Two Fires*, 14.

206. Amnesty International, *Peru*, 8.

207. For good accounts of these events, see Amnesty International, *Peru: "Disappearances", Torture and Summary Executions by Government Forces after the Prison Revolts of June 1986* (London: Amnesty International, 1987). This entire Amnesty report is devoted to the human rights violations during and after the prison riots. See also Méndez, *Human Rights in Peru*, 99–112.

208. Werlich, "Debt, Democracy and Terrorism in Peru," 36.

209. Rudolph, *Peru: The Evolution of a Crisis*, 111.

210. For a good summary of the causes and events surrounding the coup, see McClintock, "Peru's Fujimori;" Costa, "Peru's Presidential Coup;" and Mauceri, "State Reform, Coalitions, and the Neoliberal *Autogolpe* in Peru."

211. Roberts and Peceny, "Human Rights and United States Policy toward Peru," 202; and Palmer, "Introduction: History, Politics, and Shining Path in Peru," 17.

212. Maxwell Cameron, *Democracy and Authoritarianism in Peru: Political Coalitions and Social Change* (New York: St. Martin's Press, 1994), 149.

213. Cameron, *Democracy and Authoritarianism in Peru*, 150.

214. Strong, *Shining Path*, 264.

215. McClintock, "The Prospects for Democratic Consolidation," 136.

216. Mauceri, "Military Politics and Counter-Insurgency in Peru," 83. Méndez, *Tolerating Abuses*, 4, writes, "There has been virtually no democratic control of the government forces responsible for confronting the insurgent groups."

217. Cornell and Roberts, "Democracy, Counterinsurgency, and Human Rights," 530.

218. Mauceri, "State Reform, Coalitions, and the Neoliberal *Autogolpe* in Peru," 7.

219. Cornell and Roberts, "Democracy, Counterinsurgency, and Human Rights," 546.

220. Amnesty International, *Peru: Human Rights in a Climate of Terror*, 44.

221. Gorriti, *Shining Path*, xiii, writes that an independent press "has a critical role to play" in countries where democracy is tenuous.

222. Méndez, *Human Rights in Peru*, 45; and Méndez, *Tolerating Abuses*, 55.

223. Amnesty International, *Peru*, 4.

224. Méndez, *A Certain Passivity*, 42 and 43.

225. Méndez, *Human Rights in Peru*, 46. Méndez, *A Certain Passivity*, 4, writes that the military established "nearly a complete ban on access" to the emergency zones.

226. Amnesty International, *Peru: Torture and Extrajudicial Executions*, 3.

227. See Michael Reid, *Peru: Paths to Poverty* (London: Latin American Bureau, 1985), 115–117; and Strong, *Shining Path*, 135–136.

228. Werlich, "Peru: The Shadow of the Shining Path," 82.

229. Even under normal circumstances, the judiciary was the weakest and least in-dependent of the three branches of government. The judiciary was under-financed, under-trained, and subject to political manipulations. See Méndez, *Tolerating Abuses*, 33; and Brown, *In Desperate Straights*, 33.

230. Strong, *Shining Path*, 133.

231. Amnesty International, *Peru: Human Rights in a Climate of Terror*, 18.

232. Cornell and Roberts, "Democracy, Counterinsurgency, and Human Rights," 544.

233. Americas Watch, *Peru under Fire*, 26.

234. Amnesty International, *Caught between Two Fires*, 29; Americas Watch, *New Opportunity*, 23; and Méndez, *Human Rights in Peru*, 67.

235. Méndez, *Human Rights in Peru*, 72.

236. Amnesty International, *Caught between Two Fires*, 30.

237. Amnesty International, *Peru*, 9.

238. Amnesty International, *Peru: Human Rights in a State of Emergency* (New York: Amnesty International, 1989), 8.

239. Roberts and Peceny, "Human Rights and United States Policy toward Peru," 209.

240. Americas Watch, *Peru under Fire*, 43–56, recounts the reports of the following commissions: Ames, Melgar, Limo, and Mohme.

241. Americas Watch, *Peru under Fire*, 44.

242. For more on the Accomarca massacre, see Méndez, *Human Rights in Peru*, 5–8.

243. Amnesty International, *Peru: Human Rights in a Climate of Terror*, 57–58.

244. Amnesty International, *Caught between Two Fires*, 31.

245. Oddly, the military gradually but steadily lost its autonomy over a range of issue areas from 1980 until 1992 at the national level; however, it was given complete autonomy at the local or regional level to combat the Shining Path. Enrique Obando, "The Power of Peru's Armed Forces," in *Peru in Crisis: Dictatorship or Democracy?* ed. Joseph Tulchin and Gary Bland (Boulder, CO: Lynne Rienner Publishers, 1994), 109, makes this point.

246. Raúl González, "Gonzalo's Thought, Belaunde's Answer," *NACLA Report on the Americas* 20, no. 3 (June 1986), 45.

247. Bourque and Warren, "Democracy without Peace," 16; and Jo-Marie Burt, "Counterinsurgency = Impunity," *NACLA Report on the Americas* 24, no. 4 (December/January 1990/1991), 30.

248. Méndez, *Human Rights in Peru*, 2

249. Cornell and Roberts, "Democracy, Counterinsurgency, and Human Rights," 537.

250. Mauceri, "State Reform, Coalitions, and the Neoliberal *Autogolpe* in Peru," 23.

251. Amnesty International, *Peru: Torture and Extrajudicial Executions*, 3; and Amnesty International, *Caught between Two Fires*, 37.

252. Amnesty International, *Peru: Human Rights in a Climate of Terror,* 3. See also Americas Watch, *Into the Quagmire: Human Rights and U.S. Policy in Peru* 1991, 21–23; and Americas Watch, *Peru under Fire,* 114–120.

253. Cornell and Roberts, "Democracy, Counterinsurgency, and Human Rights," 541.

254. Several scholars of Peru recognize this dilemma. See McCormick, "Shining Path and Peruvian Terrorism," 124; R. Bonner, "Peru's War," 56; Woy-Hazleton and Hazleton, "Sustaining Democracy in Peru," 121; and Ronald Bruce St John, "Peru: Democracy under Siege," *The World Today* 40, no. 7 (July 1984), 304.

255. McClintock, *Revolutionary Movements in Latin America,* 94.

Chapter 7

The Tradeoff Revisited

The previous four chapters have shown that emergency powers have consequences beyond the tradeoff assumed by the conventional wisdom. In fact, the use of emergency powers can lead to four different sets of outcomes. In Chapter 2, I developed theories that attempt to explain when emergency powers are most likely to be effective as well as when they are most likely to be abused. In this final chapter, I will reassess the validity of my theories by evaluating them in terms of how well they explain all four cases. Following this, I will answer the underlying policy question that motivates this study, specifically, when should states use emergency powers? I will then turn to the issue of designing better emergency powers. The preceding empirical analysis offers insights about what types of emergency powers are most likely to be effective and which ones are most likely to be abused. Knowing which are which, we should be able to design emergency powers that are most likely to be effective and least likely to be abused. Lastly, I will consider the generalizability of my findings to other cases by considering how this study would predict the consequences of emergency powers in countries that have not yet used them against terrorism. In particular, I will focus on the United States, whether emergency powers should be used, and what their likely consequences would be.

ASSESSING THE THEORIES

How well did my theories predict the empirical findings of the four case studies? I will first discuss the effectiveness of emergency powers. Afterwards,

I will assess the different explanations for when emergency powers are most likely to be abused.

Emergency powers are more or less effective, according to my theory, depending on whether the state can capture terrorists faster than new recruits can replace them. Emergency powers, by their design, are intended to help the security forces in capturing terrorists by suspending certain liberties, such as the right not to be arrested without warrant, or held without charge, or jailed without a trial. Despite these additional powers, terrorist organizations are not easily defeated. Even as the security forces capture suspected terrorists, new recruits will join the organization and continue the fight. For emergency powers to be effective, they must not only arrest the first wave of terrorists but also the subsequent generations of terrorists. Two factors are important in determining whether emergency powers will be effective: the size of the active terrorist group in relation to its level of support, and the speed with which the security forces capture suspected terrorists. Emergency powers are most effective when the state moves quickly against a small terrorist group that has weak support.

This explanation is supported by all four cases. Where support is high, such as in Britain, Peru, and initially in Uruguay, the emergency powers were ineffective. When the terrorists were small or not well supported, such as in Canada and eventually in Uruguay, the emergency powers were effective. Likewise, when the security forces moved quickly to arrest or detain large numbers of suspected terrorists, such as in post-1972 Uruguay and in Canada, the emergency powers were effective. Conversely, when the security forces were never capable of moving quickly in capturing suspected terrorists, such as in Britain, Peru, and initially in Uruguay, the emergency powers were not effective. In every case, then, the theory I developed in Chapter 2 accurately explains whether emergency powers were effective or not.

I have argued that emergency powers are most likely to be abused when there is some agent within the state who wants to abuse the powers, and when the constitutional safeguards of the state are weak. Abuses can be both of the scope and the duration of the emergency powers. Abuses in scope are typically perpetrated by the security forces and are least likely to occur when the normative commitment to democracy among the security forces is strong, the press can monitor abuses, and the legislature or judiciary can monitor abuses and enforce the law. Abuses in the (limited) duration of emergency powers occur when the executive or the military permanently seizes greater powers for themselves. Abuses of this sort are most likely when the commitment to democracy is weak within the military or by the executive (depending on which actor commits the abuse) and when the separation of powers is unable to provide the checks and balances that protect against abuses of power.

In Uruguay and Peru, the security forces committed widespread abuses, including torture and extra-judicial killings, because they lacked a commitment to upholding individual liberties and because free speech and the separation of powers were undermined. Abuses in scope were limited in Britain, even though the security forces often tried to defeat terrorism by any means, because the press and Parliament remained strong and active in protecting against abuses. Lastly, when the security forces have a strong commitment to upholding individual liberties, such as in Canada, abuses in scope are unlikely.

Abuses in the duration of the emergency powers require that either the executive or the military desires to permanently acquire greater power. Even then, if the institutional safeguards remain strong, abuses will be less likely. In Uruguay, the norms of the military changed for the worse as they took on a greater role in fighting terrorism. Additionally, the freedom of the press and civilian oversight of the military were suspended by the emergency powers. With both a weak commitment to democracy and weak institutions, the military abused the emergency powers by launching a coup. In Peru, the military was not eager to return to power after recently returning to democratic government. Likewise, the first two democratic presidents of Peru were committed to upholding democratic procedures, although less committed to protecting human rights. President Fujimori, however, lacked a strong commitment to democracy, although his coup was an abuse of power generally and not particularly of emergency powers. On methodological grounds, these cases are not completely satisfying because each case had both weak norms *and* weak institutions. I can only argue that, hypothetically, if the institutional safeguards had been stronger, abuses of power would have been less likely. In contrast, in both Britain and Canada the military and the executive branches made no attempts to abuse their power (reflecting strong norms). Had they tried, though, the emergency powers left the institutional safeguards intact. The strength of these institutions would have made abuses more unlikely or at least harder to carry out. In sum, abuses of power can be constrained if actors have a strong normative commitment to liberty and democracy, and if institutional actors retain their ability to monitor abuses and enforce the law.

One issue that arises from this analysis concerns the relationship between norms and institutions. I have treated them as additive variables—both weak norms and weak institutions are necessary for abuses to occur. In other words, there must be both the desire and the opportunity if some actor is going to abuse emergency powers; however, perhaps norms and institutions should be treated as rivals. Maybe, in fact, the normative variable can explain the variation in abuses by itself. A more parsimonious theory could then drop the institutional variable. Moreover, strong norms are almost always correlated with strong institutions. When norms were strong, no actor attempted to abuse power and the institutional constraints were never even tested. Additionally, the coup in Peru (while not an abuse of the emergency powers) is better explained by normative variables than by institutional factors because the institutions in non-emergency zones were strong and Fujimori's normative commitment to democracy was weak. Norms, therefore, are arguably a more important variable in protecting against abuses of power and might dominate the causal consequences of institutions.

While this line of argument is somewhat valid, institutional constraints should be included in the causal explanation for the abuse of emergency powers for two reasons. Normative arguments cannot, by themselves, explain every case. In Britain, recall, the security forces in Northern Ireland were not committed to upholding the liberties and rights of suspected terrorists. Similar to many other countries, the security forces were more concerned with fighting terrorism than upholding democratic values. Yet, even *without* a strong normative commitment, the abuses of the security forces were limited by the institutional safeguards that were left intact by the emergency powers. A second reason to include institutional variables is that norms can change during the course of an emergency. In Uruguay, the norms of the military changed as they took on a greater role in fighting terrorism. If we were to predict abuses of emergency powers based on the norms of different actors *before* the emergency occurs, we would expect no abuses in Uruguay because of the strength of democratic norms. Institutional safeguards, in contrast, are only undermined by the emergency powers themselves; therefore, if we want to protect a state from abuses of power, we should want both a strong normative commitment to democracy *as well as* strong institutional safeguards in case these norms change or are weak to begin with. In sum, both weak norms and weak institutions are necessary for abuses to occur, but either strong norms or strong institutions are sufficient for protecting against abuses; therefore, both should be included as explanatory factors for when abuses occur.

LESSONS LEARNED

This study of the consequences of emergency powers was motivated by an assumed tradeoff in the literature on terrorism. So far, I have demonstrated that emergency powers have a wider range of consequences than assumed, and explained why this is so. This leaves the broader policy question—when should states use emergency powers to fight terrorism? When are the benefits (in terms of their effectiveness) worth the possible costs (in terms of abuse)? The answer depends on whether the emergency powers are expected to be effective or ineffective and abused or not.

Policy prescriptions are easiest in situations analogous to the Peru case. Emergency powers were ineffective and abused. Clearly, in cases such as this, emergency powers should not be used. The implications from the Britain and Uruguay cases, however, are more difficult to discern. These two cases can be thought of as two sides of the same coin, in terms of the tradeoff of emergency powers. Uruguay fits the conventional wisdom fairly well. Emergency powers were effective, but led to abuses of human rights and a military coup. In other words, there were benefits as well as costs to using emergency powers. Britain, on the other hand, is the opposite of this case. Emergency powers were neither effective nor abused. In a sense, then, Britain faced a reverse tradeoff. Assessing whether either state should have used emergency powers involves a similar logic. The question for both types of cases is whether the benefits (or lack thereof) of the emergency powers were worth their costs (or lack thereof). The answer is the same for both situations: Emergency powers should not have been used to fight terrorism.

In Uruguay, it is hard to imagine the benefits of emergency powers outweighing their costs, which included twelve years of a brutal military dictatorship. Even though the emergency powers helped the state defeat the Tupamaros, the citizens of Uruguay would have been better off in a democratic state plagued by terrorism than in an authoritarian state that governed through violence and fear. In Britain, emergency powers should not have been used because not only were they ineffective, they were also probably counterproductive. As argued in Chapter 3, the use of emergency powers in Northern Ireland alienated the Catholic population and increased support for the IRA. Additionally, some abuses occurred, although relatively few compared to other cases. Emergency powers were therefore doubly costly. Hypothetically, even if the emergency powers had *not* been counterproductive, but just ineffectual, they still should not have been used. If emergency powers do not increase the effectiveness of the security forces, there is no reason for using them. Even if abuses are not likely to occur, the costs to liberties from *using* emergency powers and the possibility, however remote, that some abuses might occur, is not worth the cost of using ineffective emergency powers.

The last case, Canada, should offer the clearest policy implications because emergency powers were effective and not abused. This is the desired outcome along both dimensions. In situations analogous to this case, where the state can move quickly against a small and weakly supported terrorist group, and where the norms and institutional constraints are strong, states should use emergency powers. Let me emphasize, however, that this recommendation should be taken with as much caution as possible. The emergency powers must be necessary. Recall the considerable debate in Canada over whether the War Measures Act was really necessary. Many people questioned whether the threat from the FLQ was exaggerated, and whether the police could have defeated the FLQ just as easily without the emergency powers. Ultimately, these criticisms were not justified, as argued in Chapter 5. Also, emergency powers should also be used with much reluctance and caution because of the costs associated with their *use*. Even when they are not abused, emergency powers suspend many of the liberties and due process rights of individual citizens. These suspensions, even if legal, are unwelcome in a society committed to upholding democracy and liberty. To repeat, leaders should be sure that emergency powers are necessary and should be aware that there are costs associated with them, even if they are not abused.

Some might argue that emergency powers should be used for their symbolic value, even if they are not effective. Often, governments feel pressured to "do something" after a terrorist attack, and emergency powers could be one symbol of their dedication to fighting terrorism. As a symbol, emergency powers can rally a country behind the government's efforts. This occurred in Canada following the invocation of the War Measures Act. On the other hand, if the government fails to demonstrate its resolve in fighting terrorism, it may lose credibility and legitimacy and may lose power. The leadership of a country, though, must resist this pressure. Emergency powers are too costly if abused or even if used as intended for governments to use them for symbolic purposes. If governments want to send a symbol that they are committed to fighting terrorism, pick a different symbol. Emergency powers are too costly to use for these purposes.

I have argued that emergency powers will be most effective when used against a terrorist group with low support. Perhaps, though, emergency powers can actually lower support by deterring potential terrorists from joining the organization. The emergency powers might demonstrate the resolve of the state in fighting terrorism, and also might increase the costs of becoming a terrorist by making it more likely that a new recruit will be captured and spend a longer time in prison. What, then, is the relationship between emergency powers and the support for a terrorist group? When do emergency powers increase support, and when do they decrease support? Comparing the cases of Britain and Canada helps answer this question. Recall that the British use of emergency powers, particularly their internment sweeps, increased support for the IRA, yet when Canada invoked the War Measures Act, support for the FLQ lessened. (Support for the FLQ also sharply fell because of the Laporte murder.) The difference between these two cases is in how the security forces used the emergency powers. The internment operations in Northern Ireland were seen as indiscriminate because they targeted innocent civilians as well as suspected terrorists, and because they were also directed primarily against the Catholic population. Had the sweeps been more focused or less biased, then the uninvolved Catholic community would not have felt that they were being unjustly singled out by the British. In other words, the British actions appeared to be directed more at Catholic communities than against terrorists specifically. Consequently, many Catholics turned to the IRA as their traditional protector against Unionist forces. In contrast, the police in Canada used the War Measures Act to detain approximately 500 people, most of whom were treated well while in custody and quickly released. While many innocent civilians were initially detained, the security forces did not generate any animosity from those mistakenly arrested. The use of emergency powers probably deterred future FLQ operations and undermined their support because the police used them to arrest many suspected terrorists and showed they were capable of acting effectively against future attacks. In general, then, if a state hopes to use emergency powers to cut into the support of a terrorist group and deter future recruits from joining and conducting more operations, the security forces must use the emergency powers in the most careful ways. They cannot be used to target a particular segment of the population, nor can they be seen to be indiscriminate and unnecessarily brutal. The perceptions of the public are key. If they feel the emergency powers are used legitimately, they will support the government; if not, the emergency powers will help the terrorists find new recruits.[1]

BUILDING A BETTER MOUSETRAP

We know when emergency powers are likely to be effective and abused, as well as when states should use emergency powers to fight terrorism. A question that still remains is whether emergency powers can be better designed so that they are less likely to be abused and more likely to be effective. This is possible only because certain aspects of emergency powers contribute to their effectiveness while others increase the likelihood that they will be abused. To be effective, emergency powers restrict certain liberties of suspected terrorists. The police are often permitted to conduct searches without a warrant, make arrests without charge, detain a suspect for longer before bringing charges, and hold a prisoner for longer before bringing him to trial. Measures such as these improve the effectiveness of the security forces because these extra powers make it easier for the security forces to capture terrorists and extract information from them once they are in custody.

Emergency powers also sometimes limit free speech by censoring the media and undermine the separation of powers by allowing the president to rule by decree or by giving the military autonomy in fighting terrorism. These aspects of emergency powers, however, do not contribute to the effectiveness of the security forces. For example, when Uruguay closed down newspapers, Uruguayan citizens got their news from other sources.[2] Consequently, the government could not control how the citizens thought about the Tupamaros or the government's response to them. Undermining the separation of powers also does not improve the efficacy of the security forces. In other types of emergencies, there may be more need for the executive to have greater powers, especially if decisions must be made quickly without the encumbrances of normal government.[3] In fighting terrorism, though, the inefficiencies of democratic government do not seem to be a burden. Likewise, the state may be more successful if the military is given authority to fight terrorism, but there is no reason that all civilian oversight of the military should be removed. In sum, then, only restrictions of due process rights and other liberties are necessary to improve the effectiveness of emergency powers. Other aspects of emergency powers are not necessary.

In terms of abuses of emergency powers, I have shown that the particular aspects of emergency powers that undermine the constitutional safeguards of the state contribute the most to whether they are abused. I have argued that the key constraints against abuses of power are the continued existence of a free press and the separation of powers. These institutions constrain abuses of power by monitoring alleged abuses and enforcing the law if abuses occur.

When emergency powers undermine these institutions, as they did in Peru and Uruguay, abuses are more likely. In designing emergency powers that will be least likely to be abused, therefore, the emergency powers should not include provisions that give autonomy to the military or executive branch and should not allow the state to censor the media or suspend the right to free speech in any way. Conversely, restricting due process rights may lead to some limited violations of individual liberties, but coups or widespread human rights violations are unlikely to occur.

In designing better emergency powers, we should include those powers that increase their effectiveness but are least likely to lead to abuses, and we should avoid those powers which are not effective, but do contribute to abuses. Additionally, specific aspects might increase both the effectiveness and the chance of abuse, or vice versa. In these last two cases, we would face a tradeoff (on a smaller scale) similar to the more general tradeoff of using emergency powers as discussed in Chapter 1. Conveniently, though, the different aspects of emergency powers correspond only to the first two categories. Restrictions of liberties and due process rights increase the effectiveness of the powers, but do not lead to abuses, while suspending free speech and the separation of powers does not increase the effectiveness of the emergency powers, but does lead to abuses.[4] For emergency powers to have the greatest chance of success with the lowest chance of abuse, they should be limited to restrictions of due process rights.

If all emergency powers were designed in this way, abuses would be less likely and the effectiveness of the powers would depend on the factors identified earlier (the support for the terrorist group and the speed of the government's response). In practice, though, emergency powers often include many provisions that are not really necessary, but contribute to abuses. As a result, emergency powers have the range of consequences described throughout this analysis.

EMERGENCY POWERS IN THE UNITED STATES

The theories that I developed in Chapter 2 explain the cases examined in the last four chapters, but what would my explanations predict for other cases? In general, I would expect emergency powers to be most effective when the government moves quickly against a weakly supported terrorist group. Emergency powers are more likely to be abused when free speech and the separation of powers are weak or undermined. In particular, though, what would the consequences be for the United States if it chose to use emergency powers against terrorism? Under what conditions should the United States actually use emergency powers?

Until September 11, 2001, most people thought that the United States was relatively immune from terrorism. We did not face an indigenous nationalist or separatist group demanding their own state, nor did we face the ideological terrorism common in other countries. The few attacks that occurred were the result of a few individuals (such as Timothy McVeigh or Ted Kaczynski) or were carried out by international terrorists. Confronted with terrorism of such a limited nature, emergency powers were never seriously considered. After all, emergency powers would restrict the liberties of United States citizens; against a few individuals or foreigners, such restrictions would not be necessary. None of this changed with the September 11 attacks. Nevertheless, there is renewed concern that the government might restrict certain liberties—whether temporarily or permanently—to help fight terrorism.

Hypothetically, then, what would happen if the United States used emergency powers against terrorism, as it exists today? The emergency powers would be unlikely to be abused in any way because they would not undermine any of the institutional safeguards. The only exceptional power allowed by the Constitution is the suspension of the writ of habeas corpus. If the emergency powers are limited to just suspending this one liberty, a free press and an active Congress and Supreme Court could continue to investigate and check against any abuses. Even if more extensive emergency powers are implemented, it seems unimaginable that the right to free speech would be curtailed, the military would be given autonomy, or the president would be allowed to bypass Congress. Additionally, there seems to be a strong commitment to democratic rule in the United States. As long as the safeguards remain, emergency powers would be unlikely to be abused.

Also, would the emergency powers be effective? Remember effectiveness is defined compared to what would be accomplished without emergency powers. In other words, the use of emergency powers must increase the effectiveness of the security forces. If the police can be just as effective without emergency powers, they are not necessary or effective. Against international terrorists, emergency powers would not be necessary. If the terrorists are not United States citizens, the government has a range of options to use against them. The government can tighten the requirements for acquiring a visa or deport foreigners suspected of terrorism, for example. All these measures can be directed at non-citizens, and would not require the use of emergency powers or any suspensions of liberties. Even if terrorists *are* United States citizens, emergency powers would still not be necessary because of the lack of large terrorist organizations on United States soil. At this point in time, domestic terrorists operate as individuals or in small groups. Capturing them is a task that the police or FBI are capable of accomplishing without the need for emergency powers. When terrorism is perpetrated by lone individuals, there is no danger of new recruits joining the cause. As a result, emergency powers would not be needed to help the police capture terrorists faster than new members can join the organization because there is no organization to join. In sum, with the type of terrorism the United States is facing today, emergency powers would not be necessary, but would also probably not be abused. In cases of this type, emergency powers should not be used.

Consider a different situation in which the United States faces an active right-wing domestic terrorist group. What would happen if the United States used emergency powers against this type of group? Again, the possibility of abuse remains minimal because the emergency powers would leave the institutional safeguards intact; however, the emergency powers might be necessary if the police are to be more effective. In this case, the effectiveness of the emergency powers would depend on the size and support of the terrorist group. If this hypothetical terrorist organization was relatively large with a large support base, emergency powers would be unlikely to be effective for the reasons discussed throughout this study. Conversely, if the terrorist group was not well supported, the emergency powers would be more likely to be effective. If this were the case, emergency powers *should* be used because they would be both effective and unlikely to be abused. Once again, though, they should only be used if they are necessary. If the police could be just as effective without emergency powers, the costs to liberty from *using* emergency powers are not worth the negligible benefits.

To conclude, let me return to the original issue that motivated this study. In responding to terrorism, many people fear that if a state uses emergency powers, they will face a tradeoff between the effectiveness and abuses of the emergency powers. I have shown that this tradeoff does not always materialize. Moreover, I have explained under what conditions emergency powers are abused and when they are effective. For states considering using emergency powers, they should only be used with the utmost caution, when they are necessary, when the terrorist is small and weakly supported, when the state can act quickly to capture terrorists, and when the constitutional safeguards of the state remain strong. As the United States wages its campaign against terrorism, its leaders should take these lessons to heart. Against the terrorist threat the United States now faces, emergency powers are not necessary. Using emergency powers would only further terrorize the citizens of the United States by depriving them of their liberties and freedoms.

NOTES

1. This is not to say that emergency powers will be most effective when they are used cautiously or even not abused. The effectiveness of emergency powers, as shown earlier, depends on other factors; however, everything else being equal, the way in which emergency powers are used may influence the level of support for the terrorist group and make the emergency powers more or less likely to be effective.

2. Canada did use some censorship in fighting the FLQ; however, criticism of the government was still permitted in the media. This meant that the government could not control how citizens viewed its actions against the FLQ.

3. This was the case with the Roman dictator, who was appointed to defend Rome against an invasion.

4. It might seem inconsistent that restrictions of free speech *would not* increase the effectiveness of the state, but *would* lead to abuse. If the people can gather information on the terrorists from other sources, what keeps people from gathering information to criticize the government from other sources? The difference between the two logics depends on the function of free speech. In terms of abuse, limits on free speech are dangerous because they limit or deny the opposition the ability of voicing their dissent. Information about alleged abuses is important but usually still available, just to a lesser degree. In terms of effectiveness, censorship is expected to control peoples' thoughts and ideas relating to the terrorists. In modern societies, though, even with censorship, people are still aware of the exploits of local terrorist groups and would join the terrorist organization whether or not the media is allowed to talk or write about terrorism. Limits on free speech, therefore, are likely to be ineffective, but dangerous.

Bibliography

Alexander, Yonah. *International Terrorism: National, Regional and Global Perspectives.* New York: Praeger Publishers, 1976.

Alvarez, Mike et al. "Classifying Political Regimes." *Studies in Comparative International Development* 31, no. 2 (summer 1996): 3–36.

Americas Watch. *A New Opportunity for Democratic Authority.* New York: Americas Watch Committee, 1985.

———. *Into the Quagmire: Human Rights and U.S. Policy in Peru.* New York: Human Rights Watch, 1991.

———. *Peru Under Fire: Human Rights since the Return to Democracy.* New Haven: Yale University Press, 1992.

Amnesty International. *Peru: Torture and Extrajudicial Executions.* New York: Amnesty International, 1983.

———. *Peru.* London: Amnesty International, 1985.

———. *Peru: "Disappearances", Torture and Summary Executions by Government Forces after the Prison Revolts of June 1986.* London: Amnesty International, 1987.

———. *Caught between Two Fires.* New York: Amnesty International, 1989.

———. *Peru: Human Rights in a State of Emergency.* New York: Amnesty International, 1989.

———. *Peru: Human Rights in a Climate of Terror.* New York: Amnesty International, 1991.

Andreas, Carol. "Women at War." *NACLA Report on the Americas* 24, no. 4 (December/January 1990/1991): 20–27.

Bain, George. "The Making of a Crisis." In *Power Corrupted: The October Crisis and the Repression of Quebec,* edited by Abraham Rotstein, 1–14. Toronto: new press, 1971.

Barton, Carol. "Peru: "Dirty War in Ayacucho." *NACLA Report on the Americas* 17, no. 3 (May/June 1983): 36–39.

Beaton, Leonard. "The Crisis in Quebec: Mr. Trudeau Asserts Authority." *The Round Table* no. 241 (January 1971): 147–152.

Beetham, David. "Key Principles and Indices for a Democratic Audit." In *Defining and Measuring Democracy*, edited by David Beetham, 25–43. London: Sage Publications, 1994.

———. *Democracy and Human Rights*. Cambridge: Polity Press, 1999.

Beetham, David, ed. *Defining and Measuring Democracy*. London: Sage Publications, 1994.

Bell, J. Bowyer. *A Time of Terror: How Democratic Societies Respond to Revolutionary Violence*. New York: Basic Books, 1978.

———. *The IRA 1968–2000: Analysis of a Secret Army*. London: Frank Cass Publishers, 2000.

Bennett, John. *Sendero Luminoso in Context: An Annotated Bibliography*. Lanham, MD: The Scarecrow Press, 1998.

Bennett, Philip. "Peru: Corner of the Dead." *The Atlantic* 253, no. 5 (May 1984): 18–33.

Berg, Ronald. "Peasant Responses to Shining Path in Andahuaylas." In *The Shining Path of Peru*, edited by David Scott Palmer, 101–122. New York: St. Martin's Press, 1994.

Blaustein, Albert, and Gisbert Flanz. *Constitutions of the Countries of the World*. Dobbs Ferry, NY: Oceana Publications, 1982.

Bollen, Kenneth. "Issues in the Comparative Measurement of Political Democracy." *American Sociological Review* 45 (1980): 370–390.

Bonner, David. *Emergency Powers in Peacetime*. London: Sweet and Maxwell, 1985.

———. "United Kingdom: The United Kingdom Response to Terrorism." In *Western Responses to Terrorism*, edited by Alex P. Schmid and Ronald Crelinsten, 171–205. London: Frank Cass Publishers, 1993.

Bonner, Raymond. "Peru's War." *The New Yorker*, January 4, 1988, 31–58.

Borovy, Alan. "Rebuilding a Free Society." In *Power Corrupted: The October Crisis and the Repression of Quebec*, edited by Abraham Rotstein, 97–118. Toronto: new press, 1971.

Bourque, Susan, and Kay Warren. "Democracy without Peace: The Cultural Politics of Terror in Peru." *Latin American Research Review* 24, no. 1 (1989): 7–34.

Breton, Raymond. "The Socio-Political Dynamics of the October Events." In *Quebec Society and Politics: Views from the Inside*, edited by Thomson and Dale, 213–238. Toronto: McClelland and Stewart, 1973.

Brown, Cynthia. *In Desperate Straights: Human Rights in Peru after a Decade of Democracy and Insurgency*. New York: Human Rights Watch, 1990.

Brown, Michael, and Eduardo Fernández. *War of Shadows: The Struggle for Utopia in the Peruvian Amazon*. Berkeley, CA: University of California Press, 1991.

Burt, Jo-Marie. "Counterinsurgency = Impunity." *NACLA Report on the Americas* 24, no. 4 (December/January 1990/1991): 30–31.

———. "Shining Path and the 'Decisive Battle' in Lima's *Barriadas:* The Case of Villa El Salvador." In *Shining and Other Paths: War and Society in Peru, 1980–1995*, edited by Steve Stern, 267–306. Durham, NC: Duke University Press, 1998.

Burt, Jo-Marie, and José López Ricci. "Shining Path after Guzmán." *NACLA Report on the Americas* 28, no. 3 (Nov/Dec 1994): 6–9.

Burton, Anthony. *Urban Terrorism: Theory, Practice and Response*. London: Leo Cooper, 1975.

Butler, Ross. "Terrorism in Latin America." In *International Terrorism: National, Regional and Global Perspectives*, edited by Yonah Alexander. New York: Praeger Publishers, 1976.

Cameron, Maxwell. *Democracy and Authoritarianism in Peru: Political Coalitions and Social Change.* New York: St. Martin's Press, 1994.

————. "Political and Economic Origins of Regime Change in Peru: The *Eighteenth Brumaire* of Alberto Fujimori." In *The Peruvian Labyrinth: Polity, Society, Economy,* edited by Maxwell Cameron and Philip Mauceri, 37–69. University Park, PA: The Pennsylvania State University Press, 1997.

Cameron, Maxwell, and Philip Mauceri, eds. *The Peruvian Labyrinth: Polity, Society, Economy.* University Park, PA: The Pennsylvania State University Press, 1997.

Chang-Rodríguez, Eugenio. "Origin and Diffusion of the Shining Path in Peru." In *APRA and the Democratic Challenge in Peru,* edited by Eugenio Chang-Rodríguez and Ronald Hellman, 65–90. New York: Bildner Center for Western Hemisphere Studies, 1988.

Chang-Rodríguez, Eugenio, and Ronald Hellman, eds. *APRA and the Democratic Challenge in Peru.* New York: Bildner Center for Western Hemisphere Studies, 1988.

Charney, Ann. "From Redpath Crescent to Rue des Recollets." In *Power Corrupted: The October Crisis and the Repression of Quebec,* edited by Abraham Rotstein, 15–30. Toronto: new press, 1971.

Charters, David, ed. *The Deadly Sin of Terrorism: Its Effect on Democracy and Civil Liberties in Six Countries.* Westport, CT: Greenwood Press, 1994.

Clausewitz, Carl von. *On War.* Princeton: Princeton University Press, 1976.

Clutterbuck, Richard. *Guerrillas and Terrorists.* Chicago: Ohio University Press, 1977.

————. "Peru: Cocaine, Terrorism and Corruption." *International Relations* 12, no. 5 (August 1995): 77–92.

Clutterbuck, Richard, ed. *The Future of Political Violence: Destabilization, Disorder and Terrorism.* New York: St. Martin's Press, 1986.

Collins, Eamon, and Mick McGovern. *Killing Rage.* London: Granta Books, 1997.

Combs, Cindy C. *Terrorism in the Twenty-First Century.* Upper Saddle River, NJ: Prentice Hall, 1997.

Connolly, Stephen, and Gregory Druehl. "The Tupamaros—the New Focus in Latin America." *Journal of Contemporary Revolutions* 3, no. 3 (summer 1971): 59–68.

Conroy, John. *Belfast Diary: War as a Way of Life.* Boston: Beacon Press, 1995.

Coogan, Tim Pat. *The IRA: A History.* Niwot, CO: Robert Rinehart Publishers, 1994.

Cordero, Isabel Coral. "Women in War: Impact and Responses." In *Shining and Other Paths: War and Society in Peru, 1980–1995,* edited by Steve Stern, 345–376. Durham, NC: Duke University Press, 1998.

Cornell, Angela, and Kenneth Roberts. "Democracy, Counterinsurgency, and Human Rights: The Case of Peru." *Human Rights Quarterly* 12 (1990): 529–553.

Correa, Marcial Rubio. "The Perception of the Subversive Threat." In *The Military and Democracy: The Future of Civil-Military Relations in Latin America,* edited by Louis Goodman, Johanna Mendelson and Juan Rial, 93–106. Lexington, MA: Lexington Books, 1990.

Costa, Eduardo Ferrero. "Peru's Presidential Coup." *Journal of Democracy* 3, no. 1 (January 1993): 28–40.

Crabtree, John. *Peru under García: An Opportunity Lost.* Hong Kong: University of Pittsburgh Press, 1992.

Crelinsten, Ronald. "Power and Meaning: Terrorism as a Struggle over Access to the Communication Structure." In *Contemporary Research on Terrorism,* edited by

Paul Wilkinson and Alasdair Stewart, 419–452. Aberdeen: Aberdeen University Press, 1987.

———. "The Internal Dynamics of the FLQ During the October Crisis of 1970." In *Inside Terrorist Organizations*, edited by David Rapoport, 59–89. New York: Columbia University Press, 1988.

Crenshaw, Martha. "Introduction: Reflection on the Effects of Terrorism." In *Terrorism, Legitimacy, and Power: The Consequences of Political Violence*, edited by Martha Crenshaw, 1–37. Middletown, CT: Wesleyan University Press, 1983.

———. "An Organizational Approach to the Analysis of Political Terrorism." *Orbis* 29, no. 3 (fall 1985): 465–488.

Crenshaw, Martha, ed. *Terrorism, Legitimacy, and Power: The Consequences of Political Violence*. Middletown, CT: Wesleyan University Press, 1983.

———. *Terrorism in Context*. University Park, PA: The Pennsylvania State University Press, 1995.

Dahl, Robert A. "Thinking about Democratic Constitutions: Conclusions from Democratic Experience." In *Political Order*, edited by Ian Shapiro and Russell Hardin, 175–206. New York: New York University Press, 1993.

———. *On Democracy*. New Haven: Yale University Press, 1998.

Davis, Robert. "Sendero Luminoso and Peru's Struggle for Survival." *Military Review* 70, no. 1 (January 1990): 79–88.

de la Cadena, Marisol. "From Race to Class: Insurgent Intellectuals *de provincia* in Peru, 1910–1970." In *Shining and Other Paths: War and Society in Peru, 1980–1995*, edited by Steve Stern, 22–59. Durham, NC: Duke University Press, 1998.

de Wit, Ton, and Vera Gianotten. "The Center's Multiple Failures." in *The Shining Path of Peru*, edited by David Scott Palmer, 63–76. New York: St. Martin's Press, 1994.

Degregori, Carlos Ivan. "A Dwarf Star." *NACLA Report on the Americas* 24, no. 4 (December/January 1990/1991): 10–16.

———. "Return to the Past." In *The Shining Path of Peru*, edited by David Scott Palmer, 51–62. New York: St. Martin's Press, 1994.

———. "Shining Path and Counterinsurgency Strategy since the Arrest of Abimael Guzmán." In *Peru in Crisis: Dictatorship or Democracy?* edited by Joseph Tulchin and Gary Bland, 81–100. Boulder, CO: Lynne Rienner Publishers, 1994.

———. "After the Fall of Abimael Guzmán: The Limits of Sendero Luminoso." In *The Peruvian Labyrinth: Polity, Society, Economy*, edited by Maxwell Cameron and Philip Mauceri, 179–191. University Park, PA: The Pennsylvania State University Press, 1997.

———. "Harvesting Storms: Peasant *Rondas* and the Defeat of Sendero Luminoso in Ayacucho." In *Shining and Other Paths: War and Society in Peru, 1980–1995*, edited by Steve Stern, 128–157. Durham, NC: Duke University Press, 1998.

del Pino, Ponciano. "Family, Culture, and the 'Revolution': Everyday Life with Sendero Luminoso." In *Shining and Other Paths: War and Society in Peru, 1980–1995*, edited by Steve Stern, 158–192. Durham, NC: Duke University Press, 1998.

della Porta, Donatella. "Institutional Responses to Terrorism: The Italian Case." In *Western Responses to Terrorism*, edited by Alex Schmid and Ronald Crelinsten, 151–170. London: Frank Cass Publishers, 1993.

Dempsey, James X., and David Cole. *Terrorism and the Constitution: Sacrificing Civil Liberties in the Name of National Security*. Los Angeles: First Amendment Foundation, 1999.

DeQuine, Jeanne. "The Challenge of the Shining Path." *The Nation* December 8, 1984, 610–613.

Desbarats, Peter. *René: A Canadian in Search of a Country.* Toronto: McClelland and Stewart, 1976.

Deutsch, Richard R. *Northern Ireland 1921–1974: A Select Bibliography.* New York: Garland Publishing, 1975.

Diamond, Larry, Juan Linz, and Seymour Martin Lipset, eds. *Democracy in Developing Countries: Latin America.* Boulder, CO: Lynne Rienner Publishers, 1989.

Dietz, Henry. "Peru's Sendero Luminoso as a Revolutionary Movement." *Journal of Political and Military Sociology* 18 (summer 1990): 123–150.

Dillon, Martin. *The Dirty War: Covert Strategies and Tactics Used in Political Conflicts.* New York: Routledge, 1999.

———. *God and the Gun: The Church and Irish Terrorism.* New York: Routledge, 1999.

———. *The Shankill Butchers: The Real Story of Cold-Blooded Mass Murder.* New York: Routledge, 1999.

d'Oliveira, Sergio. "Uruguay and the Tupamaro Myth." *Military Review* 53, no. 4 (April 1973): 25–36.

Donohue, Laura. *Counter-terrorist Law and Emergency Powers in the United Kingdom 1922–2000.* Dublin: Irish Academic Press, 2001.

Dowty, Alan. "Emergency Powers in Israel: The Devaluation of Crisis." In *Coping with Crises: How Governments Deal with Emergencies,* edited by Shao-chuan Leng, 1–44. Lanham, MD: University Press of America, 1990.

Drache, Daniel, ed. *Quebec—Only the Beginning: The Manifestos of the Common Front.* Toronto: new press, 1972.

Drake, Charles. "The Provisional IRA: Reorganization and the Long War." In *Terrorism's Laboratory: The Case of Northern Ireland,* edited by Alan O'Day, 87–114. Aldershot, England: Dartmouth Publishing Company, 1995.

Dror, Yehezkel. "Terrorism as a Challenge to the Democratic Capacity to Govern." In *Terrorism, Legitimacy, and Power: The Consequences of Political Violence,* edited by Martha Crenshaw, 65–90. Middletown, CT: Wesleyan University Press, 1983.

Elster, Jon. "Introduction." In *Constitutionalism and Democracy,* edited by Jon Elster and Rune Slagstad, 1–18. Cambridge: Cambridge University Press, 1988.

Elster, Jon, and Rune Slagstad, eds. *Constitutionalism and Democracy.* Cambridge: Cambridge University Press, 1988.

Encyclopedia Britannica. www.britannica.com.

Escobar, Arturo and Sonia Alvarez, eds. *The Making of Social Movements in Latin America: Identity, Strategy, and Democracy.* Boulder, CO: Westview Press, 1992.

Evans, Robert. "Terrorism and Subversion of the State: Italian Legal Responses." In *Coping with Crises: How Governments Deal with Emergencies,* edited by Shao-chuan Leng, 87–128. Lanham, MD: University Press of America, 1990.

———. "Italy and International Terrorism." In *The Deadly Sin of Terrorism: Its Effect on Democracy and Civil Liberties in Six Countries,* edited by David Charters, 73–102. Westport, CT: Greenwood Press, 1994.

Evelegh, Robin. *Peace-Keeping in a Democratic Society: The Lessons of Northern Ireland.* Montreal: McGill-Queen's University Press, 1978.

Falkenrath, Richard A., Robert D. Newman, and Bradley Thayer. *America's Achilles' Heel: Nuclear, Biological, and Chemical Terrorism and Covert Attack.* Cambridge, MA: MIT Press, 1998.

Farnsworth, Elizabeth. "Peru: A Nation in Crisis." *World Policy Journal* 5, no. 4 (fall 1988): 725–746.

Fauriol, Georges, ed. *Latin American Insurgencies.* Georgetown University Center for Strategic and International Studies, 1985.

Finch, M. H. J. "Three Perspectives on the Crisis in Uruguay." *Journal of Latin American Studies* 3, no. 2 (November 1971): 173–190.

Fitz-Simons, Daniel. "Sendero Luminoso: Case Study in Insurgency." *Parameters* 23, no. 2 (summer 1993): 64–73.

Flanz, Gisbert. "Uruguay Supplement." In *Constitutions of the Countries of the World,* edited by Albert Blaustein and Gisbert Flanz, 1–6. Dobbs Ferry, NY: Oceana Publications, 1982.

Flathman, Richard. "Liberalism and the Suspect Enterprise of Political Institutionalization: The Case of the Rule of Law." In *The Rule of Law,* edited by Ian Shapiro, 297–327. New York: New York University Press, 1994.

Foland, Frances. "A New Model for Revolution? Uruguay's Urban Guerrillas." *The New Leader* October 4, 1971, 8–11.

Friedrich, Carl. *Constitutional Government and Democracy.* Boston: Ginn and Company, 1946.

Gallagher, A. M. "Policing Northern Ireland: Attitudinal Evidence." In *Terrorism's Laboratory: The Case of Northern Ireland,* edited by Alan O'Day, 47–58. Aldershot, England: Dartmouth Publishing Company, 1995.

Gal-Or, Noemi. "Countering Terrorism in Israel." In *The Deadly Sin of Terrorism: Its Effect on Democracy and Civil Liberties in Six Countries,* edited by David Charters, 137–172. Westport, CT: Greenwood Press, 1994.

Garnett, J. C. "Emergency Powers in Northern Ireland." In *Coping with Crises: How Governments Deal with Emergencies,* edited by Shao-chuan Leng, 45–86. Lanham, MD: University Press of America, 1990.

Gaupp, Peter. "Peru: A 'Shining Path' to Darkness." *Swiss Review of World Affairs* 33, no. 10 (January 1984): 27–31.

———. "Peru on the Downslide." *Swiss Review of World Affairs* 39, no. 4 (July 1989): 21–24.

Gazit, Shlomo. "The Myth and the Reality of the PLO." In *International Terrorism: Challenge and Response,* edited by Benjamin Netanyahu. New Brunswick, NJ: Transaction Books, 1981.

Gerassi, Marysa. "Uruguay's Urban Guerrillas." *The Nation* September 29, 1969, 306–310.

Gilio, Maria Esther. *The Tupamaros.* London: Secker and Warburg, 1972.

Gillespie, Charlie. "The Breakdown of Democracy in Uruguay: Alternative Political Models." *Latin American Program, The Wilson Center, Working Papers* no. 143, (1984).

Goodman, Louis, Johanna Mendelson, and Juan Rial, eds. *The Military and Democracy: The Future of Civil-Military Relations in Latin America.* Lexington, MA: Lexington Books, 1990.

Gonzales, José. "Guerrillas and Coca in the Upper Huallaga Valley." In *The Shining Path of Peru,* edited by David Scott Palmer, 123–144. New York: St. Martin's Press, 1994.

González, Raúl. "Gonzalo's Thought, Belaunde's Answer." *NACLA Report on the Americas* 20, no. 3 (June 1986): 34–36.

———. "Coca's Shining Path." *NACLA Report on the Americas* 22, no. 6 (March 1989): 22–24.

Gordon, Scott. *Controlling the State: Constitutionalism from Ancient Athens to Today.* Cambridge, MA: Harvard University Press, 1999.

Gorriti, Gustavo. "Peru's Prophet of Terror." *Reader's Digest,* September 1992, 93–99.

———. "Shining Path's Stalin and Trotsky." In *The Shining Path of Peru,* edited by David Scott Palmer, 167–188. New York: St. Martin's Press, 1994.

———. *The Shining Path: A History of the Millenarian War in Peru.* Translated by Robin Kirk. Chapel Hill, NC: University of North Carolina Press, 1999.

Graham, Carol. *Peru's APRA: Parties, Politics, and the Elusive Quest for Democracy.* Boulder, CO: Lynne Rienner Publishers, 1992.

———. "Government and Politics." In *Peru: A Country Study,* edited by Rex Hudson, 205–258. Washington, D.C.: Federal Research Division, Library of Congress, 1993.

———. "Introduction: Democracy in Crisis and the International Response." In *Peru in Crisis: Dictatorship or Democracy,* edited by Joseph Tulchin and Gary Bland, 1–22. Boulder, CO: Lynne Rienner Publishers, 1994.

Grant, Gregory. "The Real War in Peru." *The World and I* 5, no. 8 (August 1990): 94–99.

Greer, Steven. "The Supergrass System." In *Justice under Fire: The Abuse of Civil Liberties in Northern Ireland,* edited by Anthony Jennings, 73–103. London: Pluto Press, 1990.

Greer, Steven, and Antony White. "A Return to Trial by Jury." In *Justice under Fire: The Abuse of Civil Liberties in Northern Ireland,* edited by Anthony Jennings, 47–72. London: Pluto Press, 1990.

Groenewold, Kurt. "The German Federal Republic's Response and Civil Liberties." In *Western Responses to Terrorism,* edited by Alex Schmid and Ronald Crelinsten, 136–150. London: Frank Cass Publishers, 1993.

Guillaume, Gilbert. "France and the Fight against Terrorism." In *Western Responses to Terrorism,* edited by Alex Schmid and Ronald Crelinsten, 131–135. London: Frank Cass Publishers, 1993.

Guillermoprieto, Alma. "Down the Shining Path." *The New Yorker,* February 8, 1993, 64–75.

Hadden, Tom, Kevin Boyle, and Colm Campbell. "Emergency Law in Northern Ireland: The Context." In *Justice under Fire: The Abuse of Civil Liberties in Northern Ireland,* edited by Anthony Jennings, 1–26. London: Pluto Press, 1990.

Haggart, Ron, and Aubrey Golden. *Rumours of War.* Toronto: new press, 1971.

Hall, Peter. "The Prevention of Terrorism Acts." In *Justice under Fire: The Abuse of Civil Liberties in Northern Ireland,* edited by Anthony Jennings, 144–190. London: Pluto Press, 1990.

Hamilton, Alexander, James Madison, and John Jay. *The Federalist Papers.* New York: Penguin Books, 1961.

Handbook for Volunteers of the Irish Republican Army: Notes on Guerilla Warfare. Boulder, CO: Paladin Press, 1985.

Harding, Colin. "Reporting the War in Ayacucho." *Index on Censorship* 12, no. 6 (1983): 15–17.

———. "The Rise of Sendero Luminoso." In *Region and Class in Modern Peruvian History,* edited by Rory Miller, 179–207. Liverpool: Institute of Latin American Studies, 1987.

Harrison, Michael M. "France and International Terrorism: Problem and Response." In *The Deadly Sin of Terrorism: Its Effect on Democracy and Civil Liberties in Six Countries*, edited by David Charters, 103–136. Westport, CT: Greenwood Press, 1994.

Hazleton, William, and Sandra Woy-Hazleton. "Terrorism and the Marxist Left: Peru's Struggle against Sendero Luminoso." *Terrorism* 11, no. 6 (1988): 471–490.

———. "Sendero Luminoso: A Communist Party Crosses a River of Blood." *Terrorism and Political Violence* 4, no. 2 (summer 1992): 62–83.

Hennessey, Thomas. *A History of Northern Ireland*. New York: St. Martin's Press, 1997.

Hewitt, Christopher. *The Effectiveness of Anti-Terrorist Policies*. Lanham, MD: University Press of America, 1984.

———. *Consequences of Political Violence*. Aldershot, England: Dartmouth Publishing Company Limited, 1993.

Heymann, Philip B. *Terrorism and America: A Commonsense Strategy for a Democratic Society*. Cambridge, MA: MIT Press, 1998.

Hillyard, Paddy. "Political and Social Dimensions of Emergency Law in Northern Ireland." In *Justice under Fire: The Abuse of Civil Liberties in Northern Ireland*, edited by Anthony Jennings, 191–212. London: Pluto Press, 1990.

Hinojosa, Iván. "On Poor Relations and the Nouveau Rich: Shining Path and the Radical Peruvian Left." In *Shining and Other Paths: War and Society in Peru, 1980–1995*, edited by Steve Stern, 60–83. Durham, NC: Duke University Press, 1998.

Hoffman, Bruce. *Inside Terrorism*. New York: Columbia University Press, 1998.

Holmes, Stephen. "Precommitment and the Paradox of Democracy." In *Constitutionalism and Democracy*, edited by Jon Elster and Rune Slagstad, 195–240. Cambridge: Cambridge University Press, 1988.

Holms, John Pynchon, and Tom Burke. *Terrorism: The Complete Book of Groups, Their Deadly Weapons, Their Innocent Targets and Their Terrible Crimes*. New York: Pinnacle Books, 1994.

Horowitz, Irving Louis. "The Routinization of Terrorism and Its Unanticipated Consequences." In *Terrorism, Legitimacy, and Power: The Consequences of Political Violence*, edited by Martha Crenshaw, 38–51. Middletown, CT: Wesleyan University Press, 1983.

Hsia, Tao-tai, and Wendy Zeldin. "Laws on Emergency Powers in Taiwan." In *Coping with Crises: How Governments Deal with Emergencies*, edited by Shao-chuan Leng, 173–208. Lanham, MD: University Press of America, 1990.

Hudson, Rex, ed. *Peru: A Country Study*. Washington, D.C.: Federal Research Division, Library of Congress, 1993.

Iglesias, Carlos Basombrío. "Sendero Luminoso and Human Rights: A Perverse Logic That Captured the Country." In *Shining and Other Paths: War and Society in Peru, 1980–1995*, edited by Steve Stern, 425–446. Durham, NC: Duke University Press, 1998.

Inkeles, Alex, ed. *On Measuring Democracy: Its Consequences and Concomitants*. New Brunswick, NJ: Transaction Publishers, 1991.

Isbell, Billie Jean. "Shining Path and Peasant Rebellion in Rural Ayacucho." In *The Shining Path of Peru*, edited by David Scott Palmer, 77–100. New York: St. Martin's Press, 1994.

Izaguirre, Carlos Reyna. "Shining Path in the 21st Century: Actors in Search of a New Script." *NACLA Report on the Americas* 30, no. 1 (July/August 1996): 37–38.

Janke, Peter, ed. *Terrorism and Democracy: Some Contemporary Cases.* New York: St. Martin's Press, 1992.

Jennings, Anthony. "Bullets above the Law." In *Justice under Fire: The Abuse of Civil Liberties in Northern Ireland,* edited by Anthony Jennings, 131–143. London: Pluto Press, 1990.

————. "Shoot to Kill: The Final Courts of Justice." In *Justice under Fire: The Abuse of Civil Liberties in Northern Ireland,* edited by Anthony Jennings, 104–130. London: Pluto Press, 1990.

Jennings, Anthony, ed. *Justice under Fire: The Abuse of Civil Liberties in Northern Ireland.* London: Pluto Press, 1990.

Jiménez, Fernando. "Spain: The Terrorist Challenge and the Government's Response." In *Western Responses to Terrorism,* edited by Alex Schmid and Ronald Crelinsten, 110–130. London: Frank Cass Publishers, 1993.

Kaufman, Edy. *Uruguay in Transition: From Civilian to Military Rule.* New Brunswick, NJ: Transaction Books, 1979.

Kennedy-Pipe, Caroline. *The Origins of the Present Troubles in Northern Ireland.* London: Longman, 1997.

Kim, Young. "Politics of Emergency: The Case of Korea." In *Coping with Crises: How Governments Deal with Emergencies,* edited by Shao-chuan Leng, 129–172. Lanham, MD: University Press of America, 1990.

Kirk, Robin. "Shining Path Is Gaining in Peru." *The Nation* 252, no. 16, April 29, 1991, 552–556.

Klarén, Peter. "Historical Setting." In *Peru: A Country Study,* edited by Rex Hudson, 5–58. Washington, D.C.: Federal Research Division, Library of Congress, 1993.

Kolinsky, Eva. "Terrorism in West Germany." In *The Threat of Terrorism,* edited by Juliet Lodge, 57–88. Boulder, CO: Westview Press, 1988.

Labrousse, Alain. *The Tupamaros: Urban Guerrillas in Uruguay.* London: Penguin Books, 1973.

Lane, Jan-Erik. *Constitutions and Political Theory.* Manchester: Manchester University Press, 1996.

Langguth, A. J. *Hidden Terrors: The Truth about U.S. Police Operations in Latin America.* New York: Pantheon Books, 1978.

Laqueur, Walter. *The New Terrorism: Fanaticism and the Arms of Mass Destruction.* New York: Oxford University Press, 1999.

Larson, Everette. *Sendero Luminoso: A Bibliography.* Washington, D.C.: Library of Congress, 1985.

Laufer, David. "The Evolution of Belgian Terrorism." In *The Threat of Terrorism,* edited by Juliet Lodge, 179–212. Boulder, CO: Westview Press, 1988.

The Lawyers Committee for International Human Rights. *The Generals Give Back Uruguay.* New York: The Lawyers Committee for International Human Rights, 1985.

Lee, Alfred McClung. *Terrorism in Northern Ireland.* Bayside, NY: General Hall, 1983.

Leng, Shao-chuan, ed. *Coping with Crises: How Governments Deal with Emergencies.* Lanham, MD: University Press of America, 1990.

Lesser, Ian O., Bruce Hoffman, John Arquilla, David Ronfeldt, and Michele Zanini. *Countering the New Terrorism.* Santa Monica, CA: RAND Project AIR FORCE, 1999.

Levin, Malcolm, and Christine Sylvester. *Crisis in Quebec.* Toronto: The Ontario Institute for Studies in Education, 1973.

Linfield, Michael. *Freedom under Fire: U.S. Civil Liberties in Times of War.* Boston: South End Press, 1990.

Linz, Juan J., and Alfred Stepan, eds. *The Breakdown of Democratic Regimes: Latin America.* Baltimore: Johns Hopkins University Press, 1978.

Livingstone, Neil C. *The War against Terrorism.* Lexington, MA: Lexington Books, 1982.

Lodge, Juliet, ed. *The Threat of Terrorism.* Boulder, CO: Westview Press, 1988.

Loomis, Dan. *Not Much Glory: Quelling the F.L.Q.* Toronto: Deneau Publishers, 1984.

Lopez, George, and Michael Stohl, eds. *Liberalization and Redemocratization in Latin America.* New York: Greenwood Press, 1987.

Lopez-Alves, Fernando. "Political Crises, Strategic Choices, and Terrorism: The Rise and Fall of the Uruguayan Tupamaros." *Terrorism and Political Violence* 1, no. 2 (April 1989): 202–241.

Loveman, Brian. *The Constitution of Tyranny: Regimes of Exception in Spanish America.* Pittsburgh: University of Pittsburgh Press, 1993.

Mallon, Florencia. "Chronicle of a Path Foretold? Velasco's Revolution, Vanguardia Revolucionaria, and 'Shining Omens' in the Indigenous Communities of Andahuaylas." In *Shining and Other Paths: War and Society in Peru, 1980–1995,* edited by Steve Stern, 84–120. Durham, NC: Duke University Press, 1998.

Manrique, Nelson. "Time of Fear." *NACLA Report on the Americas* 24, no. 4 (December/January 1990/1991): pp. 28–38.

———. "The Two Faces of Fujimori's Rural Policy." *NACLA Report on the Americas* 30, no. 1 (July/August 1996): 39–43.

———. "The War for the Central Sierra." In *Shining and Other Paths: War and Society in Peru, 1980–1995,* edited by Steve Stern, 193–223. Durham, NC: Duke University Press, 1998.

Marighella, Carlos. "Minimanual of the Urban Guerrilla." In "Urban Guerrilla Warfare," by Robert Moss. *Adelphi Paper* no. 79 (1971).

Marks, Tom. "Making Revolution with Shining Path." In *The Shining Path of Peru,* edited by David Scott Palmer, 209–224. New York: St. Martin's Press, 1994.

Masterson, Daniel. *Militarism and Politics in Latin America: Peru from Sánchez Cerro to Sendero Luminoso.* New York: Greenwood Press, 1991.

Mauceri, Philip. "Military Politics and Counter-Insurgency in Peru." *Journal of Interamerican Studies and World Affairs* 33, no. 4 (winter 1991): 83–109.

———. "State Reform, Coalitions, and the Neoliberal *Autogolpe* in Peru." *Latin American Research Review* 30, no. 1 (1995): 7–38.

———. *State under Siege: Development and Policy Making in Peru.* Boulder, CO: Westview Press, 1996.

———. "The Transition to 'Democracy' and the Failures of Institution Building." In *The Peruvian Labyrinth: Polity, Society, Economy,* edited by Maxwell Cameron and Philip Mauceri, 13–36. University Park, PA: The Pennsylvania State University Press, 1997.

Max, Alphonse. *Guerrillas in Latin America.* The Hague: International Document and Information Centre, 1971.

McClintock, Cynthia. "Sendero Luminoso: Peru's Maoist Guerrillas." *Problems of Communism* 32 (September-October 1983): 19–34.

———. "Why Peasants Rebel: The Case of Peru's Sendero Luminoso." *World Politics* 37, no. 1 (October 1984): 48–84.

―――. "Peru: Precarious Regimes, Authoritarian and Democratic." In *Democracy in Developing Countries: Latin America,* edited by Larry Diamond, Juan Linz and Seymour Martin Lipset, 335–386. Boulder, CO: Lynne Rienner Publishers, 1989.

―――. "The Prospects for Democratic Consolidation in a 'Least Likely' Case." *Comparative Politics* 21, no. 2 (1989): 127–148.

―――. "Peru's Fujimori: A Caudillo Derails Democracy." *Current History* 92, no. 572 (March 1993): 112–119.

―――. "Theories of Revolution and the Case of Peru." In *The Shining Path of Peru,* edited by David Scott Palmer, 243–258. New York: St. Martin's Press, 1994.

―――. *Revolutionary Movements in Latin America: El Salvador's FMLN and Peru's Shining Path.* Washington, D.C.: United States Institute of Peace Press, 1998.

McCormick, Gordon. "The Shining Path and Peruvian Terrorism." In *Inside Terrorist Organizations,* edited by David Rapoport, 109–128. New York: Columbia University Press, 1988.

McDonald, Ronald. "Electoral Politics and Uruguayan Political Decay." *Inter-American Economic Affairs* 26 (summer 1972): 25–46.

―――. "The Rise of Military Politics in Uruguay." *Inter-American Economic Affairs* 28 (spring 1975): 25–44.

McKinsey, Lauren. "Dimension of National Political Integration and Disintegration: The Case of Quebec Separatism 1960–1975." *Comparative Political Studies* 9 no. 3 (October 1976): 335–360.

Méndez, Juan. *Human Rights in Peru after Garcia's First Year.* New York: Americas Watch Committee, 1986.

―――. *A Certain Passivity: Failing to Curb Human Rights Abuses in Peru.* New York: Americas Watch Committee, 1987.

―――. *Tolerating Abuses: Violations of Human Rights in Peru.* New York: Americas Watch Committee, 1988.

Mill, John Stuart. *On Liberty.* London: Penguin Books, 1974.

Miller, Rory, ed. *Region and Class in Modern Peruvian History.* Liverpool: Institute of Latin American Studies, 1987.

Milner, Henry and Sheilagh Hodgins Milner. *The Decolonization of Quebec: An Analysis of Left-Wing Nationalism.* Toronto: McClelland and Stewart, 1973.

Mitchell, William. *Peasants on the Edge: Crop, Cult, and Crisis in the Andes.* Austin: University of Texas Press, 1991.

Montesquieu, Charles de Secondat, baron de. *The Spirit of the Laws.* Cambridge: Cambridge University Press, 1989.

Moore, Brian. *The Revolution Script.* Toronto: McClelland and Stewart, 1971.

Morf, Gustave. *Terror in Quebec: Case Studies of the FLQ.* Toronto: Clarke, Irwin and Company, 1970.

Moss, Robert. "Urban Guerrillas in Latin America." *Conflict Studies* no. 8 (October 1970): 1–15.

―――. "Urban Guerrilla Warfare." *Adelphi Papers* no. 79 (1971).

―――. "Urban Guerrillas in Uruguay." *Problems of Communism* 10 (Sept-Oct 1971): 14–23.

―――. "Uruguay: Terrorism versus Democracy." *Conflict Studies* no. 14 (August 1971): 1–10.

―――. *The War for the Cities.* New York: Coward, McCann and Geoghegan, 1972.

―――. *The Collapse of Democracy.* London: Abacus, 1975.

Moxone-Browne, Edward. "Terrorism in France." In *The Threat of Terrorism,* edited by Juliet Lodge, 213–228. Boulder, CO: Westview Press, 1988.

Muñoz, Hortensia. "Human Rights and Social Referents: The Construction of New Sensibilities." In *Shining and Other Paths: War and Society in Peru, 1980–1995,* edited by Steve Stern, 447–469. Durham, NC: Duke University Press, 1998.

NACLA Report on the Americas. "Privilege and Power in Fujimori's Peru." *NACLA Report on the Americas* 30, no. 1 (July/August 1996): 15.

Neier, Aryeh. "Peru's 'Dirty War'." *The Nation* 238, no. 5, February 11, 1984, 148–149.

Netanyahu, Benjamin. *Fighting Terrorism: How Democracies Can Defeat Domestic and International Terrorists.* New York: The Noonday Press, 1995.

Netanyahu, Benjamin, ed. *International Terrorism: Challenge and Response.* New Brunswick, NJ: Transaction Books, 1981.

———. *Terrorism: How the West Can Win.* New York: Farrar, Straus, Giroux, 1986.

Northern Ireland Office. *Guide to the Emergency Powers.* Belfast: HMSO, 1989.

Obando, Enrique. "The Power of Peru's Armed Forces." In *Peru in Crisis: Dictatorship or Democracy?* edited by Joseph Tulchin and Gary Bland, 101–124. Boulder, CO: Lynne Rienner Publishers, 1994.

———. "Fujimori and the Military: A Marriage of Convenience." *NACLA Report on the Americas* 30, no. 1 (July/August 1996): 31–36.

———. "Civil-Military Relations in Peru, 1980–1996: How to Control and Coopt the Military (and the consequences of doing so)." In *Shining and Other Paths: War and Society in Peru, 1980–1995,* edited by Steve Stern, 385–410. Durham, NC: Duke University Press, 1998.

O'Brien, Conor Cruise. "Terrorism under Democratic Conditions: The Case of the IRA." In *Terrorism, Legitimacy, and Power: The Consequences of Political Violence,* edited by Martha Crenshaw, 91–104. Middletown, CT: Wesleyan University Press, 1983.

Ochoa, Manuel Castillo. "Fujimori and the Business Class: A Prickly Partnership." *NACLA Report on the Americas* 30, no. 1 (July/August 1996): 25–30.

O'Day, Alan. "The Dilemma of Violence in Northern Ireland." In *Terrorism's Laboratory: The Case of Northern Ireland,* edited by Alan O'Day, 1–10. Aldershot, England: Dartmouth Publishing Company, 1995.

O'Day, Alan, ed. *Terrorism's Laboratory: The Case of Northern Ireland.* Aldershot, England: Dartmouth Publishing Company, 1995.

Oliart, Patricia. "Alberto Fujimori: 'The Man Peru Needed?'" In *Shining and Other Paths: War and Society in Peru, 1980–1995,* edited by Steve Stern, 411–424. Durham, NC: Duke University Press, 1998.

Palmer, David Scott. "The Sendero Luminoso Rebellion in Peru." In *Latin American Insurgencies,* edited by Georges Fauriol, 67–96. The Georgetown University Center for Strategic and International Studies, 1985.

———. "Rebellion in Rural Peru: The Origins and Evolution of Sendero Luminoso." *Comparative Politics* 18, no. 2 (January 1986): 127–146.

———. "Peru's Persistent Problems." *Current History* 89, no. 543 (January 1990): 5–34.

———. "Peru, the Drug Business and Shining Path: Between Scylla and Charybdis?" *Journal of Interamerican Studies and World Affairs* 34, no. 3 (autumn 1992): 65–88.

———. "National Security." In *Peru: A Country Study,* edited by Rex Hudson, 259–318. Federal Research Division, Library of Congress, 1993.

————. "Introduction: History, Politics, and Shining Path in Peru." In *The Shining Path of Peru*, edited by David Scott Palmer, 1–32. New York: St. Martin's Press, 1994.

————. "Conclusion: The View from the Windows." In *The Shining Path of Peru*, edited by David Scott Palmer, 259–274. New York: St. Martin's Press, 1994.

————. "The Revolutionary Terrorism of Peru's Shining Path." In *Terrorism in Context*, edited by Martha Crenshaw, 249–310. University Park, PA: The Pennsylvania State University Press, 1995.

Palmer, David Scott, ed. *The Shining Path of Peru*. New York: St. Martin's Press, 1994.

Paredes, Carlos, and Jeffrey Sachs, eds. *Peru's Path to Recovery: A Plan for Economic Stabilization and Growth*. Washington, D.C.: The Brookings Institution, 1991.

Parry, Albert. *Terrorism: From Robespierre to Arafat*. New York: Vanguard Press, 1976.

Peckenham, Nancy. "Peru: Ayacucho under Siege." *NACLA Report on the Americas* 29, no. 3 (May/June 1985): 6–8.

Pion-Berlin, David. "Military Autonomy and Emerging Democracies in South America." *Comparative Politics* 25, no. 1 (October 1992): 83–102.

Polity 98 Database. www.bsos.umd.edu/cidcm/polity/.

Pollack, Ben, and Graham Hunter. "Dictatorship, Democracy and Terrorism in Spain." In *The Threat of Terrorism*, edited by Juliet Lodge, 119–144. Boulder, CO: Westview Press, 1988.

Poole, Deborah, and Gerardo Renique. "The New Chronicles of Peru: US Scholars and their 'Shining Path' of Peasant Rebellion." *Bulletin of Latin American Research* 10, no. 2 (1991): 133–191.

Poole, Michael A. "The Spatial Distribution of Political Violence in Northern Ireland." In *Terrorism's Laboratory: The Case of Northern Ireland*, edited by Alan O'Day, 27–46. Aldershot, England: Dartmouth Publishing Company, 1995.

Porzecanski, Arturo. *Uruguay's Tupamaros: The Urban Guerrilla*. New York: Praeger Publishers, 1973.

Radu, Michael. "Terror, Terrorism, and Insurgency in Latin America." *Orbis* 28, no. 1 (spring 1984): 27–40.

Radu, Michael, and Vladimir Tismaneanu. *Latin American Revolutionaries: Groups, Goals, Methods*. Washington, D.C.: Pergamon-Brassey's International Defense Publishers, 1990.

Rapoport, David, ed. *Inside Terrorist Organizations*. New York: Columbia University Press, 1988.

Regush, Nicholas. *Pierre Vallieres: The Revolutionary Process in Quebec*. New York: Dial Press, 1973.

Reid, Michael. *Peru: Paths to Poverty*. London: Latin American Bureau, 1985.

————. "Building Bridges? Garcia Confronts Sendero." *NACLA Report on the Americas* 20, no. 3 (June 1986): 43–45.

Rénique, José Luis. "Apogee and Crisis of a 'Third Path': *Mariateguismo*, 'People's War,' and Counterinsurgency in Puno 1987–1994." In *Shining and Other Paths: War and Society in Peru, 1980–1995*, edited by Steve Stern, 307–340. Durham, NC: Duke University Press, 1998.

Rioux, Marcel. *Quebec in Question*. Translated by James Boake. Toronto: James Lewis and Samuel, 1971.

Roberts, Kenneth, and Mark Peceny. "Human Rights and United States Policy toward Peru." In *The Peruvian Labyrinth: Polity, Society, Economy*, edited by Maxwell

Cameron and Philip Mauceri, 192–222. University Park, PA: The Pennsylvania State University Press, 1997.

Robertson, Ken. "Intelligence, Terrorism, and Civil Liberties." In *Contemporary Research on Terrorism*, edited by Paul Wilkinson and Alasdair Stewart, 549–569. Aberdeen: Aberdeen University Press, 1987.

Rochabrún, Guillermo. "Deciphering the Enigmas of Alberto Fujimori." *NACLA Report on the Americas* 30, no. 1 (July/August 1996): 16–24.

Rose, Richard. *Governing without Consensus: An Irish Perspective*. Boston: Beacon Press, 1971.

Rosenau, William. "Is the Shining Path the 'New Khmer Rouge'?" *Studies in Conflict and Terrorism* 17, no. 4 (1994): 305–322.

Rospigliosi, Fernando. "Democracy's Bleak Prospects." In *Peru in Crisis: Dictatorship or Democracy*, edited by Joseph Tulchin and Gary Bland, 35–62. Boulder, CO: Lynne Rienner Publishers, 1994.

Rossiter, Clinton L. *Constitutional Dictatorship: Crisis Government in the Modern Democracies*. Princeton: Princeton University Press, 1948.

Rotstein, Abraham, and Gad Horowitz. "Quebec and Canadian Nationalism: Two Views." In *Power Corrupted: The October Crisis and the Repression of Quebec*, edited by Abraham Rotstein, 119–127. Toronto: new press, 1971.

Rotstein, Abraham, ed. *Power Corrupted: The October Crisis and the Repression of Quebec*. Toronto: new press, 1971.

Rouquié, Alain. *The Military and the State in Latin America*. Translated by Paul Sigmund. Berkeley: University of California Press, 1987.

Rudolph, James. *Peru: The Evolution of a Crisis*. Westport, CT: Praeger Publishers, 1992.

Russett, Bruce. *Grasping the Democratic Peace: Principles for a Post-Cold War World*. Princeton: Princeton University Press, 1993.

Sagasti, Francisco, and Max Hernandez. "The Crisis of Governance." In *Peru in Crisis: Dictatorship or Democracy*, edited by Joseph Tulchin and Gary Bland, 23–34. Boulder, CO: Lynne Rienner Publishers, 1994.

Salcedo, José María. "The Price of Peace: A Report from the Emergency Zone." *NACLA Report on the Americas* 20, no. 3 (June 1986): 37–42.

Saward, Michael. "Democratic Theory and Indices of Democratization." In *Defining and Measuring Democracy*, edited by David Beetham, 6–24. London: Sage Publications, 1994.

Saywell, John. *Quebec 70: A Documentary Narrative*. Toronto: University of Toronto Press, 1971.

Schmeiser, D. A. *Civil Liberties in Canada*. Glasgow: Oxford University Press, 1964.

Schmid, Alex P. "Politically-Motivated Violent Activists in the Netherlands in the 1980s." In *The Threat of Terrorism*, edited by Juliet Lodge, 145–178. Boulder, CO: Westview Press, 1988.

———. "Countering Terrorism in the Netherlands." In *Western Responses to Terrorism*, edited by Alex Schmid and Ronald Crelinsten, 79–109. London: Frank Cass Publishers, 1993.

Schmid, Alex P., et al. *Political Terrorism: A New Guide to Actors, Authors, Concepts, Data Bases, Theories, and Literature*. Amsterdam: North-Holland Publishing Company, 1988.

Schmid, Alex P., and Ronald Crelinsten, eds. *Western Responses to Terrorism*. London: Frank Cass Publishers, 1993.

Schmitt, Carl. *Political Theology: Four Chapters on the Concept of Sovereignty.* Cambridge, MA: MIT Press, 1985.

Sejersted, Francis. "Democracy and the Rule of Law: Some Historical Experiences of Contradictions in the Striving for Good Government." In *Constitutionalism and Democracy,* edited by Jon Elster and Rune Slagstad, 131–152. Cambridge: Cambridge University Press, 1988.

Seligman, Linda. *Between Reform and Revolution: Political Struggles in the Peruvian Andes, 1969–1991.* Stanford: Stanford University Press, 1995.

Seton-Watson, Christopher. "Terrorism in Italy." In *The Threat of Terrorism,* edited by Juliet Lodge, 89–118. Boulder, CO: Westview Press, 1988.

Shapiro, Ian, ed. *The Rule of Law.* New York: New York University Press, 1994.

Shapiro, Ian, and Russell Hardin, eds. *Political Order.* New York: New York University Press, 1993.

Shapiro, Samuel. "Uruguay's Lost Paradise." *Current History* (February 1972): 98–103.

Shultz, George. "The Challenge to the Democracies." In *Terrorism: How the West Can Win,* edited by Benjamin Netanyahu, 16–24. New York: Farrar, Straus, Giroux, 1986.

Slagstad, Rune. "Liberal Constitutionalism and Its Critics: Carl Schmitt and Max Weber." In *Constitutionalism and Democracy,* edited by Jon Elster and Rune Slagstad, 103–130. Cambridge: Cambridge University Press, 1988.

Smith, Denis. *Bleeding Hearts ... Bleeding Country: Canada and the Quebec Crisis.* Edmonton: M. G. Hurtig, 1971.

Smith, G. Davidson. *Combating Terrorism.* London: Routledge, 1990.

Smith, Michael. "Taking the High Ground: Shining Path and the Andes." *Terrorism, Violence, and Insurgency Report* 10, no. 3 (1991): 1–11.

———. "Shining Path's Urban Strategy: Ate Vitarte." In *The Shining Path of Peru,* edited by David Scott Palmer, 145–166. New York: St. Martin's Press, 1994.

———. "Taking the High Ground: Shining Path and the Andes." In *The Shining Path of Peru,* edited by David Scott Palmer, 33–50. New York: St. Martin's Press, 1994.

Sniderman, Paul, et al. *The Clash of Rights: Liberty, Equality, and Legitimacy in Pluralist Democracy.* New Haven: Yale University Press, 1996.

Sobieck, Stephen. "Democratic Responses to International Terrorism in Germany." In *The Deadly Sin of Terrorism: Its Effect on Democracy and Civil Liberties in Six Countries,* edited by David Charters, 43–72. Westport, CT: Greenwood Press, 1994.

St. John, Ronald Bruce. "Peru: Democracy under Siege." *The World Today* 40, no. 7 (July 1984): 299–307.

Stalling, Barbara, and Robert Kaufman, eds. *Debt and Democracy in Latin America.* Boulder, CO: Westview Press, 1989.

Starn, Orin. "'I Dreamed of Foxes and Hawks': Reflections on Peasant Protest, New Social Movements, and the *Rondas Campesinas* of Northern Peru." In *The Making of Social Movements in Latin America: Identity, Strategy, and Democracy,* edited by Arturo Escobar and Sonia Alvarez, 89–111. Boulder, CO: Westview Press, 1992.

———. "New Literature on Peru's Sendero Luminoso." *Latin American Research Review* 27, no. 2 (1992): 212–226.

———. "Maoism in the Andes: The Communist Party of Peru—Shining Path and the Refusal of History." *Journal of Latin American Studies* 27, no. 2 (May 1995): 399–421.

———. "Villagers at Arms: War and Counterrevolution in the Central-South Andes." In *Shining and Other Paths: War and Society in Peru, 1980–1995*, edited by Steve Stern, 224–260. Durham, NC: Duke University Press, 1998.

Starn, Orin, Carlos Degregori, and Robin Kirk, eds. *The Peru Reader: History, Culture, Politics*. Durham, NC: Duke University Press, 1995.

Stater, Timothy. "Sendero Luminoso's Relentless War." *Terrorism, Violence, and Insurgency* 10, no. 3 (1991): 18–23.

Stern, Peter. *Sendero Luminoso: An Annotated Bibliography of the Shining Path Guerrilla Movement, 1980–1993*. Austin, TX: SALALM, 1995.

Stern, Steve, ed. *Shining and Other Paths: War and Society in Peru, 1980–1995*. Durham, NC: Duke University Press, 1998.

Stewart, James. *The FLQ: Seven Years of Terrorism*. Ontario: Simon and Schuster, 1970.

Stokes, Susan. "Hegemony, Consciousness, and Political Change in Peru." *Politics and Society* 19, no. 3 (September 1991): 265–290.

Strong, Simon. *Shining Path: Terror and Revolution in Peru*. New York: Random House, 1992.

Sunstein, Cass. "Constitutions and Democracies: An Epilogue." In *Constitutionalism and Democracy*, edited by Jon Elster and Rune Slagstad, 327–356. Cambridge: Cambridge University Press, 1988.

Tarazona-Sevillano, Gabriela. "The Organization of Shining Path." In *The Shining Path of Peru*, edited by David Scott Palmer, 189–208. New York: St. Martin's Press, 1994.

Tarazona-Sevillano, Gabriela, and John Reuter. *Sendero Luminoso and the Threat of Narcoterrorism*. New York: Praeger Publishers, 1990.

Tarnopolsky, W. S. "Emergency Powers and Civil Liberties." *Canadian Public Administration* 15 no. 2 (summer 1972): 194–210.

Taylor, Peter. *Beating the Terrorists: Interrogation in Omagh, Gough, and Castlereagh*. New York: Penguin Books, 1980.

———. *States of Terror: Democracy and Political Violence*. London: BBC Books, 1993.

Thomson, Dale, ed. *Quebec Society and Politics: Views from the Inside*. Toronto: McClelland and Stewart, 1973.

Torrance, Judy. "The Response of Canadian Governments to Violence." *Canadian Journal of Political Science* 10, no. 3 (September 1977): 473–496.

Tulchin, Joseph S., and Gary Bland, eds. *Peru in Crisis: Dictatorship or Democracy*. Boulder, CO: Lynne Rienner Publishers, 1994.

Vallières, Pierre. *Choose!* Translated by Penelope Williams. Toronto: new press, 1972.

Vanger, Milton. *The Model Country*. Hanover, NH: University Press of New England, 1980.

Walker, Clive. *The Prevention of Terrorism in British Law*. Manchester: Manchester University Press, 1986.

Walsh, Dermont P. J. "Arrest and Interrogation." In *Justice under Fire: The Abuse of Civil Liberties in Northern Ireland*, edited by Anthony Jennings, 27–46. London: Pluto Press, 1990.

Wardlaw, Grant. *Political Terrorism: Theory, Tactics, and Counter-measures*. Cambridge: Cambridge University Press, 1989.

———. "The Democratic Framework." In *The Deadly Sin of Terrorism: Its Effect on Democracy and Civil Liberties in Six Countries*, edited by David Charters, 5–12. Westport, CT: Greenwood Press, 1994.

Warner, Bruce W. "Great Britain and the Response to International Terrorism." In *The Deadly Sin of Terrorism: Its Effect on Democracy and Civil Liberties in Six Countries*, edited by David Charters, 13–42. Westport, CT: Greenwood Press, 1994.

Watkins, Frederick Mundell. *The Failure of Constitutional Emergency Powers under the German Republic*. Cambridge, MA: Harvard University Press, 1939.

Weil, Thomas et al. *Area Handbook for Uruguay*. Washington, D.C.: Foreign Areas Studies of The American University, 1971.

Weinstein, Martin. *Uruguay: The Politics of Failure*. Westport, CT: Greenwood Press, 1975.

———. *Uruguay: Democracy at the Crossroads*. Boulder: Westview Press, 1988.

———. "Uruguay: The Legislature and the Reconstitution of Democracy." In *Legislatures and the New Democracies in Latin America*, edited by David Close, 137–150. Boulder: Lynne Rienner Publishers, 1995.

Werlich, David. "Peru: The Shadow of the Shining Path." *Current History* 83, no. 490 (February 1984): 78–90.

———. "Debt, Democracy and Terrorism in Peru." *Current History* 86, no. 516 (January 1987): 29–36.

———. "Peru: García Loses His Charm." *Current History* 87, no. 525 (January 1988): 13–37.

———. "Fujimori and the 'Disaster' in Peru." *Current History* 90, no. 553 (February 1991): 61–83.

Wheat, Andrew. "Shining Path's 'Fourth Sword' Ideology." *Journal of Political and Military Sociology* 18, no. 1 (summer 1990): 41–56.

Wilkinson, Paul. *Terrorism and the Liberal State*. London: Macmillan Press, 1977.

———. "The Orange and the Green: Extremism in Northern Ireland." In *Terrorism, Legitimacy, and Power: The Consequences of Political Violence*, edited by Martha Crenshaw, 105–123. Middletown, CT: Wesleyan University Press, 1983.

———. "Maintaining the Democratic Process and Public Support." In *The Future of Political Violence: Destabilization, Disorder and Terrorism*, edited by Richard Clutterbuck, 177–184. New York: St. Martin's Press, 1986.

———. "British Policy on Terrorism: An Assessment." In *The Threat of Terrorism*, edited by Juliet Lodge, 29–55. Boulder, CO: Westview Press, 1988.

———. *Terrorism versus Democracy: The Liberal State Response*. London: Frank Cass Publishers, 2000.

Wilkinson, Paul, and Alasdair Stewart, eds. *Contemporary Research on Terrorism*. Aberdeen: Aberdeen University Press, 1987.

Wilson, Carlos. *The Tupamaros: The Unmentionables*. Boston: Branden Press, 1974.

Wilson, J. Brent. "The United States' Response to International Terrorism." In *The Deadly Sin of Terrorism: Its Effect on Democracy and Civil Liberties in Six Countries*, edited by David Charters, 173–210. Westport, CT: Greenwood Press, 1994.

Wise, Carol. "State Policy and Social Conflict in Peru." In *The Peruvian Labyrinth: Polity, Society, Economy*, edited by Maxwell Cameron and Philip Mauceri, 70–106. University Park, PA: The Pennsylvania State University Press, 1997.

Wolf, John B. *Fear of Fear: A Survey of Terrorist Operations and Controls in Open So-cieties.* New York: Plenum Press, 1981.

———. *Antiterrorist Initiatives.* New York: Plenum Press, 1989.

Woy-Hazleton, Sandra, and William Hazleton. "Sustaining Democracy in Peru: Dealing with Parliamentary and Revolutionary Changes." In *Liberalization and Re-democratization in Latin America,* edited by George Lopez and Michael Stohl, 105–136. New York: Greenwood Press, 1987.

———. "Sendero Luminoso and the Future of Peruvian Democracy." *Third World Quarterly* (April 1990): 21–35.

———. "Shining Path and the Marxist Left." In *The Shining Path of Peru,* edited by David Scott Palmer, 225–242. New York: St. Martin's Press, 1994.

Youngers, Coletta. *After the* Autogolpe: *Human Rights in Peru and the U.S. Response.* Washington D.C., Washington Office on Latin America, 1994.

Index

About the Author

MICHAEL FREEMAN is a scholar of terrorism, international relations, and U.S. foreign policy. He was born in Indianapolis and received his B.A., M.A., and Ph.D. from the University of Chicago. He has spent several years as a political analyst for the U.S. government and is currently an independent political risk consultant.